AGENTA MILLO

Computer Graphics with OpenGL

A Beginner's Guide to 3D Graphics, Animation, and Rendering with OpenGL

Contents

Introduction to OpenGL

What is OpenGL?

OpenGL (Open Graphics Library) is a powerful, cross-platform application programming interface (API) used for rendering 2D and 3D vector graphics. It is primarily used in video games, CAD software, virtual reality, scientific simulations, and other applications where high-quality, real-time graphics are required. As a low-level graphics API, OpenGL interacts directly with the GPU (Graphics Processing Unit) to produce images, enabling the creation of interactive graphics applications.

OpenGL is a specification, not a software library. This means that OpenGL itself is a set of standards and guidelines for creating graphics, but different software vendors and developers have implemented these standards in their own ways. The most common implementation of OpenGL is by the Khronos Group, the consortium responsible for developing and maintaining OpenGL, but other companies like NVIDIA, AMD, and Intel provide their own optimized drivers and extensions for their hardware.

OpenGL enables developers to access the computational power of modern GPUs, allowing them to create real-time 3D graphics by performing complex mathematical calculations and transformations efficiently. OpenGL is used to render objects, manipulate textures, simulate lighting, and implement advanced visual effects. It also allows for the creation of intricate user interfaces, 3D models, and animations, which makes it an essential tool for graphics developers.

A Brief History and Evolution of OpenGL

The story of OpenGL begins in the late 1980s, when the graphics hardware industry was evolving rapidly. The need for a standardized API to simplify the development of high-performance graphics applications was becoming increasingly apparent.

The Early Years: OpenGL's Origins

In 1986, Silicon Graphics Inc. (SGI), a leading company in the graphics hardware industry, developed a proprietary graphics library known as **IRIS GL** (Interactive Rendering Interface System Graphics Library). IRIS GL was created for SGI's workstations, which were used for complex computer-aided design (CAD), scientific visualizations, and 3D modeling applications. It became one of the most widely used graphics APIs in the industry at the time.

As SGI's workstations gained popularity, it became clear that the industry needed a more standardized approach to graphics rendering—one that could be widely adopted across various hardware platforms. To address this, SGI and several other companies in the graphics community decided to develop a more universal graphics API.

In 1992, the **OpenGL** standard was born, under the direction of SGI, to replace IRIS GL. OpenGL was designed to be platform-independent and to allow developers to write applications that could run on different hardware, from SGI workstations to other vendors' graphics cards. The core goal of OpenGL was to establish a standard API that would enable developers to create advanced graphics applications without worrying about the underlying hardware.

The Rise of OpenGL: 1990s and Early 2000s

OpenGL quickly became the industry standard for 3D graphics. Its first major milestone was in 1993, when it was officially released as OpenGL 1.0. During this time, OpenGL was embraced by the gaming industry, software developers, and hardware manufacturers. As graphics technology progressed, OpenGL evolved to support more sophisticated rendering techniques, such as texture mapping, shading, and lighting models.

Throughout the 1990s, OpenGL was continuously updated to keep pace with the growing demands of the graphics industry. It became the go-to API for workstation graphics, and was also integrated into many consumer graphics cards. During this time, OpenGL was primarily used in high-end professional applications like CAD software, 3D modeling programs, and scientific visualization tools.

As consumer hardware improved and the gaming industry began to adopt 3D graphics, OpenGL gained widespread use in the gaming market. In 1997, the release of **OpenGL 1.1** introduced critical new features, such as support for texture mapping, stencil buffers, and multi-texturing. This allowed developers to create more realistic textures and enhanced the realism of 3D environments.

OpenGL 2.0, released in 2004, brought about the introduction of programmable shaders via **GLSL** (OpenGL Shading Language). This allowed developers to write custom shaders that could control how objects were rendered and how light interacted with surfaces in real-time, opening up new possibilities for creative graphics effects.

The Competition: DirectX and the Battle for Dominance

In the late 1990s and early 2000s, **Microsoft DirectX** became a significant competitor to OpenGL. DirectX, developed by Microsoft, was tightly integrated with Windows and gaming platforms, offering advanced graphics capabilities and a rich set of features optimized for real-time rendering. DirectX 9, released in 2002, became a major player in the gaming industry, as it was the standard API for the vast majority of Windows-based games.

OpenGL, however, remained the preferred choice for professional graphics applications, including CAD, engineering, and scientific software, as well as for cross-platform development. While DirectX was primarily tied to the Windows platform, OpenGL continued to offer cross-platform support for Linux, macOS, and other operating systems, allowing it to maintain a significant share of the professional graphics market.

By the early 2010s, however, the landscape began to shift once again with the rise of more modern and specialized graphics APIs, such as **Vulkan** and **Metal**. These new APIs were designed to give developers even finer control over the GPU, offering more efficient performance by reducing driver overhead and increasing the flexibility of rendering techniques.

OpenGL in the Modern Era

Despite the rise of new technologies, OpenGL continues to be a dominant force in the world of graphics programming, particularly in cross-platform development. While Vulkan and Metal offer more advanced features, OpenGL remains widely used because of its stability, extensive documentation, and broad hardware support.

The Khronos Group, which manages OpenGL's development, continues to release updates, with **OpenGL 4.x** introducing more powerful features such as **tessellation, geometry shaders**, and **compute shaders**, which allow for parallel computing on the GPU. These updates help OpenGL remain relevant in both professional and gaming graphics, even as newer APIs emerge.

In recent years, OpenGL has also seen extensive use in the fields of virtual reality (VR), augmented reality (AR), and scientific visualization, where high-quality 3D rendering and real-time interaction are critical. Although Vulkan and DirectX 12 are considered by some to be more efficient APIs for cutting-edge gaming, OpenGL's support for a wide range of platforms and its ability to seamlessly integrate with other technologies keeps it widely used for various types of development.

OpenGL has come a long way since its inception in the early 1990s. What began as a tool for high-end scientific applications has evolved into a critical component in the world of computer graphics, powering everything from professional CAD software to cutting-edge video games. Over the years, OpenGL has remained a standard for developers who require cross-platform graphics rendering, offering unmatched flexibility and control.

Its continued evolution, from fixed-function pipelines to modern programmable shaders, reflects the growing complexity of computer graphics

4

and the increasing demand for real-time rendering and sophisticated visual effects. Whether you are developing interactive applications, 3D simulations, or advanced visualizations, OpenGL remains an invaluable tool in the world of graphics programming.

As you continue through this book, you will learn how to harness the full power of OpenGL to create stunning 3D models, animations, and real-time visual effects. By understanding the history and evolution of OpenGL, you'll appreciate its enduring significance in the graphics industry and its capabilities in modern software development.

Why OpenGL is Still Widely Used in Graphics Programming

Despite the rise of newer graphics APIs such as DirectX 12 and Vulkan, OpenGL remains a dominant force in the world of graphics programming, with a long-standing presence in a variety of industries, from gaming and entertainment to scientific simulations and medical imaging. There are several reasons why OpenGL continues to be widely used, even in the face of competition from more modern graphics technologies.

1. Cross-Platform Compatibility

One of OpenGL's most compelling advantages is its cross-platform nature. Unlike other graphics APIs, such as DirectX (which is limited to Microsoft Windows platforms), OpenGL is supported on a wide variety of operating systems, including Windows, macOS, Linux, and others. This gives developers the flexibility to create applications that work across multiple platforms with minimal changes to the codebase.

This cross-platform capability makes OpenGL especially attractive to developers who want to create games, simulations, or applications that can run on different hardware architectures, such as desktops, laptops, and mobile devices. OpenGL's compatibility with both high-end workstations and low-power embedded devices ensures that developers can target a wide range of devices without sacrificing performance or visual quality.

For example, OpenGL's adoption in macOS has allowed developers to create powerful 3D applications for Apple's range of devices, including iPhones, iPads, and Macs, while also ensuring compatibility with Linux systems. On Windows, OpenGL is often used in professional visualization tools, CAD programs, and scientific applications that require high-quality rendering but must also run on a variety of hardware configurations.

2. Mature and Well-Documented

OpenGL has been around for more than 30 years, which has allowed it to mature into a robust, stable API. Over the years, it has been extensively documented, and there is a wealth of educational material, books, tutorials, and online resources available to developers. This makes it easy for both beginners and experienced developers to get started with OpenGL and to solve any challenges they encounter.

The long history of OpenGL also means that many bugs and performance issues have been ironed out over time, making it a reliable and trusted tool for building graphics applications. The developer community around OpenGL is large and active, and many existing OpenGL applications have been thoroughly tested across a wide range of systems and configurations, ensuring that it is a tried-and-true solution for graphics development.

Additionally, OpenGL's standardization through the **Khronos Group** ensures that its specifications remain up-to-date, while maintaining backward compatibility with older versions. This enables developers to confidently use OpenGL knowing that their applications will continue to work well across different hardware generations, as long as the correct version of the API is supported.

3. Extensive Hardware Support

OpenGL benefits from broad hardware support. Virtually all modern graphics cards from major manufacturers like NVIDIA, AMD, and Intel support OpenGL, and these companies often release drivers that are specifically optimized for OpenGL applications. This means that developers can leverage the full power of the latest GPUs while still using OpenGL as their graphics API.

Because OpenGL is widely adopted by hardware vendors, there is also a vast ecosystem of third-party tools, libraries, and middleware designed to work with OpenGL. From graphics engines and physics simulations to model loaders and shader compilers, there is no shortage of tools available to assist developers in creating high-quality OpenGL-based applications.

Moreover, OpenGL is particularly popular in embedded and mobile devices, such as smartphones, tablets, and set-top boxes, where it has been widely adopted as the standard graphics API for rendering 3D graphics. With the proliferation of mobile apps and game development on platforms like Android and iOS, OpenGL ES (a variant of OpenGL designed for embedded systems) remains a key tool in the development of graphics-heavy applications for these devices.

4. Rich Feature Set

OpenGL continues to be a highly versatile and feature-rich graphics API. It has evolved over the years to incorporate advanced rendering techniques, such as **physically-based rendering (PBR)**, **global illumination**, **real-time ray tracing**, and **high dynamic range (HDR)** imaging. These features have made OpenGL suitable for modern game development, high-end visualization, virtual reality (VR), and augmented reality (AR).

- **Shaders**: OpenGL's support for **vertex, fragment, geometry**, and **compute shaders** provides immense flexibility in how graphics are rendered. Developers can write custom shaders to achieve specific visual effects, such as lighting models, reflections, shadows, and texture mapping, all while controlling how the GPU handles computations.
- **Advanced Lighting and Effects**: OpenGL has a wide range of capabilities for implementing complex lighting effects, including **real-time lighting** (point, spot, and directional lights), **shadow mapping**, and **screen-space effects** like bloom and motion blur. These features enable developers to create photorealistic and immersive environments in games and simulations.
- **Compute Shaders**: OpenGL also supports **compute shaders**, which allow for general-purpose computation on the GPU. This capability

can be used for tasks such as physics simulations, image processing, and even artificial intelligence (AI) computations. Compute shaders provide significant performance benefits, allowing developers to offload complex computations to the GPU.

- **Real-Time Ray Tracing**: While traditionally associated with offline rendering, **real-time ray tracing** is a cutting-edge feature that OpenGL supports through extensions and integrations with modern hardware. This allows for more realistic lighting, reflections, and shadows in real-time, which is particularly beneficial for applications in VR and gaming.

5. OpenGL's Role in Education and Research

Because of its simplicity and its status as an industry-standard, OpenGL is widely used in **academic institutions** to teach computer graphics concepts. It provides an accessible entry point for students learning about 3D graphics and programming. The simplicity of OpenGL's core API allows students to focus on understanding graphics principles—such as rendering pipelines, transformations, and shaders—before delving into more complex graphics technologies.

OpenGL's role in education has also helped to establish a global community of developers who share their knowledge through forums, conferences, and open-source projects. This vibrant ecosystem fosters collaboration and the continual advancement of graphics programming as a whole.

In research, OpenGL is commonly used for scientific visualization, simulations, and data analysis. Researchers and engineers can create high-quality visualizations of complex data sets—such as molecular structures, geographic data, and fluid dynamics—using OpenGL's capabilities. OpenGL's efficiency in rendering real-time visual data makes it a valuable tool for many scientific and engineering disciplines.

6. OpenGL's Evolution: Towards Modern Graphics

While OpenGL's core functionality remains the same, it has continually evolved to meet the demands of modern graphics applications. Over the past two decades, OpenGL has undergone several revisions, introducing new features like programmable shaders, geometry shaders, tessellation, and multi-threaded rendering. These advancements have kept OpenGL relevant in the competitive world of graphics programming.

Additionally, OpenGL has adapted to support modern hardware architectures, offering tools and extensions to take full advantage of multi-core CPUs and high-performance GPUs. The introduction of **OpenGL 4.x** introduced key features like **tessellation shaders**, **transform feedback**, and **multi-sample anti-aliasing (MSAA)**, which further enhanced OpenGL's ability to handle complex 3D graphics.

While newer APIs like **Vulkan** and **DirectX 12** have emerged as low-level alternatives offering finer control over hardware, OpenGL remains a powerful choice for developers who prioritize ease of use and broad hardware compatibility. Its ability to abstract much of the complexity of modern graphics programming while still delivering high performance makes it ideal for many types of applications, from interactive media to scientific visualizations.

OpenGL vs. Other Graphics APIs (DirectX, Vulkan, Metal)

While OpenGL remains a popular choice for developers, it is not the only graphics API available. Over the years, several other APIs, such as **DirectX**, **Vulkan**, and **Metal**, have been introduced. Each of these has its own strengths and trade-offs, making them suitable for different kinds of applications, platforms, and hardware. Here, we will explore how OpenGL compares to these alternatives and why developers might still choose OpenGL over its competitors.

1. DirectX (Especially DirectX 12)

DirectX is a graphics API developed by Microsoft and is the standard for gaming on Windows PCs and Xbox consoles. DirectX was first released in 1995, and it has since evolved into a powerful, low-level API that provides developers with direct control over hardware resources and rendering pipelines. DirectX 12, the latest version, is known for its significant improvements over earlier versions, offering closer control over the GPU and better optimization for modern multi-core processors.

Comparison with OpenGL:

- **Platform Limitation**: One of the biggest differences between OpenGL and DirectX is that DirectX is exclusive to the Windows platform (and Xbox), while OpenGL is cross-platform, supporting Windows, macOS, Linux, and others. This makes OpenGL the better option for developers who need to target multiple platforms.
- **Performance**: DirectX 12 is designed for maximum performance and is considered by many to be a more efficient API than OpenGL, especially when it comes to low-level hardware control. It allows developers to take full advantage of modern GPUs and multi-core CPUs by minimizing CPU bottlenecks and enabling more parallel processing. For applications where performance is critical, such as AAA games, DirectX 12 might be the better choice, especially on Windows.
- **Ease of Use**: While DirectX 12 offers great power and flexibility, it is also more complex and difficult to learn than OpenGL. OpenGL has been around longer, and many developers are already familiar with it, making it easier to implement for projects that don't require the deep-level optimizations provided by DirectX 12. DirectX 12's API is lower-level and requires more effort from developers to manage memory, resources, and synchronization.
- **Market**: DirectX has a stronger foothold in the gaming market, particularly for PC and console games. For developers targeting Windows-based applications, particularly in the gaming industry, DirectX remains the dominant API. However, for cross-platform applications or applications aimed at multiple operating systems, OpenGL is often the better choice.

2. Vulkan

Vulkan, also developed by the Khronos Group (the same organization that maintains OpenGL), is a modern, low-level graphics API designed to give developers even more control over the hardware than OpenGL. It is positioned as a successor to OpenGL, offering higher performance and efficiency by providing low-level access to GPU hardware and allowing more direct control over memory management, multi-threading, and synchronization.

Comparison with OpenGL:

- **Performance and Efficiency**: Vulkan was specifically designed to offer lower CPU overhead and more efficient use of multi-core CPUs compared to OpenGL. Vulkan's architecture is more modern than OpenGL's, with better handling of multi-threading, reduced CPU bottlenecks, and better control over how commands are issued to the GPU. For performance-critical applications like high-end games or VR, Vulkan can often outperform OpenGL, particularly on multi-core systems.

- **Complexity**: While Vulkan offers many performance improvements over OpenGL, it comes at the cost of increased complexity. Vulkan is a lower-level API, which means developers must manage more aspects of memory allocation, synchronization, and resource management manually. This makes Vulkan more difficult to learn and use effectively compared to OpenGL, which abstracts away many of these complexities.

- **Cross-Platform Support**: Just like OpenGL, Vulkan is a cross-platform API that works on Windows, Linux, and macOS. Vulkan also supports mobile platforms, including Android, making it an appealing choice for developers who need to create applications that run on multiple devices and operating systems. However, Vulkan has not yet been integrated into as many platforms as OpenGL, which has a longer history of widespread adoption.

- **Adoption**: Vulkan is relatively new, and while it has been adopted by many AAA game studios and hardware manufacturers (particularly for modern gaming and VR applications), it has not yet reached the same level of support and maturity as OpenGL. For developers who need a well-established, tried-and-true API with a wealth of resources and documentation, OpenGL may still be the preferred option.

3. Metal

Metal is Apple's proprietary graphics API, designed for iOS, macOS, and other Apple platforms. It is a high-performance, low-level API that provides developers with direct access to the GPU and is optimized for Apple's hardware. Metal was introduced in 2014 as a more efficient alternative to OpenGL and OpenCL, which Apple had previously supported.

Comparison with OpenGL:

- **Platform Exclusivity**: One of the key differences between Metal and OpenGL is that Metal is exclusive to Apple platforms, including macOS, iOS, iPadOS, tvOS, and watchOS. This makes Metal an ideal choice for developers building applications specifically for Apple devices. OpenGL, on the other hand, is cross-platform, meaning that it can run on a variety of operating systems and hardware configurations, including non-Apple devices. For developers targeting only Apple devices, Metal may offer superior performance and features.
- **Performance**: Metal is designed to take full advantage of Apple's hardware, including their custom-built A-series chips and the latest M-series processors. Because Metal is tailored to the Apple ecosystem, it often delivers superior performance on Apple devices compared to OpenGL, which is more generalized. Metal provides more fine-grained control over GPU resources, multi-threading, and memory management, making it an excellent choice for high-performance applications on Apple devices.
- **Ease of Use**: While Metal offers high performance, it also requires more work from developers to manage resources and optimize their code for Apple's hardware. OpenGL, with its broad cross-platform support and more mature ecosystem, may still be preferred for cross-platform applications, or when a simpler, higher-level API is desired.

- **Adoption**: Metal has been the preferred graphics API for Apple's ecosystem since its introduction. As such, it is the go-to choice for iOS game development, augmented reality (AR) apps, and graphics-intensive applications targeting Apple platforms. However, for developers targeting multiple platforms (e.g., both Windows and macOS), OpenGL remains the more practical choice due to its platform-agnostic nature.

In the battle between OpenGL, DirectX, Vulkan, and Metal, each API has its own strengths and weaknesses, and the best choice depends on the specific needs of the project. OpenGL remains a popular and versatile choice because of its cross-platform support, extensive documentation, and maturity as an API. However, for developers targeting specific platforms, such as Windows or Apple devices, DirectX or Metal may offer advantages in terms of performance and optimization. Vulkan, while still relatively new, promises cutting-edge performance and efficiency, especially for multi-core CPUs, but it comes with added complexity.

Ultimately, the choice of graphics API should be guided by the project's platform requirements, performance needs, and the developer's familiarity with the technology. While newer APIs may offer better performance or more control, OpenGL's broad adoption, ease of use, and cross-platform support ensure that it will remain a valuable tool for graphics developers for years to come.

Setting Up Your Development Environment

Before diving into writing OpenGL code, it's essential to set up your development environment properly. OpenGL itself is just an API specification—it requires other libraries to work effectively in a modern development environment. These libraries help you interface with the GPU, manage windows and events, load graphics resources, and work with shaders and rendering pipelines.

In this section, we will cover the installation process of OpenGL and its commonly used supporting libraries: **GLFW** for window management and handling user input, and **GLEW** for managing OpenGL extensions. We will also walk through setting up your first basic OpenGL project, creating a simple window, and rendering a basic object, like a triangle, to get you started with OpenGL development.

Installing OpenGL and Related Libraries (GLFW, GLEW)

Setting up your environment can vary slightly depending on your operating system (Windows, macOS, or Linux). However, the process is generally similar across platforms. Let's break down the steps for each platform.

Windows Setup

Install a C++ Compiler and IDE: OpenGL development typically requires a C++ development environment. One of the most common and versatile options for C++ development on Windows is **Microsoft Visual Studio**. Visual Studio provides everything you need for compiling and debugging your OpenGL projects. It also integrates well with additional tools and libraries like GLFW and GLEW.

- Download and install Visual Studio (Community edition is free) from the official Microsoft website.
- During installation, ensure you select the **Desktop development with C++** workload to install the necessary compilers and libraries.

Install GLFW: GLFW is a library that provides an interface for creating windows, handling input (keyboard, mouse), and managing other window-related tasks. It is a lightweight, cross-platform library ideal for OpenGL applications.

- Download the GLFW binaries for Windows from the official GLFW website.
- After downloading, extract the contents and place them in an appropriate folder, such as C:\Libraries\GLFW.

Install GLEW: GLEW (OpenGL Extension Wrangler Library) is another library that helps with managing OpenGL extensions and provides easy access to newer OpenGL functionality.

- Download GLEW from the official website.
- Extract the files and copy them into a folder, for example, C:\Libraries\GLEW.
- You'll need to link to these libraries in your Visual Studio project to use them.

Set Up the Project in Visual Studio:

- Open Visual Studio and create a new **Console Application** project in C++.
- Add the GLFW and GLEW header files and library files to your project. To do this:
- Right-click on the project in the **Solution Explorer**, select **Properties**, and navigate to the **VC++ Directories** tab.
- Under **Include Directories**, add the path to the include folders for both GLFW and GLEW (e.g., C:\Libraries\GLFW\include).
- Under **Library Directories**, add the path to the lib folders for GLFW and GLEW (e.g., C:\Libraries\GLFW\lib).
- In the **Linker** settings, add the respective .lib files for GLFW and GLEW to the **Additional Dependencies** under **Input** (e.g., glfw3.lib, glew32.lib).

Test the Setup: After setting up your environment, it's time to test your configuration. A simple OpenGL program to create a window and render a colored triangle will help you confirm everything is working properly.

macOS Setup

Install Xcode: On macOS, you'll need to install **Xcode** to get the necessary development tools. You can download Xcode from the **App**

Store.

- After installing Xcode, open **Xcode** and go to **Preferences > Locations** to ensure the command-line tools are installed.

Install GLFW and GLEW: The easiest way to install GLFW and GLEW on macOS is by using **Homebrew**, a popular package manager for macOS.

- Install Homebrew by running the following command in the terminal:

bash

```
/bin/bash -c "$(curl -fsSL
https://raw.githubusercontent.com/Homebrew/install/HEAD/install.sh)"
```

- Once Homebrew is installed, run the following commands to install GLFW and GLEW:

bash

```
brew install glfw
brew install glew
```

Create the Project: You can use **Xcode** or **Terminal** with a text editor (like Sublime Text or VSCode) to set up your project. If you're using **Xcode**:

- Create a new **Command Line Tool** project in C++.
- Use **CMake** to manage dependencies or manually link GLFW and GLEW by adding the paths to the libraries in your Xcode project settings.

Test the Setup: Like on Windows, it's essential to test the installation by creating a simple OpenGL program that opens a window and renders a basic shape. OpenGL support on macOS can be tricky at times due to its reliance on **Metal** (Apple's proprietary graphics API). Therefore, make sure that you're using the correct OpenGL version compatible with your macOS version.

Linux Setup

Install Development Tools: On Linux, most distributions come with the necessary development tools, but you might need to install additional libraries and tools.

- On **Ubuntu** or **Debian-based** systems, run the following commands to install the tools:

```bash
sudo apt-get update
sudo apt-get install build-essential cmake libglfw3-dev
libglew-dev libglm-dev
```

Install GLFW and GLEW: If you don't want to rely on package managers like apt, you can manually install GLFW and GLEW by downloading the source code and compiling them from source.

- For **GLFW**:

```bash
sudo apt-get install libglfw3-dev
```

- For **GLEW**:

```bash
bash

sudo apt-get install libglew-dev
```

Create the Project:

- In your terminal, create a new directory for your OpenGL project and navigate into it:

```bash
bash

mkdir MyOpenGLProject
cd MyOpenGLProject
```

- Create your main.cpp file, where you will write your OpenGL code. You can also create a **CMakeLists.txt** file to handle compiling and linking dependencies.

Test the Setup: A simple OpenGL program that opens a window and renders a triangle will confirm that GLFW and GLEW are properly linked.

Setting Up Your First OpenGL Project

Once you have installed the necessary libraries, it's time to set up your first OpenGL project. Let's write a simple program that opens a window using GLFW, initializes OpenGL using GLEW, and renders a basic colored triangle.

Here's a basic example in **C++**:

```cpp
cpp
```

```cpp
#include <GL/glew.h>
#include <GLFW/glfw3.h>
#include <iostream>

// Function to initialize OpenGL
bool initOpenGL()
{
    // Initialize GLFW
    if (!glfwInit())
    {
        std::cerr << "GLFW initialization failed!" << std::endl;
        return false;
    }

    // Create a GLFW windowed mode window and its OpenGL context
    GLFWwindow* window = glfwCreateWindow(800, 600, "OpenGL
    Setup", nullptr, nullptr);
    if (!window)
    {
        std::cerr << "Failed to open GLFW window!" << std::endl;
        glfwTerminate();
        return false;
    }

    // Make the window's context current
    glfwMakeContextCurrent(window);
    glfwSwapInterval(1); // Enable vsync

    // Initialize GLEW
    if (glewInit() != GLEW_OK)
    {
        std::cerr << "GLEW initialization failed!" << std::endl;
        return false;
    }

    return true;
}

int main()
{
```

```
if (!initOpenGL())
{
    return -1;
}

// Rendering loop
while (!glfwWindowShouldClose(window))
{
    glClearColor(0.2f, 0.3f, 0.3f, 1.0f); // Set clear color
    glClear(GL_COLOR_BUFFER_BIT); // Clear the screen

    // Draw your objects here (like a triangle)

    glfwSwapBuffers(window); // Swap buffers
    glfwPollEvents(); // Poll for input events
}

glfwTerminate(); // Clean up and close the window
return 0;
}
```

In this code, we initialize GLFW to create a window, make an OpenGL context, and then initialize GLEW to handle OpenGL extensions. This is the basic structure for starting OpenGL applications, and you can build upon it to add more complex rendering.

By following these steps, you can set up your development environment to begin working with OpenGL, enabling you to create cross-platform, high-performance graphical applications. With GLFW handling window management and GLEW managing OpenGL extensions, you're now ready to start rendering 3D graphics and building more advanced OpenGL-based applications.

The Basics of 3D Graphics

Understanding 3D Graphics Fundamentals

At the heart of any 3D graphics application is the representation of objects and scenes in three-dimensional space. Unlike 2D graphics, where shapes are positioned along two axes (X and Y), 3D graphics operate in a world defined by three axes: **X**, **Y**, and **Z**. These axes represent the width, height, and depth of objects in the world. The challenge of 3D graphics is to take the complex mathematical concepts that define how objects move, interact, and are displayed in 3D space, and convert them into visually engaging scenes rendered on a 2D screen.

Understanding the basic principles of 3D graphics, including coordinate systems, transformations, and vector mathematics, is essential for anyone developing 3D applications, whether in games, simulations, or computer-aided design (CAD). In this section, we will break down the core concepts needed to understand 3D graphics and start working with them in OpenGL.

Coordinate Systems (World, View, and Screen Space)

In 3D graphics, objects exist in space, and how they are represented and transformed depends on different **coordinate systems**. Each system has a different purpose, and understanding the relationships between them is key to transforming and rendering objects correctly.

World Space: This is the "global" coordinate system, the ultimate 3D space in which all objects in your scene exist. In world space, every object, camera, light, and other elements have a position, orientation, and scale.

For example, the position of a tree in a 3D game world is defined in world coordinates, such as (x, y, z) relative to an origin point in the scene.

- In OpenGL, you usually define your 3D objects in world space. Once an object is created and placed in the world, its transformations (like rotation and translation) are applied in this coordinate system.
- The world space is global for all objects in the scene, meaning that objects can interact with each other based on their positions relative to each other in this shared coordinate space.

View Space (Camera Space): This is a local coordinate system used to represent the scene from the perspective of the camera. In the view space, the camera is typically treated as the origin (0, 0, 0) and looking down the negative Z-axis.

- When rendering a scene, OpenGL transforms each object from world space into view space. This transformation simulates the effect of the camera moving around the world and viewing different parts of the scene.
- The **view matrix** is used to represent this transformation. It moves the entire world into a view of the camera, ensuring that objects in the scene are correctly positioned relative to the camera's viewpoint.

Screen Space (Clip Space): This is the final stage of the rendering pipeline where 3D objects are mapped to a 2D screen. The objects in view space are projected onto a 2D surface (your screen), and their positions are converted to screen coordinates based on the resolution and aspect ratio of the display.

- The projection matrix is used to transform objects from view space to clip space. After projection, the coordinates are mapped to screen space, and a final transformation (often involving viewport adjustments) ensures that the objects are placed correctly on the screen.
- Objects are then clipped, and anything outside the viewing frustum

(the cone of vision of the camera) is discarded before rendering.

The relationship between these three spaces is crucial to understanding how 3D objects are rendered on the screen. The process flows from **world space** (defining the objects), to **view space** (transforming the objects based on the camera's position and orientation), and finally to **screen space** (where the objects are mapped to 2D coordinates for display).

Vectors, Matrices, and Transformations

The key to manipulating and transforming objects in 3D space is understanding **vectors**, **matrices**, and how they work together to perform operations like translation, scaling, and rotation.

Vectors: A vector is a mathematical object that describes a point or direction in space. In 3D graphics, vectors are used to represent positions, directions, and movement in the 3D world. A 3D vector typically has three components: (x, y, z).

- **Position Vectors**: These represent the location of a point in space. For example, a position vector of (3, 5, -2) places a point 3 units along the X-axis, 5 units along the Y-axis, and -2 units along the Z-axis (in front of the camera, assuming the camera looks down the negative Z-axis).
- **Direction Vectors**: These represent the direction of movement or orientation in space. They are often normalized to have a length of 1, which is called a unit vector. For example, a direction vector of (0, 1, 0) might represent a direction straight up along the Y-axis.

Matrices: Matrices are 4x4 arrays of numbers that are used to perform transformations in 3D space. They are particularly useful for handling multiple operations at once, such as rotating, scaling, and translating an object. In OpenGL, matrices are used to transform objects from one coordinate space to another (for example, from world space to view space).

23

- **Transformation Matrices**: These matrices allow us to apply various transformations to objects. For example:
- **Translation Matrix**: Moves an object from one position to another.
- **Scaling Matrix**: Resizes an object in space.
- **Rotation Matrix**: Rotates an object around a specific axis.

A matrix is applied to a vector (representing an object or a point) by multiplying the matrix with the vector. The result is a transformed vector.

- For example, a translation matrix might look like this:

```css
[ 1   0   0   tx ]
[ 0   1   0   ty ]
[ 0   0   1   tz ]
[ 0   0   0   1  ]
```

- This matrix translates an object by (tx, ty, tz) along the X, Y, and Z axes, respectively.
- **Homogeneous Coordinates**: In 3D graphics, we often use **homogeneous coordinates**, which extend the concept of 2D coordinates by adding an extra dimension. This allows matrices to represent translation operations, which aren't possible with just 3x3 matrices. Homogeneous coordinates are represented as (x, y, z, w), where w is usually set to 1 for positions in space.

Transformations (Translation, Scaling, and Rotation): Transformations are operations that change the position, size, or orientation of objects in 3D space. In OpenGL, these transformations are applied to the vertices of objects to position them within the world and to manipulate how they are displayed.

24

- **Translation**: This transformation shifts an object from one position to another without changing its shape or orientation. A translation matrix is used to apply a displacement vector to an object's coordinates.
- Example: Moving a cube by (2, 3, -5) shifts the cube 2 units along the X-axis, 3 units along the Y-axis, and -5 units along the Z-axis.
- **Scaling**: This transformation changes the size of an object, making it larger or smaller. A scaling matrix is applied to an object's vertices, scaling them along the X, Y, and Z axes.
- Example: Scaling a cube by (2, 2, 2) doubles the size of the cube in all three dimensions.
- **Rotation**: This transformation rotates an object around a specific axis (X, Y, or Z). Rotation matrices are used to rotate an object by a given angle around a specific axis.
- Example: Rotating an object by 45 degrees around the Y-axis can be represented by a rotation matrix that changes the object's orientation in space, but not its position.

These transformations are essential for manipulating objects in a 3D world. They are typically combined together to perform complex operations. For example, a 3D model of a car might first be scaled to its correct size, then rotated to face the camera, and finally translated to a new position in the world.

In OpenGL, these transformations are applied using **model, view, and projection matrices**:

- **Model Matrix**: Defines the transformation applied to an object in world space (translation, scaling, and rotation).
- **View Matrix**: Defines the camera's transformation, converting world space to view space.
- **Projection Matrix**: Converts view space to clip space, allowing 3D objects to be projected onto the 2D screen.

By combining these matrices in the correct order, you can manipulate and render complex 3D scenes in a consistent and predictable manner.

In summary, understanding these fundamental concepts—coordinate systems, vectors, matrices, and transformations—forms the foundation of working with 3D graphics in OpenGL. These principles enable you to define and manipulate the positions, sizes, and orientations of objects in a 3D world and are critical for creating immersive, interactive visual experiences. In the next sections of this book, we will explore how to implement these concepts in OpenGL and apply them to create engaging 3D applications.

Creating Your First OpenGL Program: A Simple Window and Triangle

Now that you have a fundamental understanding of 3D graphics concepts, it's time to jump into creating a simple OpenGL program. This example will involve setting up a basic OpenGL window using the **GLFW** library, and rendering a simple 2D triangle. This serves as the foundation for more complex projects, allowing you to build upon the basic window management and rendering process.

We will follow these steps:

1. **Set up the development environment** (covered in the previous chapter).
2. **Create an OpenGL context** using GLFW.
3. **Initialize GLEW** to access OpenGL extensions.
4. **Write a basic shader program**.
5. **Render a simple triangle** in the OpenGL window.

Let's go through each step in detail.

Step 1: Setting Up the Window with GLFW

To begin, we need to create an OpenGL window where our 3D scene will be rendered. This is done using the **GLFW** library, which provides functions to create windows and handle user input.

1. **Create a New Project**: Open your C++ IDE (such as Visual Studio or Code::Blocks) and create a new console application project.
2. **Include OpenGL and GLFW Libraries**: Make sure that you have added the appropriate header files for **GLFW** and **GLEW** to your project. As mentioned previously, you need to link to the library directories and add the respective .lib files to your project settings.
3. **Create the OpenGL Window**: The following code initializes GLFW, creates a window, and sets up a basic OpenGL context.

cpp

```cpp
#include <GLFW/glfw3.h>
#include <iostream>

// Window dimensions
const GLuint WIDTH = 800, HEIGHT = 600;

int main() {
    // Initialize GLFW
    if (!glfwInit()) {
        std::cerr << "GLFW Initialization Failed!" << std::endl;
        return -1;
    }

    // Create a windowed mode window and its OpenGL context
    GLFWwindow* window = glfwCreateWindow(WIDTH, HEIGHT, "First
    OpenGL Program", nullptr, nullptr);
    if (!window) {
        std::cerr << "Window Creation Failed!" << std::endl;
        glfwTerminate();
        return -1;
    }

    // Make the window's context current
    glfwMakeContextCurrent(window);

    // Main loop
```

```
while (!glfwWindowShouldClose(window)) {
    // Poll events
    glfwPollEvents();

    // Render here
    glClear(GL_COLOR_BUFFER_BIT); // Clear the screen to
    black

    // Swap buffers
    glfwSwapBuffers(window);
}

// Clean up
glfwDestroyWindow(window);
glfwTerminate();

return 0;
}
```

In this simple program, the following happens:

- **GLFW initialization**: Initializes the GLFW library to set up the environment.
- **Window creation**: Creates a window with a specific width and height and an OpenGL context.
- **Main loop**: The window remains open and responsive, polling for events (like keyboard and mouse inputs). Inside the loop, OpenGL commands to render the scene can be placed (e.g., clearing the screen).
- **Clean-up**: When the window is closed, GLFW is properly shut down to free up resources.

Step 2: Initializing GLEW

GLEW is used to access OpenGL extensions. It makes sure that you are able to use the latest OpenGL features, regardless of the version of OpenGL supported by the graphics card.

To initialize **GLEW**, add the following steps to the program after creating the OpenGL window:

Add GLEW Header: At the top of your program, include the GLEW header file:

cpp

```
#include <GL/glew.h>
```

Initialize GLEW: After calling glfwMakeContextCurrent(window), initialize GLEW to ensure that OpenGL functions are available. This should be done before calling any OpenGL functions:

cpp

```
if (glewInit() != GLEW_OK) {
    std::cerr << "GLEW Initialization Failed!" << std::endl;
    return -1;
}
```

GLEW checks whether the OpenGL functions can be loaded and ensures that the correct extensions are available for use.

Step 3: Creating Shaders

Shaders are small programs written in GLSL (OpenGL Shading Language) that run on the GPU. In this example, we will write two basic shaders: a **vertex shader** and a **fragment shader**.

Vertex Shader: The vertex shader processes each vertex of the triangle and performs transformations such as translation, scaling, and rotation.

cpp

```
const char* vertexShaderSource = R"(
    #version 330 core
    layout(location = 0) in vec3 position;
```

```
    void main() {
        gl_Position = vec4(position.x, position.y, position.z,
        1.0);
    }
)";
```

The vertex shader takes in the position of each vertex (position), and simply passes it to the next stage (gl_Position), which will be used in the next stage of the pipeline (the fragment shader).

Fragment Shader: The fragment shader determines the color of each pixel in the triangle.

cpp

```
const char* fragmentShaderSource = R"(
    #version 330 core
    out vec4 FragColor;
    void main() {
        FragColor = vec4(1.0f, 0.5f, 0.2f, 1.0f); // Set color
        to orange
    }
)";
```

This shader outputs a constant color (orange) for each pixel inside the triangle.

Step 4: Compiling and Linking Shaders

Next, you need to compile these shaders and link them into a shader program. Here's how you can do this:

Compile the Shaders:

cpp

```
GLuint vertexShader = glCreateShader(GL_VERTEX_SHADER);
glShaderSource(vertexShader, 1, &vertexShaderSource, nullptr);
```

```cpp
glCompileShader(vertexShader);

GLuint fragmentShader = glCreateShader(GL_FRAGMENT_SHADER);
glShaderSource(fragmentShader, 1, &fragmentShaderSource,
nullptr);
glCompileShader(fragmentShader);
```

Check for Compilation Errors:

You should always check if the shaders compiled successfully. If not, print out the error messages.

Link the Shaders into a Program:

cpp

```cpp
GLuint shaderProgram = glCreateProgram();
glAttachShader(shaderProgram, vertexShader);
glAttachShader(shaderProgram, fragmentShader);
glLinkProgram(shaderProgram);
```

1. **Clean Up**: After linking, the individual shaders can be deleted as they are no longer needed.

cpp

```cpp
glDeleteShader(vertexShader);
glDeleteShader(fragmentShader);
```

Step 5: Defining Vertices for the Triangle

We need to define the vertices for the triangle and upload them to the GPU.

cpp

```
GLfloat vertices[] = {
     0.0f,  0.5f, 0.0f,   // Top vertex
    -0.5f, -0.5f, 0.0f,   // Bottom left vertex
     0.5f, -0.5f, 0.0f    // Bottom right vertex
};
```

This array defines three vertices for a triangle, each with a position in 3D space (X, Y, Z).

Step 6: Rendering the Triangle

Now that everything is set up, it's time to render the triangle. Here's how you can do it inside the main loop:

cpp

```cpp
// Create a Vertex Array Object (VAO) and Vertex Buffer Object
(VBO)
GLuint VAO, VBO;
glGenVertexArrays(1, &VAO);
glGenBuffers(1, &VBO);

// Bind the VAO and VBO
glBindVertexArray(VAO);
glBindBuffer(GL_ARRAY_BUFFER, VBO);
glBufferData(GL_ARRAY_BUFFER, sizeof(vertices), vertices,
GL_STATIC_DRAW);

// Specify the vertex attributes
glVertexAttribPointer(0, 3, GL_FLOAT, GL_FALSE, 3 *
sizeof(GLfloat), (GLvoid*)0);
glEnableVertexAttribArray(0);

// Unbind the VAO
glBindVertexArray(0);
```

To render the triangle, use the following commands:

cpp

```cpp
// Use the shader program
glUseProgram(shaderProgram);

// Clear the screen
glClear(GL_COLOR_BUFFER_BIT);

// Draw the triangle
glBindVertexArray(VAO);
glDrawArrays(GL_TRIANGLES, 0, 3);

// Swap buffers
glfwSwapBuffers(window);
```

This code sets up the rendering pipeline, clears the screen, draws the triangle, and then swaps the buffer to display the results.

With these steps, you have successfully created your first OpenGL program that renders a triangle on the screen. This basic foundation opens the door for more complex 3D graphics programming, allowing you to create sophisticated scenes, manipulate objects, and implement real-time visual effects. As you move forward in this book, you'll continue building on this foundation to incorporate more advanced OpenGL features, including shaders, textures, lighting, and more.

Understanding the OpenGL Rendering Pipeline

The **OpenGL rendering pipeline** is a series of stages through which 3D data is processed and transformed into pixels that are rendered on the screen. It is a fundamental part of how OpenGL processes geometry and produces images. The pipeline involves transforming 3D vertices, applying shaders, and ultimately rendering them to a 2D viewport. Understanding the various stages of the pipeline will help you write more efficient and effective OpenGL code.

The OpenGL pipeline can be broken down into several key stages, each of which performs a specific function. These stages work in sequence, starting with raw 3D data (such as vertices) and ending with the final color output that will appear on the screen.

Below, we'll walk through each stage of the OpenGL pipeline and explain how they work.

1. Vertex Processing

The first step in the OpenGL pipeline is **vertex processing**, where the raw vertex data is taken and transformed into a form that can be further processed in the pipeline. This includes applying transformations (such as rotation, scaling, and translation), lighting calculations, and preparing data for the next stage.

- **Input**: The vertex data, which typically includes positions, normals, colors, and texture coordinates.
- **Transformation**: During vertex processing, various transformations are applied to the vertices. These transformations are performed using **model, view, and projection matrices**:
- **Model Transformation**: This moves vertices from object space (local coordinates) into world space.
- **View Transformation**: Converts world space into camera (view) space. The camera is treated as the origin of the scene in this space.
- **Projection Transformation**: Converts view space into clip space, where a perspective projection is applied to simulate the 3D depth.
- Shaders are commonly used in this stage, especially **vertex shaders**, which process each vertex's data before it moves to the next stage. A vertex shader is responsible for transforming vertex positions, calculating lighting, applying texture coordinates, and any other per-vertex calculations.
- **Example**: A vertex shader might apply the model-view-projection (MVP) matrix to each vertex, transforming the coordinates into clip space.

2. Clipping

Once the vertices are processed in view space and projected into clip space, the **clipping** stage occurs. In this stage, any geometry that falls outside of the **view frustum** (the cone of vision seen by the camera) is removed. This is necessary to avoid wasting processing resources on geometry that will never be seen in the final image.

- **Clip Space**: This is the coordinate system used to determine which geometry should be visible. The vertices that lie within the near and far planes of the camera's view are kept, while others are discarded.
- **Output**: The remaining vertices that are within the visible frustum are passed on to the next stage of the pipeline.

3. Rasterization

After clipping, the next stage in the OpenGL pipeline is **rasterization**, where the remaining primitives (such as triangles, lines, and points) are converted into fragments (potential pixels). This is where 3D data is first converted into 2D pixels for display on the screen.

- **Primitives**: Primitives are the basic building blocks of a scene (e.g., triangles, lines, and points). In OpenGL, triangles are the most common primitive used to represent 3D geometry.
- **Fragment**: A fragment is an intermediate data structure that contains information about the potential pixel: its position on the screen, color, depth, texture coordinates, and other attributes.

During rasterization, the geometry is "broken down" into a grid of fragments corresponding to the pixels on the screen. If a triangle covers several pixels on the screen, each pixel becomes a fragment, and the pipeline computes the color of each fragment.

4. Fragment Processing (Pixel Shader)

After rasterization, each fragment enters the **fragment processing** stage.

Here, the attributes of each fragment are used to calculate the final pixel color that will appear on the screen. This stage is where **fragment shaders** (also known as pixel shaders) come into play.

Fragment shaders are programs that operate on individual fragments and calculate their final color, which is then written to the framebuffer (the memory area where the final image is stored). Fragment shaders have access to data like texture maps, lighting information, and the results of earlier pipeline stages.

- **Inputs**: The fragment shader receives information from the vertex shader, such as the interpolated vertex data (position, color, normals, and texture coordinates) for each fragment.
- **Outputs**: The final color for each fragment, which will be written to the frame buffer. This is where operations like texturing, lighting, shading, and blending are applied.

For example, in a simple **phong shading model**, the fragment shader would compute the color of each fragment by using light sources and the normal at that fragment's position.

5. Depth and Stencil Testing

Before the final color is written to the framebuffer, OpenGL performs **depth testing** and **stencil testing** to ensure that fragments are drawn in the correct order and that visibility issues (like overlapping objects) are properly handled.

- **Depth Testing**: This ensures that fragments that are behind other geometry are not rendered. It compares the depth value of the current fragment to the depth value already stored in the depth buffer. If the current fragment is further away from the camera, it will be discarded.
- Depth testing is essential for ensuring proper object occlusion in a 3D scene. Without depth testing, objects could incorrectly appear in front of other objects, making the scene look incorrect.

- **Stencil Testing**: The stencil buffer is used for more advanced effects like shadows, masking, and reflections. Stencil tests can prevent certain areas of the screen from being drawn, depending on the stencil values.

6. Blending

Once the depth and stencil tests have been performed, **blending** takes place. Blending is the process of combining the color of the fragment with the color already stored in the framebuffer. This is particularly important for rendering transparent objects or achieving special effects.

For example, when rendering a semi-transparent object, the colors of the object and the background are blended together to create a final result. OpenGL allows you to control how this blending is done using various blending modes (e.g., additive blending, alpha blending).

- **Input**: The color of the fragment and the color already in the framebuffer.
- **Output**: The final color that is written to the framebuffer.

7. Final Output (Framebuffer)

The final output of the OpenGL pipeline is the image that is displayed on the screen. After the fragment is processed, blended, and passed through depth and stencil tests, the resulting color is written to the **framebuffer**, which stores the final pixel values for the image.

The framebuffer is a 2D array of pixels, and once all the fragments are processed and written to it, the image is sent to the screen for display. This is typically done by swapping the framebuffer with the one currently being displayed.

The OpenGL rendering pipeline is a complex, multi-stage process that converts 3D geometry into the final image shown on screen. By understanding each stage of the pipeline—vertex processing, clipping, rasterization, fragment processing, depth and stencil testing, blending, and final output—you can more effectively control how your 3D scene is rendered, optimize performance, and create realistic, visually stunning graphics.

In the next chapters, we'll dive deeper into the specific components of the OpenGL pipeline, such as shaders, textures, lighting models, and more, enabling you to create sophisticated 3D applications.

The OpenGL Graphics Pipeline

The **OpenGL graphics pipeline** is a series of stages through which the data that represents a 3D scene is processed and ultimately transformed into a 2D image that appears on the screen. The pipeline is designed to be flexible and efficient, allowing developers to create visually complex scenes while optimizing the performance of the underlying hardware.

The pipeline consists of several stages, each performing a specific operation on the data as it passes through. Understanding the flow of this data and the role of each stage is crucial for writing efficient and effective OpenGL programs. In this chapter, we will explore the major stages of the OpenGL pipeline, focusing on **Vertex Processing**, **Shading**, and **Rasterization**.

1. Vertex Processing

Vertex processing is the first step in the graphics pipeline, and it plays a vital role in transforming 3D models into something that can be rendered in a 2D space. The process begins with raw vertex data (points in 3D space) and applies transformations, lighting calculations, and other operations to position the vertices correctly in camera space and to prepare them for rasterization.

Key Concepts in Vertex Processing:

- **Vertex Shader**: The vertex shader is the heart of vertex processing. It is a programmable shader that processes each vertex individually. It takes the vertex attributes, such as position, color, normal, and texture coordinates, and applies transformations, lighting, and other effects. The primary operations performed by the vertex shader are:

- **Transformation**: The vertex position is typically transformed from model space (the object's local coordinate system) to world space, then to camera space (view space), and finally to clip space through a series of matrix multiplications (using the model, view, and projection matrices).

- **Lighting Calculations**: The vertex shader can also compute basic lighting effects, such as ambient, diffuse, and specular lighting, by using the vertex normal and light positions. This gives the vertices a realistic appearance by simulating how light interacts with the surfaces of the 3D models.

- **Texture Coordinates**: If the model uses textures, the vertex shader will pass texture coordinates to the fragment shader so that textures can be applied during rasterization.

- **Model, View, and Projection Matrices**:

- **Model Matrix**: This matrix transforms the object's local coordinates to world space, placing the object in the scene.

- **View Matrix**: Also known as the camera matrix, it transforms the world space coordinates to camera space, positioning the camera at the origin and orienting it to view the scene.

- **Projection Matrix**: The projection matrix transforms the coordinates from camera space into clip space, applying perspective or orthogonal projection to simulate depth.

At the end of vertex processing, each vertex has been transformed, and its attributes (such as color and texture coordinates) are ready to be passed to the next stage of the pipeline.

Example of a Vertex Shader:

```c

#version 330 core
```

```
layout(location = 0) in vec3 position;      // Vertex position
layout(location = 1) in vec3 color;         // Vertex color
layout(location = 2) in vec2 texCoord;      // Texture
coordinates

uniform mat4 model; // Model transformation matrix
uniform mat4 view;  // View transformation matrix
uniform mat4 projection; // Projection transformation matrix

out vec3 fragColor; // Color passed to fragment shader
out vec2 fragTexCoord; // Texture coordinates passed to fragment
shader

void main() {
    // Apply the model, view, and projection transformations
    gl_Position = projection * view * model * vec4(position,
    1.0);

    // Pass the color and texture coordinates to the fragment
    shader
    fragColor = color;
    fragTexCoord = texCoord;
}
```

In this shader, the vertex position is transformed using the model, view, and projection matrices, and the color and texture coordinates are passed along to the fragment shader for use in later stages.

2. Shading

Shading is the next key stage in the OpenGL pipeline, and it is where the appearance of each pixel is determined. After vertex processing, the graphics pipeline enters the **fragment shader** stage, where the lighting and color calculations are applied to individual fragments (potential pixels) before they are written to the frame buffer.

Key Concepts in Shading:

- **Fragment Shader**: The fragment shader is a programmable stage that processes each fragment (essentially a potential pixel) that is generated by rasterization. The fragment shader receives data from the vertex shader, such as transformed vertex positions, texture coordinates, and colors, and performs calculations to determine the final color and other attributes of each pixel.

- **Lighting**: One of the primary tasks of the fragment shader is to apply lighting calculations, which simulate how light interacts with the surface of 3D objects. Common types of lighting models used in fragment shaders include:
- **Phong Reflection Model**: This model calculates the color of a pixel based on ambient, diffuse, and specular lighting. It takes into account the light source's position, the surface normal, and the camera's position to create realistic lighting effects.
- **Blinn-Phong**: A variation of Phong that is often used for performance reasons, offering a more efficient way of calculating specular highlights.
- **Textures**: The fragment shader can also apply textures to the surface of objects. A texture is a 2D image that is mapped onto a 3D model to provide more detailed visual information. The fragment shader uses the texture coordinates passed from the vertex shader to fetch the corresponding pixel color from a texture.
- **Shadowing and Reflection**: Advanced techniques such as shadows, reflections, and refractions can also be calculated in the fragment shader. Shadows can be implemented through techniques such as **shadow mapping**, where the depth of each pixel is compared to a depth buffer to determine whether it is in shadow.

At the end of the shading stage, the fragment shader has computed the final color for each fragment, which is then passed to the next stage in the pipeline—**fragment operations** (also known as pixel operations).

Example of a Simple Fragment Shader:

```c

#version 330 core

in vec3 fragColor;      // Color passed from vertex shader
in vec2 fragTexCoord;   // Texture coordinates passed from
vertex shader

uniform sampler2D textureSampler; // Texture to be applied
out vec4 FragColor;     // Final color output

void main() {
    // Fetch the texture color from the texture map
    vec4 texColor = texture(textureSampler, fragTexCoord);

    // Combine texture color with the passed color
    FragColor = texColor * vec4(fragColor, 1.0);  // Simple
    texture and color blending
}
```

In this example, the fragment shader fetches a texture using texture coordinates and combines it with the vertex color. The final output is the pixel's color, which will be displayed on the screen.

3. Rasterization

Rasterization is the process where the geometry is transformed into fragments (potential pixels). This stage converts the geometric shapes (such as triangles) into pixels that can be displayed on the screen. Rasterization determines which pixels (fragments) will be affected by a particular primitive (e.g., a triangle) and interpolates the attributes for each pixel.

Key Concepts in Rasterization:

- **Primitives**: In OpenGL, the most common primitive is the triangle. Each triangle is defined by three vertices. When the GPU rasterizes a triangle, it determines which pixels (or fragments) are inside the triangle and generates the corresponding fragments.

- **Interpolation**: During rasterization, the attributes of the vertices—such as color, texture coordinates, and normals—are interpolated across the pixels inside the triangle. This means that for each fragment, the GPU computes the values for attributes based on the values of the vertices at the triangle's corners.
- **Depth and Stencil Testing**: Once the fragments are generated, they must be tested to ensure they are in the correct order (depth testing) and adhere to any stencil operations. For example, depth testing checks whether a fragment is closer to the camera than the current pixel in the frame buffer, discarding fragments that are behind others.

Example of Depth Testing:

When rendering a scene with multiple objects, depth testing ensures that the closest objects are visible while the farther ones are obscured. This test is usually performed after rasterization but before fragment coloring.

The **OpenGL graphics pipeline** is a highly optimized sequence of stages that transforms raw 3D data into a rendered image. By understanding the roles of **vertex processing**, **shading**, and **rasterization**, developers can gain a deeper appreciation for how OpenGL works and how to write more efficient shaders and rendering code. Each stage in the pipeline allows for customization, and by leveraging this flexibility, you can create stunning graphics and optimize performance across different platforms and hardware.

Detailed Breakdown of Each Pipeline Stage

In OpenGL, the rendering pipeline consists of several stages that each perform specific tasks on the data as it moves through. Each stage is programmable, allowing developers to control exactly how data is processed at every step, providing flexibility for achieving complex visual effects.

This section will break down each key stage of the OpenGL graphics pipeline in detail, focusing on **Vertex Processing**, **Shading**, **Rasterization**, and the final steps of **Drawing** and **Color Computation**.

Vertex Processing Stage

Vertex Processing is the first major stage in the pipeline. It involves taking raw vertex data and transforming it into a format that can be understood by subsequent stages. The most important part of this stage is the **vertex shader**, which is a programmable shader that handles the transformation of vertex data.

Vertex Shader Explained

The vertex shader processes each vertex individually, performing the following tasks:

Transformation: The primary job of the vertex shader is to apply various transformations to the vertex data. The transformations involve moving objects from one coordinate system to another (model space to world space, world space to view space, and view space to clip space).

- **Model Transformation**: This transformation applies to the object's position and takes the vertex from object space (local coordinates) to world space.
- **View Transformation**: The view transformation converts world space into camera space (or view space), where the camera is considered the origin of the world.
- **Projection Transformation**: The projection matrix transforms coordinates from camera space into **clip space**, applying a perspective to simulate depth and create the illusion of 3D space on a 2D screen.

Lighting Calculations: Basic lighting can be applied in the vertex shader, especially in simpler shading models like **Phong shading**. The vertex shader can calculate how light interacts with an object based on its normal vector and the position of light sources in the scene. The result of this can be passed to the fragment shader for further refinement.

45

Passing Data to the Fragment Shader: After transforming the vertex data, the vertex shader will pass it to the next stage, which is **fragment processing**. This includes passing along attributes such as the transformed position, texture coordinates, and any lighting or color information.

Setting Clip Space Coordinates: Once the transformations are complete, the vertex shader sets the **clip space coordinates** for each vertex. Clip space is a normalized coordinate system used by OpenGL to determine which parts of the scene are visible (i.e., inside the camera's view).

Example Vertex Shader Code:

```c
#version 330 core

layout(location = 0) in vec3 position;  // Vertex position
layout(location = 1) in vec3 color;     // Vertex color
layout(location = 2) in vec2 texCoord;  // Texture coordinates

uniform mat4 model;      // Model transformation matrix
uniform mat4 view;       // View transformation matrix
uniform mat4 projection; // Projection transformation matrix

out vec3 fragColor;  // Output to fragment shader
out vec2 fragTexCoord; // Texture coordinates to pass to
fragment shader

void main() {
    // Apply transformations
    gl_Position = projection * view * model * vec4(position,
    1.0);

    // Pass color and texture coordinates to fragment shader
    fragColor = color;
    fragTexCoord = texCoord;
}
```

Shading Stage: Vertex and Fragment Shaders

The **Shading** stage involves the **fragment shader**, which processes each fragment (potential pixel) generated by the rasterization stage. This shader determines the final color and properties of the pixels that will appear on the screen.

Fragment Shader Explained

The fragment shader, often called a **pixel shader**, is responsible for determining the color of individual pixels based on the interpolated attributes passed from the vertex shader. These attributes can include color, texture coordinates, and normal vectors. The fragment shader is executed for each fragment (potential pixel) that results from rasterization, and its output is written to the frame buffer.

Texture Mapping: The fragment shader can apply textures to the geometry by using texture coordinates that were passed from the vertex shader. It fetches the appropriate texture data using these coordinates and combines it with lighting and other attributes to generate the final pixel color.

Lighting: The fragment shader computes the lighting for each fragment, often using a lighting model like **Phong shading**. This model accounts for ambient, diffuse, and specular reflections:

- **Ambient**: The constant light that affects all surfaces equally.
- **Diffuse**: The light scattered in many directions after hitting a surface. It is based on the angle between the light source and the surface normal.
- **Specular**: The light that reflects off a surface in a shiny, concentrated direction, typically used to simulate highlights on shiny objects.

Transparency and Blending: If the object is partially transparent, the fragment shader can calculate the transparency of each pixel and combine it with the existing pixels in the frame buffer using a blending mode (e.g., alpha blending).

Post-Processing Effects: The fragment shader can also be used for various post-processing effects like bloom, motion blur, and depth of field, depending on the needs of the application.

Example Fragment Shader Code:

```c
#version 330 core

in vec3 fragColor;      // Color passed from vertex shader
in vec2 fragTexCoord;   // Texture coordinates passed from
vertex shader

uniform sampler2D textureSampler; // The texture to sample from
out vec4 FragColor;      // Final pixel color

void main() {
    // Fetch the texture color from the texture map
    vec4 texColor = texture(textureSampler, fragTexCoord);

    // Combine the texture color with the fragment color
    FragColor = texColor * vec4(fragColor, 1.0); // Simple color
    and texture blending
}
```

In this example, the fragment shader combines the color passed from the vertex shader with a texture, resulting in a final color for each pixel.

Rasterization Stage

Rasterization is the stage where the geometric primitives (such as triangles) are converted into fragments that correspond to individual pixels on the screen. It is one of the most critical stages of the pipeline, as it takes 3D geometry and projects it onto the 2D plane of the screen.

1. **Primitive Generation**: After the vertex shader, the geometric primitives (such as points, lines, or triangles) are formed from the transformed vertices. The most common primitive used in OpenGL

is the triangle, which is the building block for all other complex shapes in 3D rendering.

2. **Fragment Generation**: Each primitive generated during rasterization is broken down into fragments, which are potential pixels. The GPU determines which screen pixels are covered by the primitive and generates corresponding fragments for those pixels.

3. **Interpolation**: During rasterization, the vertex attributes—such as position, color, and texture coordinates—are interpolated across the fragments. This means that the vertex attributes of the triangle's three vertices are calculated at each fragment's position, based on their relative position within the triangle. This allows for smooth transitions between attributes like color and texture.

4. **Depth and Stencil Testing**: Rasterization also prepares the data for depth and stencil testing, which ensures that fragments are properly occluded (i.e., objects closer to the camera block those that are further away). These tests help ensure proper visibility of objects in the final rendered scene.

How OpenGL Handles Drawing and Color Computation

Once the fragment data has been generated and passed through the fragment shader, OpenGL performs the final operations to compute the final color values for each fragment and handle drawing operations. These operations ensure that the correct fragments are drawn and that the final output is accurate.

Color Computation:

- The **final color** for each fragment is computed by blending the fragment shader's output with the existing data in the frame buffer (if necessary). This can involve operations like alpha blending (for transparency), gamma correction, or other color adjustments depending on the settings in OpenGL.

- In a typical rendering pipeline, the computed fragment color is written to the frame buffer. The frame buffer is a memory area that holds the final pixel values for the image. Each fragment's color is stored in the appropriate location of the frame buffer based on its screen coordinates.

Depth Testing:

- Depth testing ensures that only the closest fragments are drawn. Each fragment has a depth value, which represents its distance from the camera. Depth testing compares this value with the depth of the existing fragment in the frame buffer, discarding the fragment if it is farther away from the camera than the existing fragment.

Stencil Testing:

- The stencil buffer is used to restrict drawing to specific areas of the screen. Stencil testing can be used for special effects like shadows, reflections, or masking parts of the scene. If a fragment passes the stencil test, it will proceed to the final color computation.

Blending:

- For transparent objects, OpenGL uses **blending** to combine the color of the incoming fragment with the color already in the frame buffer. The blending equation typically uses the alpha channel (opacity) to determine how much of the existing color and new color should contribute to the final output.

The OpenGL graphics pipeline is a powerful, flexible system that allows developers to control every stage of the rendering process. **Vertex processing** handles transformations and basic lighting, **shading** applies complex effects like texture mapping and advanced lighting, and **rasteri-**

zation converts geometry into fragments that are mapped to the screen. Understanding how each stage functions—and how they interconnect— empowers developers to create highly optimized and visually stunning 3D applications.

As you progress in your OpenGL journey, you'll work more intimately with each of these stages, learning how to leverage shaders, control blending modes, and optimize rendering to create rich, interactive graphics.

Understanding Shaders: From GLSL Basics to Advanced Techniques

Shaders are the backbone of modern computer graphics programming. These small programs run on the GPU and are responsible for determining how an object is rendered on the screen. OpenGL allows developers to write custom shaders, providing fine-grained control over the rendering process. At the core of this control is GLSL (OpenGL Shading Language), a high-level language designed for writing shaders.

In this section, we'll explore the fundamentals of shaders in OpenGL, beginning with the basic structure of GLSL and moving through to more advanced techniques like custom lighting models, post-processing effects, and optimization strategies.

Introduction to GLSL (OpenGL Shading Language)

GLSL is a C-like language designed specifically for writing shaders that execute on the GPU. GLSL is used to write both **vertex shaders** and **fragment shaders**, and more recently, **geometry shaders, tessellation shaders**, and **compute shaders**.

The basic syntax and structure of GLSL are similar to C, but with special functions and types designed for graphics programming. GLSL programs are executed in parallel on many GPU cores, which makes them incredibly efficient for rendering tasks.

GLSL Shader Types

OpenGL supports various shader types, each serving a different role in the graphics pipeline:

1. **Vertex Shaders**: These are responsible for transforming 3D vertex data into 2D coordinates that can be projected onto the screen. Vertex shaders also pass additional information to the fragment shader, such as color, normals, and texture coordinates.
2. **Fragment Shaders**: These handle the final color of each pixel. The fragment shader calculates lighting, applies textures, and decides the final color of each fragment based on various inputs.
3. **Geometry Shaders**: Geometry shaders are used to generate new geometry from existing primitives. They are not used as frequently as vertex and fragment shaders but can be helpful for creating things like point clouds, particle systems, or procedurally generated geometry.
4. **Tessellation Shaders**: These shaders are used for subdividing geometry into smaller patches. Tessellation can be used to improve the appearance of objects by dynamically adding detail based on distance from the camera or other criteria.
5. **Compute Shaders**: Compute shaders allow general-purpose computing on the GPU. While not directly related to the graphics pipeline, they can be used for complex computations like physics simulations, image processing, or any task that can be parallelized.

Each of these shaders is executed at a different stage in the OpenGL pipeline, and together they offer an immense amount of flexibility in creating sophisticated graphics effects.

Basic GLSL Syntax and Structure

A typical GLSL program consists of two primary components: **Shader Code** and **Uniforms/Attributes**.

Shader Code

Each shader in GLSL is written in a specific version of the language. For example:

```glsl
#version 330 core
```

This version directive specifies which version of GLSL is being used. OpenGL 3.3 or later is commonly used for modern graphics programming, and the version will define the available features and syntax.

Here's a basic example of a vertex shader:

```glsl
#version 330 core

layout(location = 0) in vec3 position;  // Vertex position input
layout(location = 1) in vec3 color;     // Color input

out vec3 fragColor;  // Output to fragment shader

uniform mat4 model;      // Model matrix for transformations
uniform mat4 view;       // View matrix (camera)
uniform mat4 projection; // Projection matrix

void main() {
    // Apply transformations
    gl_Position = projection * view * model * vec4(position,
    1.0);
    fragColor = color;  // Pass color to fragment shader
}
```

This vertex shader applies the model, view, and projection transformations to the input vertex position and passes the color data to the fragment shader.

And here's a simple fragment shader:

```glsl
```

```
#version 330 core

in vec3 fragColor;  // Color passed from the vertex shader
out vec4 FragColor;  // Final output color

void main() {
    FragColor = vec4(fragColor, 1.0);  // Set the output color
}
```

In the fragment shader, the output color is determined by the color passed from the vertex shader.

Advanced GLSL Techniques

After mastering the basics of GLSL, you can move on to more advanced techniques that enhance the visual quality and realism of your 3D scenes. Some of the most common advanced shader techniques include **custom lighting models, environment mapping, shadow mapping, post-processing effects**, and **optimization strategies**.

Custom Lighting Models

Lighting is one of the most important aspects of rendering realistic scenes, and GLSL allows you to create complex lighting models. One of the simplest and most common lighting models is **Phong shading**, which calculates lighting based on three main components:

1. **Ambient Light**: A constant light that affects all surfaces equally.
2. **Diffuse Light**: Light scattered in many directions after hitting a surface, dependent on the angle between the light source and the surface normal.
3. **Specular Reflection**: The light that reflects off a surface in a concentrated, shiny spot.

Here's a basic Phong lighting model implemented in GLSL:

```glsl
#version 330 core

in vec3 fragColor;
in vec3 fragNormal;
in vec3 fragPosition;
out vec4 FragColor;

uniform vec3 lightPosition;
uniform vec3 viewPosition;
uniform vec3 lightColor;
uniform vec3 objectColor;

void main() {
    // Normalize the normal and light direction
    vec3 norm = normalize(fragNormal);
    vec3 lightDir = normalize(lightPosition - fragPosition);
    vec3 viewDir = normalize(viewPosition - fragPosition);
    vec3 reflectDir = reflect(-lightDir, norm);

    // Ambient lighting
    vec3 ambient = 0.1 * lightColor;

    // Diffuse lighting
    float diff = max(dot(norm, lightDir), 0.0);
    vec3 diffuse = diff * lightColor;

    // Specular lighting
    float spec = pow(max(dot(viewDir, reflectDir), 0.0), 32.0);
    vec3 specular = spec * lightColor;

    // Combine the results
    vec3 result = (ambient + diffuse + specular) * objectColor;
    FragColor = vec4(result, 1.0);
}
```

This shader calculates lighting using the **ambient**, **diffuse**, and **specular** terms, with the result producing more realistic lighting effects. You can extend this model to support multiple light sources, shadows, and more advanced techniques.

Post-Processing Effects

Post-processing is the technique of applying effects to a scene after the initial rendering. These effects can add visual flair and realism, or they can simulate real-world phenomena like motion blur or bloom.

Some common post-processing effects include:

- **Bloom**: Adds a glowing effect to bright parts of the image, simulating overexposed light.
- **Motion Blur**: Creates a blur effect to simulate fast-moving objects.
- **Depth of Field**: Simulates the blur that occurs in the background or foreground when focusing on a specific object.
- **Tone Mapping**: Adjusts the contrast and brightness of an image to match the human eye's perception of light.

In OpenGL, post-processing is typically done in a **framebuffer**. The final scene is rendered to a texture, and then the texture is passed to a fragment shader where the effects are applied.

Here's a simple example of applying a bloom effect:

```glsl
#version 330 core

in vec2 fragTexCoord;
out vec4 FragColor;

uniform sampler2D sceneTexture; // The final scene texture

void main() {
    vec3 color = texture(sceneTexture, fragTexCoord).rgb;

    // Simple bloom: brighten the image
    color *= 1.5;  // Increase brightness
```

```
    FragColor = vec4(color, 1.0);
}
```

This fragment shader brightens the colors of the scene, simulating a bloom effect.

Optimization Techniques in GLSL

As powerful as shaders are, they can become a bottleneck in performance if not written efficiently. OpenGL allows you to harness the power of parallel processing on the GPU, but poorly written shaders can cause unnecessary computations. Here are some optimization tips:

1. **Avoid Redundant Computations**: If a calculation does not change across multiple fragments (e.g., the result of a transformation or lighting calculation), compute it in the vertex shader and pass the result to the fragment shader instead of recalculating it for every fragment.

2. **Minimize Texture Fetches**: Texture lookups can be slow, so avoid performing unnecessary texture fetches in your shaders. If possible, try to use a lower resolution for textures or use techniques like **texture atlases** to reduce the number of texture fetches.

3. **Use Early Z-Culling**: Depth tests can be performed early in the pipeline, discarding fragments that are behind other geometry. This can help improve performance by avoiding expensive fragment shader computations on fragments that won't be visible.

4. **Use GPU-specific Extensions**: OpenGL has many extensions and features tailored for specific GPUs that can help optimize performance. Use these where possible to take advantage of the hardware capabilities.

Shaders are a core component of modern 3D graphics, allowing for flexible and programmable control over the rendering process. From the basics of GLSL to advanced techniques like custom lighting models, post-processing effects, and optimization strategies, shaders unlock a wide range of possibilities for creating visually stunning graphics.

By mastering GLSL and understanding how to write efficient and powerful shaders, you can create everything from simple 3D games to complex simulations and visual effects. The key is to experiment, learn, and constantly push the limits of what's possible with shaders.

Transformations and Camera Setup

Introduction to Transformations (Translation, Rotation, Scaling)

In 3D graphics, transformations are the key operations that modify the position, orientation, and size of objects in the 3D space. These transformations allow us to manipulate objects, place them in the correct position relative to each other, and make them behave according to the scene's requirements. Without transformations, objects in a 3D scene would be static, and there would be no way to animate or interact with them.

Transformations are mathematically expressed using **matrices**, which are used to perform operations like **translation**, **rotation**, and **scaling**. These operations are fundamental to the creation of 3D graphics and are essential for virtually all graphical applications—from video games to simulations and visualizations. In this chapter, we'll delve into each of these transformation operations and explain how they are applied in OpenGL.

Understanding Transformations in 3D Graphics

In the context of 3D graphics, transformations modify the **model** or **world space** of objects. These operations are typically performed in a sequence to achieve the desired effect. To manipulate objects effectively in 3D, it's crucial to understand how objects are represented mathematically in space, which leads us to the concept of **transform matrices**.

A **transformation matrix** is a 4x4 matrix used to perform operations on objects' coordinates. These matrices can represent several transformations, including translation, rotation, and scaling, and are typically combined into a single matrix. When applied to the vertices of an object, these matrices alter their positions, orientations, and sizes.

Translation

Translation is the process of moving an object from one position to another in space. In a 3D coordinate system, this means adding a constant value to each coordinate of the object, effectively shifting it along the X, Y, and Z axes.

When an object is translated, its original coordinates $(x,y,z)(x, y, z)(x,y,z)$ are altered by a vector $(tx,ty,tz)(tx, ty, tz)(tx,ty,tz)$, which specifies the amount of movement along each axis. The translation is represented by the following transformation matrix:

$$T = \begin{pmatrix} 1 & 0 & 0 & tx \\ 0 & 1 & 0 & ty \\ 0 & 0 & 1 & tz \\ 0 & 0 & 0 & 1 \end{pmatrix}$$

Here:

- tx, ty, tz represent the amount of translation along the X, Y, and Z axes, respectively.
- The other values (except the bottom row) are set to 1s to preserve the object's orientation.

The translation matrix is then multiplied by the object's vertices to move them from one position to another.

Example: Translating a Cube

Let's say we have a cube at the position $(1,1,1)(1, 1, 1)(1,1,1)$, and we want to move it to the new position $(3,4,5)(3, 4, 5)(3,4,5)$. The translation vector is $(2,3,4)(2, 3, 4)(2,3,4)$. The matrix multiplication will shift each of the cube's vertices by this vector, and the object will now be in its new position.

Rotation

Rotation is the process of rotating an object around one of the three axes (X, Y, or Z). Rotation is essential for creating dynamic animations or for changing the orientation of objects. In 3D graphics, rotations are usually performed using **rotation matrices**.

There are three main types of rotations:

- **Rotation around the X-axis**
- **Rotation around the Y-axis**
- **Rotation around the Z-axis**

Each of these rotations has its own matrix, and applying them to an object rotates it by a given angle in space. Let's look at each of these rotation matrices in more detail.

Rotation Around the X-axis

A rotation around the X-axis changes the Y and Z coordinates of the object while leaving the X-coordinate unchanged. The rotation matrix for this operation is:

$$R_x(\theta) = \begin{pmatrix} 1 & 0 & 0 & 0 \\ 0 & \cos(\theta) & -\sin(\theta) & 0 \\ 0 & \sin(\theta) & \cos(\theta) & 0 \\ 0 & 0 & 0 & 1 \end{pmatrix}$$

Here, θ is the angle of rotation in radians. This matrix will rotate an object around the X-axis by the given angle.

Rotation Around the Y-axis

A rotation around the Y-axis changes the X and Z coordinates of the object while leaving the Y-coordinate unchanged. The rotation matrix for this operation is:

$$R_y(\theta) = \begin{pmatrix} \cos(\theta) & 0 & \sin(\theta) & 0 \\ 0 & 1 & 0 & 0 \\ -\sin(\theta) & 0 & \cos(\theta) & 0 \\ 0 & 0 & 0 & 1 \end{pmatrix}$$

Rotation Around the Z-axis

A rotation around the Z-axis affects the X and Y coordinates of the object while leaving the Z-coordinate unchanged. The rotation matrix for this operation is:

$$R_z(\theta) = \begin{pmatrix} \cos(\theta) & -\sin(\theta) & 0 & 0 \\ \sin(\theta) & \cos(\theta) & 0 & 0 \\ 0 & 0 & 1 & 0 \\ 0 & 0 & 0 & 1 \end{pmatrix}$$

Combining Rotations

In most cases, rotations are not limited to a single axis. Instead, you may need to apply rotations around multiple axes to achieve the desired effect. This is done by multiplying the individual rotation matrices in the correct order. Matrices are applied in a specific sequence, so the order of multiplication is important.

For example, to rotate an object first around the X-axis and then around the Y-axis, the combined transformation matrix would be the product of the rotation matrices:

$$R = R_y(\theta_y) \cdot R_x(\theta_x)$$

Scaling changes the size of an object, either by enlarging or shrinking it along one or more axes. Scaling is typically represented by a diagonal matrix, where the scaling factors for each axis are placed on the diagonal.

The scaling matrix looks like this:

$$S = \begin{pmatrix} sx & 0 & 0 & 0 \\ 0 & sy & 0 & 0 \\ 0 & 0 & sz & 0 \\ 0 & 0 & 0 & 1 \end{pmatrix}$$

Where:

- sx, sy, sz are the scaling factors for the X, Y, and Z axes.
- A value greater than 1 scales the object up, while a value between 0 and 1 scales it down.

Example: Scaling a Cube

Let's say we have a cube with a scaling factor of 2 along the X-axis, 0.5 along the Y-axis, and 1 along the Z-axis. The scaling matrix would be:

$$S = \begin{pmatrix} 2 & 0 & 0 & 0 \\ 0 & 0.5 & 0 & 0 \\ 0 & 0 & 1 & 0 \\ 0 & 0 & 0 & 1 \end{pmatrix}$$

This matrix would scale the object twice as large along the X-axis, half as small along the Y-axis, and leave the Z-axis unchanged.

Combining Transformations

In 3D graphics, transformations are typically combined to create complex effects. For instance, to move (translate) an object, rotate it, and then scale it, you would apply all three transformations in a specific order. Matrices are multiplied together to combine these transformations.

In OpenGL, transformations are often applied in this order:

1. **Scaling**: First, we scale the object.
2. **Rotation**: Next, we apply any rotation to the object.
3. **Translation**: Finally, we move the object to the desired location.

This combined transformation is then used to modify the object's vertices during rendering.

The order of these operations is critical. For example, scaling an object and then rotating it will yield a different result than rotating it first and then scaling it. The order of transformations must be carefully chosen based on the desired effect.

Understanding the fundamental transformations—translation, rotation, and scaling—is essential for creating dynamic and interactive 3D graphics. These transformations enable you to manipulate objects in space, create animations, and set up a 3D scene that behaves as expected. In OpenGL, transformations are applied using 4x4 matrices, and their power comes from the ability to combine them in a sequence. Mastery of these concepts is critical to building more complex systems, such as camera setups, animations, and even physics simulations, as you move forward with OpenGL development.

By applying transformations, you can move from a static, unanimated world to one filled with motion, perspective, and interactivity, laying the foundation for all subsequent visual experiences in 3D graphics.

Setting up and Controlling the Camera in OpenGL

As we discussed earlier, the camera in OpenGL is not a physical object like in real-world photography; instead, it's represented mathematically through **view** and **projection** matrices. These matrices define the viewpoint of the camera (where it is, where it's looking, and how the scene is projected onto the screen). In this section, we will explore in greater detail how to control camera movement and user interaction in OpenGL, as well as how to simulate navigation through a 3D world using the camera.

Using the Camera for 3D Scene Navigation

To allow users to navigate through a 3D scene, you need to control the movement of the camera in a way that feels intuitive and responsive. OpenGL does not provide built-in functions for direct camera control, so we rely on **camera transformations**—which are controlled by modifying the **view matrix**. We'll look into some basic camera movements, such as translating the camera (moving it through the scene), rotating it (changing the viewing angle), and zooming (changing the field of view). These transformations are mapped to user input, like keyboard or mouse actions, to provide interactive navigation.

1. Camera Translation (Moving the Camera)

Camera translation refers to moving the camera along the X, Y, and Z axes. In OpenGL, this can be achieved by adjusting the **eye** position in the **view matrix**.

For instance, if you want the camera to move forward, backward, left, or right, you'll modify the **eye** vector, which determines the position of the camera in world space.

Example of Camera Translation:

Let's say you want to move the camera forward by a certain amount. You can do this by subtracting from or adding to the **eye** position along the Z-axis (assuming the camera is moving along the Z-axis in the world space).

```cpp
// Forward and backward movement
float cameraSpeed = 0.05f;  // Speed of camera movement
if (moveForward) {
    eye.z -= cameraSpeed;  // Move the camera forward
}
if (moveBackward) {
    eye.z += cameraSpeed;  // Move the camera backward
}
```

Similarly, for left and right movement, you can adjust the **eye.x** or **eye.y** values:

```cpp
// Left and right movement
if (moveLeft) {
    eye.x -= cameraSpeed;  // Move the camera left
}
if (moveRight) {
    eye.x += cameraSpeed;  // Move the camera right
}
```

In a typical 3D navigation setup, the camera's movement might be controlled by user input, like arrow keys or WASD keys. You can map the movement of the camera to such keys to simulate intuitive 3D navigation, similar to how first-person shooters control their viewpoint.

2. Camera Rotation (Changing the View Direction)

In addition to translating the camera (moving it around the scene), you can also rotate it to change the direction in which it's looking. This is done by altering the **view matrix** to reflect a change in the camera's orientation, allowing it to "look" at different parts of the scene.

Rotation can be achieved using **quaternions** or **Euler angles** (pitch, yaw, and roll). However, for simplicity, we'll focus on rotating the camera with Euler angles, which represent rotations around the **X, Y,** and **Z** axes.

Example of Camera Rotation Using Euler Angles:

Let's assume you have two angles, yaw and pitch, that control the camera's rotation around the Y-axis (left/right) and X-axis (up/down), respectively. The rotation of the camera will update the **view matrix** to reflect the new orientation.

cpp

```cpp
float yaw = 0.0f;  // Rotation around Y-axis (left/right)
float pitch = 0.0f;  // Rotation around X-axis (up/down)

if (rotateLeft) {
    yaw -= 1.0f;  // Rotate left
}
if (rotateRight) {
    yaw += 1.0f;  // Rotate right
}
if (rotateUp) {
    pitch += 1.0f;  // Rotate up
}
if (rotateDown) {
    pitch -= 1.0f;  // Rotate down
}

// Recalculate the camera's direction vectors
glm::vec3 front;
front.x = cos(glm::radians(yaw)) * cos(glm::radians(pitch));
front.y = sin(glm::radians(pitch));
front.z = sin(glm::radians(yaw)) * cos(glm::radians(pitch));
cameraFront = glm::normalize(front);

// Recalculate the camera's view matrix
viewMatrix = glm::lookAt(cameraPos, cameraPos + cameraFront,
cameraUp);
```

In this example:

- **Yaw** controls the left-right rotation (turning the camera horizontally).
- **Pitch** controls the up-down rotation (tilting the camera vertically).
- We calculate the new direction (front vector) based on the yaw and pitch angles and update the **view matrix** accordingly.

You can map these rotations to mouse movements to create a more immersive experience. For example, moving the mouse horizontally could increase the yaw (left or right), and moving it vertically could change the pitch (up or down).

3. Zooming the Camera (Adjusting Field of View)

Zooming is another important aspect of camera control. In 3D graphics, zooming typically involves adjusting the **field of view (FoV)**, which determines how wide or narrow the camera's viewing angle is. A smaller FoV simulates a zoom-in effect, making objects appear closer, while a larger FoV simulates a zoom-out effect, making objects appear farther away.

In OpenGL, the **projection matrix** governs the FoV, and changing this matrix will allow you to zoom in or out. When the user scrolls the mouse wheel or presses a zoom button, you can update the **FoV** angle and recompute the **projection matrix**.

Example of Zooming:

Let's implement zooming by adjusting the **FoV** based on user input (such as scrolling the mouse wheel):

```cpp
float fov = 45.0f; // Default field of view

if (zoomIn) {
    fov -= 1.0f; // Decrease FoV to zoom in
}
if (zoomOut) {
    fov += 1.0f; // Increase FoV to zoom out
```

```cpp
}

// Constrain the FoV to prevent extreme values
if (fov < 1.0f) fov = 1.0f;
if (fov > 45.0f) fov = 45.0f;

// Recompute the projection matrix with the updated FoV
projection = glm::perspective(glm::radians(fov), aspect,
nearPlane, farPlane);
```

In this case:

- The **zoom** is controlled by adjusting the **FoV**.
- The new **projection matrix** is computed every time the **FoV** changes.
- We use glm::perspective to update the projection matrix and apply the zoom effect.

Combining Translation, Rotation, and Zoom for Full Navigation

In a typical 3D application, you'll want to combine **translation**, **rotation**, and **zoom** to allow users to fully navigate a 3D scene. For instance, you might use the WASD keys for translation, the mouse for rotation, and the scroll wheel for zooming. The following is a basic example of how these transformations can be combined for complete scene navigation:

cpp

```cpp
// Handle keyboard input for translation (WASD keys)
if (moveForward) eye += cameraSpeed * cameraFront;
if (moveBackward) eye -= cameraSpeed * cameraFront;
if (moveLeft) eye -= glm::normalize(glm::cross(cameraFront,
cameraUp)) * cameraSpeed;
if (moveRight) eye += glm::normalize(glm::cross(cameraFront,
cameraUp)) * cameraSpeed;

// Handle mouse movement for rotation
```

```
yaw += deltaX * sensitivity;
pitch -= deltaY * sensitivity; // Invert pitch if necessary
if (pitch > 89.0f) pitch = 89.0f;  // Prevent the camera from
flipping over
if (pitch < -89.0f) pitch = -89.0f;

// Update camera's front vector based on yaw and pitch
glm::vec3 front;
front.x = cos(glm::radians(yaw)) * cos(glm::radians(pitch));
front.y = sin(glm::radians(pitch));
front.z = sin(glm::radians(yaw)) * cos(glm::radians(pitch));
cameraFront = glm::normalize(front);

// Handle zoom input (mouse scroll)
if (zoomIn) fov -= 1.0f;
if (zoomOut) fov += 1.0f;
fov = glm::clamp(fov, 1.0f, 45.0f);

// Update view and projection matrices
viewMatrix = glm::lookAt(eye, eye + cameraFront, cameraUp);
projection = glm::perspective(glm::radians(fov), aspect,
nearPlane, farPlane);
```

In this example, the camera translation, rotation, and zoom all operate simultaneously, giving the user full control over the viewpoint. The **view matrix** (for positioning and orientation) and the **projection matrix** (for zooming and field of view) are both updated based on the user's input.

Setting up and controlling the camera in OpenGL is an essential part of developing 3D applications. By using transformations like translation, rotation, and zooming, you can provide users with intuitive navigation through the 3D space. While OpenGL doesn't have a built-in camera object, the flexibility of the **view** and **projection matrices** allows you to design camera systems that offer a rich user experience.

In this chapter, we've explored how to move and rotate the camera, how to zoom in and out, and how to integrate these controls to navigate through 3D scenes. These foundational concepts will serve as the basis for more complex camera systems and user interactions as we progress through this book.

Implementing a First-Person Camera Control System

A first-person camera control system provides users with an immersive experience by allowing them to move and look around in a 3D world just like they would in real life. In this section, we'll walk through how to implement a simple first-person camera control system in OpenGL. This will involve user inputs to control camera movements (forward, backward, strafe left/right) and look directions (mouse movement for yaw and pitch rotations). We'll use basic keyboard and mouse input handling to simulate the typical FPS camera system.

1. Overview of First-Person Camera Movement

In a typical first-person shooter (FPS) game or 3D simulation, the camera behaves as if the player is the camera, looking around and moving through the world. The camera is positioned at an eye-level perspective, and its movement is driven by input devices, like the keyboard (for movement) and the mouse (for rotation).

Key aspects of the first-person camera include:

- **Translation**: Moving the camera forward/backward and strafing left/right, controlled by the keyboard.
- **Rotation**: Changing the direction the camera is looking, controlled by the mouse's X and Y movements (yaw and pitch).
- **Zooming**: Optional, but it may be implemented by changing the camera's field of view (FoV).

In OpenGL, you would manipulate the **view matrix** to translate and rotate the camera, and use the **projection matrix** to adjust the zoom (FoV).

Let's break down the necessary steps to implement a first-person camera system.

2. Camera Translation: Moving the Camera

To move the camera forward, backward, or sideways, you will modify its position along the X, Y, and Z axes in world space. Typically, for a first-person camera, forward and backward movements are along the camera's view direction, while strafe movements are perpendicular to that direction.

- **Move Forward/Backward**: Move along the camera's "forward" direction (the vector the camera is looking at).
- **Strafe Left/Right**: Move along the camera's right direction (the perpendicular vector).

To implement this, you will use the **cameraFront** vector for forward/backward movement, and the **cameraRight** vector (which is the normalized cross product of **cameraFront** and **cameraUp**) for strafing.

```cpp
// Assuming camera position and movement variables have been
declared
glm::vec3 cameraPos = glm::vec3(0.0f, 0.0f, 3.0f);  // Camera
start position
glm::vec3 cameraFront = glm::vec3(0.0f, 0.0f, -1.0f); // Camera
front direction
glm::vec3 cameraUp = glm::vec3(0.0f, 1.0f, 0.0f);    // Camera
up direction
glm::vec3 cameraRight = glm::normalize(glm::cross(cameraFront,
cameraUp)); // Right direction
float cameraSpeed = 0.05f; // Movement speed

// Camera translation logic based on user input (WASD keys)
if (moveForward) cameraPos += cameraSpeed * cameraFront;
if (moveBackward) cameraPos -= cameraSpeed * cameraFront;
if (moveLeft) cameraPos -= cameraSpeed * cameraRight;
if (moveRight) cameraPos += cameraSpeed * cameraRight;
```

In this example:

- **moveForward** increases the camera's position along its front direction (i.e., moves the camera closer to the world's origin).
- **moveBackward** moves the camera in the opposite direction (away from the origin).
- **moveLeft** and **moveRight** allow strafing by modifying the camera's position along its right vector.

3. Camera Rotation: Looking Around

To rotate the camera (change the direction it's facing), we adjust the **yaw** and **pitch** values based on mouse movements. The yaw controls left/right movement, and pitch controls up/down movement. This rotation can be mapped to the mouse's X and Y movements.

- **Yaw**: Rotating the camera left or right around the Y-axis.
- **Pitch**: Rotating the camera up or down around the X-axis.

We need to prevent the camera from rotating too far up or down (i.e., to avoid flipping upside down), so we limit the **pitch** between -89° and +89°.

```cpp
// Yaw and pitch angles to control the rotation
float yaw = -90.0f;  // Initial yaw (camera starts looking
straight ahead)
float pitch = 0.0f;  // Initial pitch (camera starts level)

// Camera rotation based on mouse movement
float sensitivity = 0.1f; // Sensitivity of mouse movement

// Calculate the new cameraFront based on yaw and pitch
yaw += deltaX * sensitivity;  // X movement of the mouse affects
yaw
pitch -= deltaY * sensitivity; // Y movement of the mouse
affects pitch
```

```
// Clamp pitch to prevent the camera from flipping upside down
if (pitch > 89.0f) pitch = 89.0f;
if (pitch < -89.0f) pitch = -89.0f;

// Calculate new cameraFront vector based on updated yaw and
pitch
glm::vec3 front;
front.x = cos(glm::radians(yaw)) * cos(glm::radians(pitch));
front.y = sin(glm::radians(pitch));
front.z = sin(glm::radians(yaw)) * cos(glm::radians(pitch));

// Normalize the front vector to avoid scaling issues
cameraFront = glm::normalize(front);

// Update view matrix with the new camera position and direction
viewMatrix = glm::lookAt(cameraPos, cameraPos + cameraFront,
cameraUp);
```

Here, we calculate the **cameraFront** vector based on the **yaw** and **pitch** angles. As the user moves the mouse, the yaw and pitch values change, updating the **cameraFront** direction. The **lookAt** function is then used to recompute the **view matrix**.

4. Zooming: Adjusting the Field of View (FoV)

Zooming is implemented by changing the **field of view** (FoV) of the camera. This controls how much of the scene is visible at any given time. In FPS games, zooming is often used to simulate the effect of looking through a scope or camera lens.

You can zoom in by decreasing the **FoV** (making things appear closer) or zoom out by increasing the **FoV** (making things appear farther).

cpp

```
// Default field of view
float fov = 45.0f;
```

```
// Adjust the FoV based on mouse wheel scroll or other input
if (zoomIn) fov -= 1.0f;  // Zoom in
if (zoomOut) fov += 1.0f; // Zoom out

// Limit the FoV to avoid extreme values
fov = glm::clamp(fov, 1.0f, 45.0f);

// Update the projection matrix with the new FoV
projection = glm::perspective(glm::radians(fov), aspectRatio,
nearPlane, farPlane);
```

The **projection matrix** is updated every time the **FoV** changes, adjusting how much of the scene is visible in the camera's view.

5. Handling User Input

In a first-person camera control system, you need to handle user input from the keyboard and mouse. For keyboard input (WASD keys for movement), you would capture key presses and adjust the camera position accordingly. For mouse input, you need to track mouse movement to rotate the camera and possibly mouse scroll for zooming.

In **GLFW** (or other libraries), you can use the following functions for input handling:

- glfwSetCursorPosCallback(): Tracks mouse movement to change the yaw and pitch.
- glfwGetKey(): Checks for key presses like WASD to move the camera.
- glfwSetScrollCallback(): Adjusts the **FoV** when the mouse wheel is scrolled.

6. Putting It All Together

Here's a basic example that combines all of the concepts we've discussed for a first-person camera system in OpenGL:

cpp

```cpp
// Camera input and movement
if (glfwGetKey(window, GLFW_KEY_W) == GLFW_PRESS) moveForward =
true;
if (glfwGetKey(window, GLFW_KEY_S) == GLFW_PRESS) moveBackward =
true;
if (glfwGetKey(window, GLFW_KEY_A) == GLFW_PRESS) moveLeft =
true;
if (glfwGetKey(window, GLFW_KEY_D) == GLFW_PRESS) moveRight =
true;

// Mouse input for rotation
glfwGetCursorPos(window, &lastX, &lastY);
deltaX = lastX - mouseX;
deltaY = lastY - mouseY;
lastX = mouseX;
lastY = mouseY;

if (glfwGetKey(window, GLFW_KEY_SPACE) == GLFW_PRESS) zoomIn =
true;
if (glfwGetKey(window, GLFW_KEY_LEFT_SHIFT) == GLFW_PRESS)
zoomOut = true;

// Update camera position, rotation, and zoom
updateCamera();
```

In this example:

- We check for keyboard input (WASD keys) to translate the camera.
- We capture mouse movement to update yaw and pitch.
- We adjust the **FoV** when the user zooms in or out.

This setup allows users to move around and look around a 3D scene with smooth, interactive controls, typical of first-person navigation in games or simulations.

Implementing a first-person camera system in OpenGL is a critical part of creating immersive 3D environments. By using transformations, controlling the camera's view matrix, and updating the projection matrix, you can simulate realistic navigation through 3D spaces. Whether you're building a game, a simulation, or any other interactive application, the first-person camera system is a core component that enriches the user experience. As you continue with this book, you will learn how to optimize and extend the camera system to handle more complex scenarios, such as adding collision detection, custom camera movements, and integration with other parts of your rendering pipeline.

Debugging Common Errors in Transformations

Transformations are one of the most fundamental components in any 3D graphics application, and they can often be the source of frustration when things don't appear as expected. Whether it's a translation error that causes objects to appear in the wrong place, or an unexpected rotation behavior, debugging transformation issues is a key skill for any OpenGL developer. In this section, we'll explore some common errors related to transformations and provide strategies for identifying and fixing them.

1. Incorrect Object Positioning (Translation Issues)

One of the most frequent issues when working with transformations is incorrect object positioning. This happens when an object doesn't appear where you expect it to in the world space. The root cause of such problems is usually related to the way the **model matrix** is set up or applied.

Common Causes:

- **Using incorrect translation values**: If the translation vector is not set properly, the object might appear off-screen or in an unexpected location.

- **Incorrect use of the model matrix**: When creating the model matrix for an object, you might have missed applying the correct translation order or neglected to multiply matrices properly.

Solutions:

- **Check the translation vector**: Ensure that the translation values are appropriate for the scene. For instance, an object might appear off-screen if it's placed outside the visible region of the camera's view frustum.

cpp

```cpp
glm::mat4 model = glm::mat4(1.0f);
// Correct translation
model = glm::translate(model, glm::vec3(2.0f, 0.0f, -5.0f));
```

- **Review matrix multiplication order**: When applying transformations, the order of matrix multiplication is crucial. OpenGL applies transformations in a specific order (model → view → projection). Ensure that your transformations are applied in the right order for the desired effect.

cpp

```cpp
// Apply transformations in the correct order
glm::mat4 model = glm::translate(glm::mat4(1.0f),
glm::vec3(2.0f, 0.0f, -5.0f));
glm::mat4 view = glm::lookAt(cameraPos, cameraPos + cameraFront,
cameraUp);
glm::mat4 projection = glm::perspective(glm::radians(fov),
aspectRatio, nearPlane, farPlane);

// Apply the correct transformation hierarchy
```

```
glm::mat4 mvp = projection * view * model;
```

- **Debugging Tip**: Add debug logging or visual markers at key points in the pipeline. For instance, after each transformation step, log the resulting model matrix to the console or use simple shapes (like a colored cube) to visualize the object at intermediate stages.

2. Unexpected Rotation Behavior

Rotation is another area where errors are common. It can be difficult to ensure the object is rotating around the correct axis or in the expected direction. Incorrect rotation behavior can manifest as objects spinning wildly or rotating in unintended ways.

Common Causes:

- **Wrong axis of rotation**: A common issue when working with rotation is misunderstanding which axis the object is rotating around.
- **Matrix multiplication order**: As with translation, the order in which you apply rotations can impact the final result. This is especially true if you're rotating an object in multiple axes.

Solutions:

- **Check the axis of rotation**: When rotating an object, ensure that the axis is specified correctly. In OpenGL, the rotation matrix is created with the glm::rotate function. The axis vector should be normalized, and it should correctly represent the direction around which you want to rotate.

cpp

COMPUTER GRAPHICS WITH OPENGL

```cpp
glm::mat4 model = glm::mat4(1.0f);
// Correct rotation around Y-axis
model = glm::rotate(model, glm::radians(45.0f), glm::vec3(0.0f,
1.0f, 0.0f));
```

- **Use multiple rotations carefully**: If applying multiple rotations, be mindful of the order. OpenGL applies transformations in the reverse order they are provided, meaning if you first rotate an object around the Z-axis and then the X-axis, it will rotate around the X-axis with respect to the rotated Z position.

cpp

```cpp
// Rotation order can cause unexpected results
glm::mat4 model = glm::mat4(1.0f);
model = glm::rotate(model, glm::radians(30.0f), glm::vec3(0.0f,
0.0f, 1.0f)); // Z-axis
model = glm::rotate(model, glm::radians(45.0f), glm::vec3(1.0f,
0.0f, 0.0f)); // X-axis
```

- **Debugging Tip**: To verify the behavior of your rotations, visualize the object from different angles using the camera and debug the orientation visually. If the rotation is still incorrect, try simplifying the transformation chain by rotating along one axis first to isolate the issue.

3. Scaling Issues

Scaling can be tricky, especially when it leads to unexpected object stretching or shrinking. These issues are often caused by incorrect scale values, either too large or too small, or by applying non-uniform scaling unintentionally.

Common Causes:

- **Using uniform vs. non-uniform scaling**: Uniform scaling scales an object equally in all directions, while non-uniform scaling can stretch the object disproportionately.
- **Negative scaling factors**: If negative scaling values are used, objects may be flipped or mirror-imaged in ways that are not intended.

Solutions:

- **Verify the scaling factors**: Ensure that the scaling factors are positive and correctly represent the desired scale. Uniform scaling requires equal scaling factors in all axes, while non-uniform scaling allows for different factors for each axis.

cpp

```
glm::mat4 model = glm::mat4(1.0f);
// Correct uniform scaling
model = glm::scale(model, glm::vec3(2.0f, 2.0f, 2.0f)); //
Uniform scaling

// Non-uniform scaling
model = glm::scale(model, glm::vec3(2.0f, 1.0f, 1.0f)); //
Stretch only along X-axis
```

- **Debugging Tip**: If an object appears flipped or distorted, check for negative scaling values in the model matrix. If applying non-uniform scaling, verify that each axis is scaled as expected.

4. Gimbal Lock in Rotations

Gimbal lock occurs when you lose one degree of freedom in a 3D rotation system. This happens when two of the rotation axes align, and it can cause

unpredictable behavior, especially when using Euler angles for rotations.
Common Causes:

- **Using Euler angles for rotation**: When applying rotations using Euler angles, gimbal lock can occur if two axes of rotation become aligned. This is especially problematic in complex animations or camera systems.

Solutions:

- **Use quaternions instead of Euler angles**: Quaternions are a more robust way to represent rotations in 3D space and avoid gimbal lock. While they are more complex to understand initially, they offer smooth, continuous rotations without the issues of gimbal lock.

cpp

```cpp
glm::quat rotation = glm::quat(glm::vec3(glm::radians(30.0f),
glm::radians(45.0f), 0.0f));
glm::mat4 model = glm::mat4_cast(rotation);
```

- **Debugging Tip**: If you notice erratic rotation behavior, especially when rotating through multiple axes, try switching to quaternions. This will help maintain smooth and predictable rotations.

5. Transformation Pipeline Debugging

When working with transformations in OpenGL, it is crucial to remember that the entire pipeline (model → view → projection) works together. If any of these steps are incorrect or out of order, your scene might not render as expected.
Common Causes:

- **Incorrect view matrix setup**: If the camera's position or orientation is wrong, the entire scene can appear from an unintended perspective, making it seem like transformations are incorrect.
- **Projection matrix misalignment**: A misconfigured projection matrix (for example, using an incorrect near/far plane or field of view) can distort the scene and make objects appear far too small or too large.

Solutions:

- **Review the transformation chain**: Always double-check the matrix multiplications. Ensure that you are applying the correct transformation hierarchy: model matrix → view matrix → projection matrix.
- **Verify the camera setup**: Confirm that your camera's position, up vector, and direction vectors are correctly defined and updated.

cpp

```cpp
// Correctly apply transformations in order
glm::mat4 model = glm::mat4(1.0f);  // Identity matrix
model = glm::translate(model, glm::vec3(2.0f, 0.0f, -5.0f)); //
Apply translation

glm::mat4 view = glm::lookAt(cameraPos, cameraPos + cameraFront,
cameraUp); // View matrix
glm::mat4 projection = glm::perspective(glm::radians(fov),
aspectRatio, nearPlane, farPlane); // Projection matrix

// Final transformation matrix
glm::mat4 mvp = projection * view * model;
```

- **Debugging Tip**: Visualize each transformation step. Render objects with simple colors or in wireframe mode to make sure the transformations are applied correctly at each stage.

Debugging transformations is a key part of mastering OpenGL and 3D graphics programming. By methodically checking each transformation step, ensuring the correct order of operations, and using appropriate debugging tools, you can identify and fix errors quickly. Understanding how translation, rotation, and scaling interact within the graphics pipeline will lead to a more efficient and accurate rendering process. As you continue to develop more complex 3D scenes, mastering these debugging techniques will save you time and frustration.

Drawing and Manipulating 3D Objects

Creating and drawing 3D objects is one of the foundational tasks in computer graphics, and OpenGL provides the tools needed to manipulate basic shapes such as cubes, spheres, and pyramids. These fundamental geometric shapes form the building blocks for more complex objects, and understanding how to efficiently render and manipulate them is essential for any 3D graphics developer. In this chapter, we will cover the process of creating, drawing, and transforming basic 3D shapes in OpenGL. By the end of this section, you'll be equipped with the skills to render 3D shapes and transform them for use in games, simulations, and other graphical applications.

1. Introduction to Basic 3D Shapes

In 3D graphics, objects are often modeled by combining simple geometric shapes. The most common of these are cubes, spheres, and pyramids. Each of these shapes can be described mathematically and rendered using OpenGL's pipeline. Understanding how to draw and manipulate these shapes is a fundamental skill that lays the groundwork for more advanced techniques such as texturing, lighting, and animation.

We'll break down the process of creating each of these shapes, starting from their mathematical descriptions to how we can use OpenGL to render them. These basic shapes are often used as primitives to build complex 3D models by combining them or transforming them into more elaborate forms.

2. Drawing a Cube in OpenGL

The cube, or rectangular prism, is one of the simplest 3D shapes and is widely used in 3D graphics. In OpenGL, a cube can be represented by six faces, each with four vertices, and each vertex having a position in 3D space. A cube's vertices can be defined explicitly and passed into OpenGL as a vertex buffer, which is then drawn to the screen using OpenGL's rendering pipeline.

Creating the Cube Vertices

A cube has 8 unique vertices, but these vertices are shared by multiple faces, so the total number of vertices required for the cube is 36 (6 faces × 2 triangles per face × 3 vertices per triangle). Here's how we can define the vertices for a cube:

cpp

```cpp
GLfloat vertices[] = {
    // Positions
    -0.5f, -0.5f, -0.5f,  // 0
     0.5f, -0.5f, -0.5f,  // 1
     0.5f,  0.5f, -0.5f,  // 2
    -0.5f,  0.5f, -0.5f,  // 3
    -0.5f, -0.5f,  0.5f,  // 4
     0.5f, -0.5f,  0.5f,  // 5
     0.5f,  0.5f,  0.5f,  // 6
    -0.5f,  0.5f,  0.5f,  // 7
};

// Indices to draw 2 triangles for each face
GLuint indices[] = {
    0, 1, 2, 2, 3, 0,    // Bottom
    4, 5, 6, 6, 7, 4,    // Top
    0, 1, 5, 5, 4, 0,    // Front
    2, 3, 7, 7, 6, 2,    // Back
    1, 2, 6, 6, 5, 1,    // Right
    0, 3, 7, 7, 4, 0     // Left
};
```

Rendering the Cube

Once the vertices are defined, we can upload them to the GPU using a Vertex Buffer Object (VBO), and an Element Buffer Object (EBO) for the indices, which represent how the vertices should be connected to form triangles. Here's a basic example of setting up the cube for rendering:

cpp

```cpp
GLuint VBO, VAO, EBO;
glGenVertexArrays(1, &VAO);
glGenBuffers(1, &VBO);
glGenBuffers(1, &EBO);

glBindVertexArray(VAO);

glBindBuffer(GL_ARRAY_BUFFER, VBO);
glBufferData(GL_ARRAY_BUFFER, sizeof(vertices), vertices,
GL_STATIC_DRAW);

glBindBuffer(GL_ELEMENT_ARRAY_BUFFER, EBO);
glBufferData(GL_ELEMENT_ARRAY_BUFFER, sizeof(indices), indices,
GL_STATIC_DRAW);

glVertexAttribPointer(0, 3, GL_FLOAT, GL_FALSE, 3 *
sizeof(GLfloat), (GLvoid*)0);
glEnableVertexAttribArray(0);

glBindBuffer(GL_ARRAY_BUFFER, 0);
glBindVertexArray(0);
```

Rendering Loop

To render the cube, simply call glDrawElements() within the render loop:

cpp

```cpp
glUseProgram(shaderProgram);
glBindVertexArray(VAO);
glDrawElements(GL_TRIANGLES, 36, GL_UNSIGNED_INT, 0);
```

```
glBindVertexArray(0);
```

3. Drawing a Sphere in OpenGL

A sphere is a more complex shape than a cube, and representing it mathematically requires a bit more work. A common method for rendering spheres is to use **parametric equations** or to build a sphere from **latitude-longitude lines** (similar to how a globe is divided). We can generate a sphere using the **UV Sphere** approach.

Generating Sphere Vertices

A UV sphere is constructed by parametrically creating vertices based on the angles θ (theta) and φ (phi) that traverse latitude and longitude lines, respectively.

```cpp
// Number of segments and rings for the sphere
int stacks = 20; // latitude lines
int sectors = 20; // longitude lines

float radius = 1.0f;
std::vector<GLfloat> vertices;

// Generate vertices based on spherical coordinates
for (int i = 0; i <= stacks; ++i) {
    float stackAngle = glm::pi<float>() * i / stacks; // from 0
    to pi
    float xy = radius * sin(stackAngle); // x and y scale
    float z = radius * cos(stackAngle); // z coordinate

    for (int j = 0; j <= sectors; ++j) {
        float sectorAngle = 2 * glm::pi<float>() * j / sectors;
        // from 0 to 2*pi
        float x = xy * cos(sectorAngle); // x position
        float y = xy * sin(sectorAngle); // y position

        vertices.push_back(x);
```

```cpp
        vertices.push_back(y);
        vertices.push_back(z);
    }
}
```

Creating Indexes for Sphere

Just like with the cube, the sphere's surface is made up of triangles. After generating the vertices, we can calculate the appropriate indices to form these triangles.

4. Drawing a Pyramid in OpenGL

A pyramid is another simple 3D shape consisting of a square base and four triangular faces. It can be represented using a small number of vertices, just like the cube. A basic pyramid has 5 vertices: one at the apex and four at the corners of the base.

Creating Pyramid Vertices

cpp

```cpp
GLfloat pyramidVertices[] = {
    // Positions
     0.0f,  0.5f,  0.0f, // Apex (Top)
    -0.5f, -0.5f,  0.5f, // Base front-left
     0.5f, -0.5f,  0.5f, // Base front-right
     0.5f, -0.5f, -0.5f, // Base back-right
    -0.5f, -0.5f, -0.5f  // Base back-left
};
```

Drawing the Pyramid

To draw the pyramid, we can similarly create a vertex buffer and index buffer, ensuring the indices are set correctly for the faces of the pyramid. The pyramid can be rendered as a collection of triangles using glDrawElements().

5. Manipulating and Transforming 3D Objects

Now that we can render basic shapes, the next step is to manipulate and transform them in 3D space. We can apply **translation**, **scaling**, and **rotation** transformations to each of these objects.

Applying Transformations

We can combine the model matrix with transformations such as translation, rotation, and scaling. For example, to translate the pyramid along the x-axis and rotate it around the y-axis, we could do the following:

cpp

```
// Create the model matrix
glm::mat4 model = glm::mat4(1.0f);
model = glm::translate(model, glm::vec3(2.0f, 0.0f, 0.0f)); //
Translate along x-axis
model = glm::rotate(model, glm::radians(45.0f), glm::vec3(0.0f,
1.0f, 0.0f)); // Rotate around y-axis
```

Applying the Model Matrix

Once we've calculated the transformations, we pass the model matrix to the shader program to apply these transformations to the object:

cpp

```
// Pass the model matrix to the shader
GLuint modelLoc = glGetUniformLocation(shaderProgram, "model");
glUniformMatrix4fv(modelLoc, 1, GL_FALSE, glm::value_ptr(model));
```

In this chapter, we covered the essentials of creating and drawing basic 3D geometric shapes such as cubes, spheres, and pyramids. We learned how to define vertices, index buffers, and render these shapes to the screen using OpenGL. Additionally, we explored how to manipulate these shapes with transformations such as translation, scaling, and rotation to position them in 3D space. Mastering these techniques is critical to building more complex 3D scenes and forms the backbone of 3D object manipulation in OpenGL.

Understanding Vertex Buffers, Index Buffers, and Vertex Arrays

In OpenGL, efficient handling of data is crucial for rendering high-performance graphics. To achieve this, OpenGL provides mechanisms such as **Vertex Buffers**, **Index Buffers**, and **Vertex Array Objects (VAOs)**. These concepts are foundational for managing and optimizing the drawing of 3D objects in your application. Understanding how to use these buffers and arrays will significantly improve both the performance and organization of your code.

Let's dive deeper into each of these components, starting with vertex buffers, then moving to index buffers, and concluding with vertex array objects.

1. Vertex Buffers (VBOs)

A **Vertex Buffer Object (VBO)** is an OpenGL feature that allows you to store vertex data (such as positions, colors, normals, and texture coordinates) directly in the GPU's memory, rather than sending this data from the CPU every frame. This greatly improves performance because it eliminates the need to constantly transfer data from the CPU to the GPU during each frame render.

Why Use Vertex Buffers?

Vertex buffers provide several advantages:

- **Performance Optimization**: Storing vertex data on the GPU reduces the overhead of sending this data over the bus each time OpenGL draws an object.
- **Batching Draw Calls**: By storing multiple objects' vertex data in a single buffer, you can batch your drawing commands, which further reduces performance overhead.
- **Memory Management**: The GPU has its own high-speed memory (VRAM), which is optimized for handling the large amounts of data involved in rendering 3D objects.

Creating and Using Vertex Buffers

A VBO is created by generating a buffer object, binding it, and then uploading vertex data to the GPU. Here's how to do it in OpenGL:

```cpp
GLuint VBO;
glGenBuffers(1, &VBO);                    // Generate a buffer
object
glBindBuffer(GL_ARRAY_BUFFER, VBO);       // Bind the buffer as a
vertex buffer
glBufferData(GL_ARRAY_BUFFER, sizeof(vertices), vertices,
GL_STATIC_DRAW);  // Upload the vertex data
```

- **glGenBuffers()** creates one or more buffer objects.
- **glBindBuffer()** binds the buffer so that subsequent operations target this buffer.
- **glBufferData()** uploads the actual vertex data to the buffer.

Once a VBO is created and the data is uploaded, you can link the VBO to the vertex attributes in your vertex shader, which allows OpenGL to use the buffer data during rendering.

2. Index Buffers (EBOs)

An **Element Buffer Object (EBO)** is used to store indices that refer to vertices stored in a VBO. When rendering geometric primitives, like triangles, instead of specifying all the vertex data every time, OpenGL can simply refer to the vertex indices in the EBO to assemble triangles, saving memory and improving performance.

Why Use Index Buffers?

- **Memory Efficiency**: When a shape (like a cube) has shared vertices between multiple faces, using indices ensures that we don't duplicate vertex data. Instead, we can refer to the same vertex multiple times, leading to smaller data sizes.

- **Improved Performance**: Using EBOs helps in reducing redundancy, especially for shapes that share vertices between multiple faces (such as a cube, where each corner is shared by three faces).

Creating and Using Index Buffers

Here's how you create and use an EBO in OpenGL:

cpp

```
GLuint EBO;
glGenBuffers(1, &EBO);                      // Generate an EBO
glBindBuffer(GL_ELEMENT_ARRAY_BUFFER, EBO); // Bind the buffer
as an index buffer
glBufferData(GL_ELEMENT_ARRAY_BUFFER, sizeof(indices), indices,
GL_STATIC_DRAW); // Upload the index data
```

- **glGenBuffers()** generates a new EBO.
- **glBindBuffer()** binds the EBO so that subsequent operations affect it.
- **glBufferData()** uploads the index data to the GPU.

The index buffer references the vertex data stored in the VBO, meaning each element of the index buffer points to a specific vertex in the VBO. This way, instead of repeating vertex data for each triangle face, we use indices to reuse vertices efficiently.

Using the EBO During Rendering

Once the index buffer is set up, it can be used during rendering with the glDrawElements() function, which specifies how OpenGL should use the indices to draw primitives:

cpp

93

```
glBindVertexArray(VAO);  // Bind the vertex array object
glDrawElements(GL_TRIANGLES, 36, GL_UNSIGNED_INT, 0); // Draw
using indices
glBindVertexArray(0);    // Unbind the VAO
```

- **glDrawElements()** tells OpenGL to use the indices stored in the EBO to assemble the triangles. The second argument (36 in this case) is the number of indices to be used.

3. Vertex Array Objects (VAOs)

A **Vertex Array Object (VAO)** is an OpenGL object that encapsulates the configuration of vertex buffers, element buffers, and vertex attribute pointers. The VAO stores all the state related to the vertex buffers and attributes, so once it's set up, you don't need to repeatedly bind individual buffers or set attribute pointers for each frame.

Why Use Vertex Arrays?

- **Organization**: VAOs allow you to organize your buffers and vertex attribute configurations. Instead of needing to rebind multiple buffers every frame, you can just bind the VAO, which includes all the necessary data and state.
- **Performance**: VAOs reduce the overhead of setting up the rendering pipeline. Once a VAO is set up, switching between different objects is as simple as binding the appropriate VAO.
- **Code Cleanliness**: VAOs help in separating data setup and rendering logic, making the code more modular and easier to maintain.

Creating and Using a VAO

Here's how to create a VAO and associate it with your VBO and EBO:

cpp

```
GLuint VAO;
glGenVertexArrays(1, &VAO);              // Generate a VAO
glBindVertexArray(VAO);                  // Bind the VAO

// Bind the VBO and EBO as before
glBindBuffer(GL_ARRAY_BUFFER, VBO);
glBindBuffer(GL_ELEMENT_ARRAY_BUFFER, EBO);

// Set the vertex attribute pointers
glVertexAttribPointer(0, 3, GL_FLOAT, GL_FALSE, 3 *
sizeof(GLfloat), (GLvoid*)0);
glEnableVertexAttribArray(0);

// Unbind the VAO (you can do this as soon as it is set up)
glBindVertexArray(0);
```

- **glGenVertexArrays()** generates a VAO.
- **glBindVertexArray()** binds the VAO.
- **glVertexAttribPointer()** and **glEnableVertexAttribArray()** link the vertex data to the appropriate vertex shader attribute.

Once the VAO is set up, it can be bound and used for rendering. This encapsulates all the buffer bindings and attribute configurations into a single object.

cpp

```
glBindVertexArray(VAO);
glDrawElements(GL_TRIANGLES, 36, GL_UNSIGNED_INT, 0); // Draw
using VAO and indices
glBindVertexArray(0); // Unbind the VAO after drawing
```

4. Best Practices for Buffer Management

While vertex buffers, index buffers, and VAOs are powerful tools, it's essential to manage them efficiently. Here are some best practices:

1. Use Static Data Appropriately

If you have objects that don't change often, use **static** buffer objects with the GL_STATIC_DRAW flag. This tells OpenGL that the data will not change frequently and can be stored in a way that's optimized for drawing.

2. Minimize Buffer State Changes

Switching between different VBOs, EBOs, and VAOs can be costly, especially when done too frequently. Try to batch your objects or group them by their buffer requirements to minimize state changes.

3. Keep Data in GPU Memory

Use **persistent mapping** or **streaming** techniques if you need to modify buffer data frequently (e.g., for animation or simulations). This helps to keep the data closer to the GPU for quicker access.

4. Clean Up Resources

OpenGL doesn't automatically manage memory, so you must ensure to properly delete buffers and VAOs when they're no longer needed. Use glDeleteBuffers() and glDeleteVertexArrays() to free memory.

Understanding and using **Vertex Buffers**, **Index Buffers**, and **Vertex Array Objects (VAOs)** is crucial for optimizing and structuring your OpenGL rendering code. VBOs allow you to efficiently upload vertex data to the GPU, while EBOs save memory by reusing vertices across multiple faces. VAOs organize and encapsulate this data for streamlined rendering, reducing the need for redundant setup. By following best practices and understanding the roles of these objects, you can significantly improve the performance, scalability, and maintainability of your OpenGL projects. Mastering these concepts is key to becoming proficient in 3D graphics programming with OpenGL.

Loading and Displaying 3D Models with OpenGL

In real-world applications, 3D graphics typically go beyond basic geometric shapes like cubes, spheres, or pyramids. To create more complex and realistic scenes, you need to load 3D models from external files. These models can be anything from simple static objects to animated characters, landscapes, or entire game levels.

OpenGL itself doesn't provide a built-in mechanism for loading 3D models, so you'll need to rely on external libraries for importing model data into your application. In this section, we'll explore how to load and display 3D models in OpenGL, focusing on the process of importing model data (such as vertices, textures, and normals) and rendering it on the screen.

1. Understanding 3D Model Formats

Before diving into the process of loading 3D models, it's essential to understand the types of data that make up a 3D model. Most 3D models consist of several components:

- **Vertices**: These are the fundamental building blocks of any 3D model. Each vertex contains information about the position (coordinates), color, and other properties (such as normals or texture coordinates).
- **Indices**: For efficiency, models are often stored with indices that refer to the vertices, instead of storing vertex data repeatedly for each face.
- **Normals**: These vectors are perpendicular to the surfaces of the model and are used for lighting calculations.
- **Texture Coordinates**: These define how 2D textures are applied to the 3D surface.
- **Textures**: Textures are images applied to the surface of 3D models, such as diffuse maps, normal maps, or specular maps, giving models detail and realism.

Common file formats for 3D models include:

- **OBJ**: A widely-used, simple text-based format that stores vertex data, normals, texture coordinates, and faces.
- **FBX**: A more advanced and feature-rich format that supports animations, skeletal structures, and more.
- **GLTF**: A JSON-based format optimized for modern web applications and real-time rendering.
- **STL**: Commonly used for 3D printing, this format only stores vertex positions and faces, without support for textures or advanced features.

For simplicity, we will focus on the **OBJ format** in this chapter, as it is widely supported and easy to work with. We'll also use the **Assimp (Open Asset Import Library)** to load these models into OpenGL.

2. Setting Up Assimp for Model Loading

Assimp is a popular open-source library that helps you load 3D model files into your application. Assimp supports multiple formats, including OBJ, FBX, 3DS, COLLADA, and many others, making it an excellent tool for handling diverse model types.

Installing Assimp

First, you need to install Assimp. Here's how you can install Assimp on different platforms:

- **Windows**: Download precompiled binaries from the Assimp website or compile the source code using CMake.
- **Linux (Ubuntu)**: Use the following command to install Assimp from the package manager:

```bash
sudo apt-get install libassimp-dev
```

• **macOS**: You can install Assimp using Homebrew:

```bash
brew install assimp
```

Once Assimp is installed, you can link the library to your OpenGL project by including the Assimp header and linking to the library during the build process.

3. Loading 3D Models with Assimp

Assimp provides a simple API for loading 3D models. Here's a step-by-step guide to loading a 3D model into OpenGL using Assimp.

Loading the Model Data

To load a 3D model file, you need to call Assimp's aiImportFile() function, which returns an aiScene structure containing all the model data (e.g., meshes, materials, textures).

Here's an example of loading a 3D model from an OBJ file:

```cpp
#include <assimp/Importer.hpp>
#include <assimp/scene.h>
#include <assimp/postprocess.h>

Assimp::Importer importer;

// Load the model using Assimp
const aiScene* scene =
importer.ReadFile("path/to/your/model.obj",
                                    aiProcess_Triangulate |
                                    aiProcess_FlipUVs |
                                    aiProcess_GenNormals);
```

```
// Check if the scene was loaded successfully
if (!scene || !scene->HasMeshes()) {
    std::cerr << "Error: Failed to load model!" << std::endl;
    return;
}
```

- **aiProcess_Triangulate** ensures that the model's faces are converted into triangles, which is what OpenGL expects.
- **aiProcess_FlipUVs** is used to flip the texture coordinates in case they are stored in a different orientation.
- **aiProcess_GenNormals** generates normals for the model if they're missing.

Extracting Mesh Data

Once the model is loaded, you need to extract the mesh data (vertices, normals, textures, etc.) and store it in the appropriate OpenGL buffers. Below is a simplified version of how you can extract the vertices and indices from an Assimp model.

```cpp
std::vector<Vertex> vertices;
std::vector<GLuint> indices;

for (unsigned int i = 0; i < scene->mNumMeshes; i++) {
    aiMesh* mesh = scene->mMeshes[i];

    // Process vertices
    for (unsigned int j = 0; j < mesh->mNumVertices; j++) {
        aiVector3D pos = mesh->mVertices[j];
        aiVector3D normal = mesh->mNormals[j];
        aiVector3D texCoord = mesh->mTextureCoords[0] ?
        mesh->mTextureCoords[0][j] : aiVector3D(0.0f, 0.0f,
        0.0f);
```

```
        Vertex vertex = { glm::vec3(pos.x, pos.y, pos.z),
                          glm::vec3(normal.x, normal.y,
                          normal.z),
                          glm::vec2(texCoord.x, texCoord.y) };

        vertices.push_back(vertex);
    }

    // Process indices
    for (unsigned int j = 0; j < mesh->mNumFaces; j++) {
        aiFace face = mesh->mFaces[j];
        for (unsigned int k = 0; k < face.mNumIndices; k++) {
            indices.push_back(face.mIndices[k]);
        }
    }
}
```

In this code:

- We loop over each mesh in the scene, and for each mesh, we loop through all vertices to extract their positions, normals, and texture coordinates.
- We then extract the indices, which describe how to assemble the vertices into triangles.

At this point, you should have two arrays:

- **vertices**: Contains the data for each vertex (position, normal, and texture coordinates).
- **indices**: Contains the indices that define how the vertices form the mesh.

Creating OpenGL Buffers

Once the model data is extracted, you can upload it to the GPU using OpenGL's buffer objects. Here's how to create and bind the buffers for the vertices and indices:

```cpp
cpp

GLuint VAO, VBO, EBO;
glGenVertexArrays(1, &VAO);
glGenBuffers(1, &VBO);
glGenBuffers(1, &EBO);

glBindVertexArray(VAO);

// Upload vertex data to the GPU
glBindBuffer(GL_ARRAY_BUFFER, VBO);
glBufferData(GL_ARRAY_BUFFER, vertices.size() * sizeof(Vertex),
&vertices[0], GL_STATIC_DRAW);

// Upload index data to the GPU
glBindBuffer(GL_ELEMENT_ARRAY_BUFFER, EBO);
glBufferData(GL_ELEMENT_ARRAY_BUFFER, indices.size() *
sizeof(GLuint), &indices[0], GL_STATIC_DRAW);

// Enable vertex attribute pointers
glVertexAttribPointer(0, 3, GL_FLOAT, GL_FALSE, sizeof(Vertex),
(GLvoid*)0); // Position
glEnableVertexAttribArray(0);

glVertexAttribPointer(1, 3, GL_FLOAT, GL_FALSE, sizeof(Vertex),
(GLvoid*)offsetof(Vertex, normal)); // Normal
glEnableVertexAttribArray(1);

glVertexAttribPointer(2, 2, GL_FLOAT, GL_FALSE, sizeof(Vertex),
(GLvoid*)offsetof(Vertex, texCoords)); // TexCoords
glEnableVertexAttribArray(2);

// Unbind the VAO (you can bind it again during rendering)
glBindVertexArray(0);
```

This code creates the necessary buffers and binds the vertex and index data to the GPU. It also sets up vertex attribute pointers to tell OpenGL how to interpret the vertex data.

4. Rendering the Model

Once the model is loaded and the buffers are set up, rendering the model is as simple as binding the VAO and issuing a draw call:

cpp

```
// Bind the VAO and render the model
glBindVertexArray(VAO);
glDrawElements(GL_TRIANGLES, indices.size(), GL_UNSIGNED_INT, 0);
glBindVertexArray(0);
```

This draws the model by using the indices to assemble triangles from the vertex data stored in the VAO.

5. Handling Textures

If your model has textures, you will need to load and bind those as well. Here's a brief overview of how to load textures in OpenGL:

- Use libraries like **STB Image** or **Assimp** to load image files (e.g., PNG, JPEG) as textures.
- Bind the texture and set texture parameters before rendering the model.
- Ensure the correct texture is applied to the correct part of the model, based on the texture coordinates stored in the model data.

In this section, we explored how to load and display 3D models using OpenGL and the Assimp library. We covered:

- The basics of 3D model formats and their components (vertices, normals, textures).
- How to load models with Assimp and extract the relevant data.
- How to upload the model data to the GPU using OpenGL buffer objects.

- Rendering the model on the screen.

This is a fundamental process for creating 3D applications, such as games or simulations, where you want to import and render complex models in a 3D environment.

Working with Lighting Models: Ambient, Diffuse, and Specular Lighting

Lighting is a crucial component of 3D graphics, as it significantly impacts the realism and visual appeal of your scene. In real life, light interacts with surfaces in various ways, and simulating these interactions is essential to creating believable 3D graphics. OpenGL provides several ways to simulate lighting effects, with the most basic lighting models focusing on three key components: **ambient**, **diffuse**, and **specular** lighting.

In this section, we'll explore these three types of lighting, how they work together, and how you can implement them in OpenGL to create realistic lighting effects.

1. The Basics of Lighting in 3D Graphics

In 3D graphics, lighting is typically modeled using the **Phong Reflection Model**, which breaks down light interaction into three components:

1. **Ambient Light**: This is the general illumination that fills the environment. It's a uniform light that doesn't depend on the position or orientation of objects or light sources. Ambient light ensures that no part of a scene is completely dark, even when no other light sources are present.
2. **Diffuse Reflection**: This represents the light that bounces off a rough surface and scatters in many directions. It's dependent on the angle between the light source and the surface normal. The intensity of the diffuse reflection decreases as the angle between the surface and the light source increases.
3. **Specular Reflection**: This simulates the bright spots of light that

appear on shiny surfaces when light reflects off them. The amount of specular reflection depends on the viewing angle and the surface's shininess or glossiness.

Together, these three components make up the **Phong lighting model**, which is one of the most commonly used models in computer graphics.

2. Ambient Lighting

Ambient light is a constant, non-directional light that affects all objects in the scene equally, regardless of their position or orientation. Ambient light simulates the effect of indirect light that is scattered throughout the environment, filling in the shadows that would otherwise exist.

In OpenGL, you can simulate ambient lighting by applying a constant color to all surfaces. This color is not affected by the light source's direction or distance, and it ensures that the scene remains visible even when no direct light is hitting an object.

Ambient Light Equation:

```plaintext
I_ambient = ambient_color * material_ambient
```

Where:

- I_ambient: The resulting ambient light intensity.
- ambient_color: The color of the ambient light in the scene (usually a dim white or light color).
- material_ambient: The material's ambient reflection property (defines how much ambient light the surface reflects).

In OpenGL, the ambient light can be set as a uniform value in your shader, typically using a light color value and a global light intensity.

Example:

```cpp
// Shader fragment for ambient lighting
vec3 ambient = lightColor * material.ambient;
```

This is a simplified representation, where the light color is multiplied by the material's ambient reflection property.

3. Diffuse Lighting

Diffuse lighting is the result of light striking a rough surface and scattering in multiple directions. The amount of diffuse reflection depends on the angle between the light source and the surface's normal vector. The greater the angle between the light and the surface (i.e., the more perpendicular the light is to the surface), the more intense the diffuse reflection.

The intensity of the diffuse light is calculated using the **Lambertian reflection model**, which involves taking the dot product of the surface normal and the normalized vector pointing to the light source. The result of the dot product determines how much light is reflected in that direction.

Diffuse Lighting Equation:

```plaintext
I_diffuse = diffuse_color * max(0, dot(normal, light_direction))
```

Where:

- I_diffuse: The resulting diffuse light intensity.
- diffuse_color: The color of the light source.
- dot(normal, light_direction): The dot product of the surface normal and the light source direction vector.

The max(0, …) part ensures that no light is reflected in the opposite direction of the light source (i.e., when the dot product is negative, the surface is in shadow).

In OpenGL, you would calculate the diffuse reflection in the fragment shader, similar to the following code:

cpp

```
// Shader fragment for diffuse lighting
vec3 norm = normalize(normal);
vec3 lightDir = normalize(lightPosition - fragPosition);
float diff = max(dot(norm, lightDir), 0.0);
vec3 diffuse = diff * lightColor * material.diffuse;
```

This code calculates the angle between the light source and the surface, and then scales the diffuse color by the intensity of the diffuse reflection.

4. Specular Lighting

Specular lighting represents the bright spots of light that appear on shiny or smooth surfaces, where the reflection of the light source is concentrated. The intensity of the specular highlight depends on the angle between the viewer, the surface, and the light source. A perfect mirror-like reflection will result in a sharp highlight, while rougher surfaces will have a more diffused reflection.

Specular lighting is controlled by two factors:

1. The angle between the reflection vector and the viewer's position.
2. The material's shininess, which controls how tightly the specular highlight is concentrated. This is often represented by a **shininess** coefficient.

The specular reflection is computed using the **Blinn-Phong reflection model**, which is an extension of the Phong model and uses the **halfway vector** between the light direction and the view direction.

Specular Lighting Equation:

plaintext

```
I_specular = specular_color * pow(max(0, dot(normal, halfway)),
shininess)
```

Where:

- I_specular: The resulting specular light intensity.
- specular_color: The color of the specular light.
- shininess: A material property that controls the sharpness of the specular highlight.
- halfway: The normalized vector halfway between the light direction and the view direction, calculated as:

cpp

```
vec3 halfway = normalize(lightDir + viewDir);
```

In OpenGL, the specular component is calculated similarly to the diffuse component, but using the dot product of the normal and the halfway vector. The shininess value controls the power of the resulting reflection.

cpp

```
// Shader fragment for specular lighting
vec3 viewDir = normalize(viewPosition - fragPosition);
vec3 halfwayDir = normalize(lightDir + viewDir);
float spec = pow(max(dot(norm, halfwayDir), 0.0),
material.shininess);
vec3 specular = spec * lightColor * material.specular;
```

This code computes the specular reflection by using the angle between the light, normal, and viewer directions, then raising the result to the power of the material's shininess.

5. Combining the Lighting Components

To simulate realistic lighting in a scene, we combine all three lighting components: ambient, diffuse, and specular. Each component contributes to the overall color of a surface, and the final lighting color is a sum of these contributions.

Total Lighting Equation:

```plaintext
I_total = I_ambient + I_diffuse + I_specular
```

In the shader, you can combine these components as follows:

```cpp
// Combined lighting in shader
vec3 ambient = lightColor * material.ambient;
vec3 diffuse = diff * lightColor * material.diffuse;
vec3 specular = spec * lightColor * material.specular;

vec3 result = ambient + diffuse + specular;
FragColor = vec4(result, 1.0);
```

This code computes the total lighting by adding the contributions of the ambient, diffuse, and specular components, and then applies the final color to the fragment.

In this section, we explored the fundamental concepts behind **ambient**, **diffuse**, and **specular** lighting. These components, when combined, create the realistic lighting effects that make 3D scenes come alive. We learned how each lighting model works, how to implement them in OpenGL shaders, and how to combine them to simulate the full range of light interactions with 3D objects.

By understanding these basic lighting models and how they are implemented, you'll be able to create more visually appealing and realistic 3D scenes. As you progress, you can explore more advanced lighting techniques such as **normal mapping**, **reflection/refraction**, and **global illumination** to further enhance the lighting in your OpenGL applications.

Shaders and Advanced Rendering Techniques

Shaders are a critical part of the OpenGL graphics pipeline, enabling developers to manipulate the appearance of objects and effects within a 3D scene. Whether you're creating realistic lighting, special effects, or intricate visual styles, shaders allow you to control how your graphics are rendered at the pixel, vertex, and even fragment level. In this chapter, we will dive deep into the **OpenGL Shading Language (GLSL)**, a powerful tool for writing shaders that interact with OpenGL's rendering pipeline. We'll guide you through writing your first vertex and fragment shaders, and explore the fundamental role of shaders in the pipeline.

1. What is GLSL?

The **OpenGL Shading Language (GLSL)** is a high-level programming language specifically designed for writing shaders in OpenGL. GLSL allows you to write programs that run directly on the GPU, enabling real-time graphics computations. These programs are used to define the behavior of your graphics pipeline stages, particularly the vertex processing, fragment processing, and more.

GLSL is similar to C in syntax and is designed to be both efficient and easy to use for 3D graphics programming. It offers a set of built-in functions and data types that make working with vectors, matrices, and colors straightforward. There are several types of shaders that GLSL can be used to create, but the two most important for beginners are:

- **Vertex Shaders**: Responsible for transforming vertex data (positions, colors, normals, etc.) into screen-space coordinates.
- **Fragment Shaders**: Handle the color and texture of individual pixels (or fragments) that make up the final image.

GLSL is closely tied to the OpenGL pipeline, allowing you to programmatically alter how vertices and pixels are processed, thus enabling a high degree of control over the final output.

2. Writing Your First Vertex and Fragment Shaders

In OpenGL, shaders are written in GLSL and are compiled and executed on the GPU. Let's begin by writing a basic vertex shader and fragment shader.

Vertex Shader:

The vertex shader is responsible for processing vertex attributes (e.g., position, color, normal vectors) and transforming them into a 2D space for display on the screen. It's executed once for each vertex of an object, and its main task is to calculate the final screen position of each vertex.

A basic vertex shader might look like this:

```c
#version 330 core  // GLSL version
layout(location = 0) in vec3 aPosition;  // Vertex position input
layout(location = 1) in vec3 aColor;  // Vertex color input

out vec3 vertexColor;  // Output variable for fragment shader

uniform mat4 model;  // Model transformation matrix
uniform mat4 view;   // View transformation matrix
uniform mat4 projection;  // Projection matrix

void main()
{
    // Apply transformations: Model, View, Projection
```

```
    gl_Position = projection * view * model * vec4(aPosition,
    1.0);

    // Pass the vertex color to the fragment shader
    vertexColor = aColor;
}
```

Explanation:

- layout(location = X): Specifies the attribute locations for the vertex data (in this case, aPosition and aColor).
- uniform mat4 model, view, projection: These are transformation matrices that handle object, camera, and projection space transformations.
- gl_Position: This built-in GLSL variable stores the final transformed position of the vertex in clip space.
- vertexColor: The color of the vertex, passed along to the fragment shader for further processing.

Fragment Shader:

The fragment shader is executed for every pixel (or fragment) that will be drawn to the screen. It determines the final color of the pixel, applying lighting, textures, and other effects to achieve the desired look.

A simple fragment shader might look like this:

```c
#version 330 core   // GLSL version

in vec3 vertexColor;   // Color from vertex shader

out vec4 FragColor;   // Final color output to framebuffer

void main()
{
    // Set the final fragment color
```

```
    FragColor = vec4(vertexColor, 1.0);  // RGB color with full
    opacity
}
```

Explanation:

- in vec3 vertexColor: This is the color value passed from the vertex shader.
- out vec4 FragColor: This is the final color output that will be written to the framebuffer, used to display the pixel on screen.
- FragColor = vec4(vertexColor, 1.0): The final fragment color is set to the vertex color with an alpha value of 1.0 (fully opaque).

3. Understanding Shaders' Roles in the Pipeline

Shaders play a vital role in the OpenGL rendering pipeline. To better understand their function, let's walk through how each shader fits into the overall process of rendering a 3D scene.

Vertex Processing: Vertex Shader

The first step in the OpenGL pipeline is **vertex processing**, where each vertex of a 3D object is transformed from its local object coordinates to screen coordinates. This is where the **vertex shader** comes into play. It takes each vertex's position, along with any additional data (such as normals or texture coordinates), and applies transformations (model, view, and projection matrices) to position the vertices on the screen.

Once the vertex shader has processed the data, the next step is typically **clipping**, where OpenGL determines if the transformed vertex is within the visible area of the screen. If the vertex is outside the visible area, it is discarded.

Primitive Assembly and Rasterization:

After vertex processing, the transformed vertices are grouped into primitives (such as triangles, lines, or points). These primitives are then passed to the **rasterizer**, which determines which pixels on the screen correspond to the current primitive. Rasterization is the process of determining which pixels are covered by the primitive and generating fragments (potential pixels).

Fragment Processing: Fragment Shader

After rasterization, each fragment is processed by the **fragment shader**. The fragment shader is responsible for computing the color of each pixel in the scene. This can involve applying lighting models (ambient, diffuse, specular), textures, and other effects. The output of the fragment shader is the final color that will be written to the screen.

This step occurs after the vertex data has been transformed, so the fragment shader operates on a pixel-by-pixel basis, rather than vertex-by-vertex.

4. Shaders in Action: The OpenGL Pipeline

To understand the flow of data, here is a simplified breakdown of how shaders are used in the OpenGL rendering pipeline:

Vertex Shader:

- Input: Vertex data (positions, colors, normals, etc.).
- Transformation: Applies model, view, and projection transformations.
- Output: Transformed vertices and interpolated data (such as colors or texture coordinates).

Primitive Assembly:

- Groups vertices into primitives (triangles, lines, etc.).
- Passes the primitives to the rasterizer.

Rasterization:

- Converts primitives into fragments (potential pixels).

- Determines which pixels are affected by the primitive.

Fragment Shader:

- Input: Fragments (pixel data, including interpolated data from the vertex shader).
- Color computation: Applies lighting, texturing, or other effects to compute the final color.
- Output: Final pixel color written to the framebuffer.

Framebuffer:

- Stores the final rendered image after all shaders have processed the data.

This is the core sequence of events in OpenGL's graphics pipeline, with vertex and fragment shaders playing the central role in transforming geometry and generating final pixel values.

5. Debugging and Optimizing Shaders

Writing shaders is an art and science, and sometimes things don't go as expected. Shader bugs, such as artifacts, incorrect colors, or performance issues, can arise for many reasons. To help debug and optimize your shaders:

- **Check for errors**: OpenGL provides functions to check for shader compilation and linking errors. Make sure you use these to catch common issues like syntax errors or incorrect shader programs.

cpp

```
GLint success;
GLchar infoLog[512];
glGetShaderiv(shader, GL_COMPILE_STATUS, &success);
if (!success) {
    glGetShaderInfoLog(shader, 512, NULL, infoLog);
    std::cout << "ERROR::SHADER_COMPILATION_ERROR of type: " <<
    type << "\n" << infoLog << "\n";
}
```

- **Use debugging tools**: OpenGL offers several tools for debugging, such as **gDEBugger** and **RenderDoc**, which allow you to step through your shaders and examine their output.
- **Optimize for performance**: Avoid unnecessary computations in shaders and aim to minimize the amount of data passed between shaders. For example, use simple mathematical expressions, minimize texture fetches, and use efficient lighting calculations.

In this chapter, we explored the fundamental concepts behind **GLSL** (OpenGL Shading Language) and learned how to write basic **vertex** and **fragment shaders**. We discussed the critical role that shaders play in the OpenGL pipeline, from transforming vertex data to computing the final color of fragments.

Writing shaders allows you to create custom visual effects, implement advanced rendering techniques, and gain deeper control over the graphics pipeline. As you continue exploring OpenGL, you'll build on this foundation to create more complex shaders and effects such as **normal mapping**, **shadow mapping**, and **post-processing** effects. Mastering shaders is essential for anyone looking to push the boundaries of 3D graphics programming.

Advanced Shader Techniques

As we move beyond the basics of writing vertex and fragment shaders, we enter the realm of advanced rendering techniques that can dramatically enhance the visual realism and complexity of a 3D scene. In this section, we will delve into some of the most commonly used advanced shader techniques, including **lighting models**, **texture mapping**, and more sophisticated techniques like **bump mapping**, **parallax mapping**, and **environment mapping**.

These techniques are essential for creating immersive, visually rich 3D graphics, and are widely used in modern games and applications to achieve effects like realistic lighting, surface detail, and reflections.

1. Lighting Models: Phong, Blinn-Phong, and Lambertian

Lighting models are the backbone of realistic graphics, simulating how light interacts with surfaces. The two main types of lighting are **ambient lighting** (light that is present everywhere in the scene) and **direct lighting** (light that comes from specific sources, such as the sun or a light bulb). The way light interacts with surfaces is computed through **shading**, and advanced models allow for better approximation of real-world lighting phenomena.

Phong Lighting Model

The **Phong lighting model** is one of the most widely used lighting models in computer graphics. It calculates the color of a surface based on three components:

1. **Ambient Lighting**: A constant color applied uniformly across the entire scene, representing light that has scattered throughout the environment. It doesn't change based on the surface's orientation or position.

2. **Diffuse Lighting**: Simulates the light that hits a surface and scatters in all directions. The amount of light received depends on the angle between the surface normal and the light source. It creates the base color for the object.

3. **Specular Lighting**: Simulates the reflection of light off shiny surfaces, creating highlights. It depends on the angle between the viewer's

position, the light direction, and the surface normal.

The Phong model is calculated using the following formula:

$$I = I_a + I_d \cdot (L \cdot N) + I_s \cdot (R \cdot V)^\alpha$$

Where:

- I_a is the ambient light intensity.
- I_d is the diffuse light intensity.
- I_s is the specular light intensity.
- L is the light direction vector.
- N is the surface normal vector.
- R is the reflection vector.
- V is the view direction vector.
- α is the shininess factor (controls the size and sharpness of specular highlights).

Blinn-Phong Lighting Model

The **Blinn-Phong model** is an extension of the Phong model that improves the efficiency of calculating specular highlights, particularly in real-time graphics. Instead of using the reflection vector RRR, Blinn-Phong uses a **halfway vector**, which is the normalized vector halfway between the light direction and the view direction. This change reduces the number of operations required for specular calculations, making it more efficient while producing visually similar results.

The formula for Blinn-Phong is:

$$I = I_a + I_d \cdot (L \cdot N) + I_s \cdot (H \cdot N)^\alpha$$

Where:

- H is the halfway vector between the light and view vectors.
- The other variables are the same as in the Phong model.

119

Blinn-Phong is widely used in games and real-time rendering because of its speed and simplicity without sacrificing too much visual fidelity.

Lambertian Lighting Model

The **Lambertian** model is a simple and efficient model for calculating diffuse lighting. Unlike Phong and Blinn-Phong, Lambertian shading assumes that light is scattered uniformly across a surface, meaning that the amount of light hitting a surface is directly proportional to the cosine of the angle between the surface normal and the light direction. This model is computationally simple and very effective for representing matte surfaces (surfaces without gloss or reflection).

The Lambertian reflection is given by:

$$I_d = I_0 \cdot max(0, L \cdot N)$$

Where:

- I_0 is the diffuse light intensity.
- L is the light direction.
- N is the surface normal.
- $max(0, L \cdot N)$ ensures that light is only received from the side of the surface facing the light.

Lambertian shading doesn't account for reflections or specular highlights, but it is useful for rendering basic, non-shiny surfaces such as walls or other matte objects.

2. Texture Mapping: Diffuse, Specular, and Normal Maps

Textures are one of the most powerful ways to add realism to 3D objects by defining the appearance of their surfaces. In OpenGL, textures are applied to models through **texture mapping**, which involves mapping a 2D texture (an image) onto a 3D surface.

Diffuse Maps

A **diffuse map** (or albedo map) is the base texture that defines the color of a surface. It is applied to the object's surface and provides the general appearance of the material. Diffuse maps are used to simulate the surface detail of a material, including its natural color and patterns (e.g., wood, stone, fabric).

In GLSL, the diffuse texture is usually sampled in the fragment shader like this:

```glsl
uniform sampler2D diffuseTexture; // Diffuse texture
in vec2 texCoord; // Texture coordinates passed from vertex
shader

void main() {
    vec4 diffuseColor = texture(diffuseTexture, texCoord);
    FragColor = diffuseColor;
}
```

Specular Maps

A **specular map** defines the shininess and reflective qualities of a surface. It controls how much light is reflected at each pixel based on the material's properties. For example, a metal surface will reflect more light than a plastic one, and the specular map can define this behavior. In many cases, the specular map stores values that control the intensity of the specular reflection.

In GLSL, the specular map can be combined with the lighting calculation in the fragment shader:

```glsl
uniform sampler2D specularTexture; // Specular texture
in vec2 texCoord; // Texture coordinates

void main() {
    vec4 specular = texture(specularTexture, texCoord);
```

```
    vec3 reflection = specular.rgb * specularIntensity;
    FragColor = reflection * specularColor;
}
```

Normal Maps

A **normal map** is used to simulate complex surface details by altering the surface normals of a model. Rather than modifying the geometry, a normal map alters how light interacts with the surface. This allows for highly detailed textures without adding additional polygons to the model. A normal map encodes RGB values that represent the x, y, and z components of a normal vector at each pixel.

In GLSL, a normal map can be applied by modifying the surface normal in the fragment shader:

```glsl
glsl

uniform sampler2D normalMap; // Normal map texture
in vec2 texCoord; // Texture coordinates

void main() {
    vec3 normal = texture(normalMap, texCoord).rgb;
    // Use normal in lighting calculations
    FragColor = vec4(normal, 1.0);
}
```

3. Advanced Mapping Techniques

Beyond basic texture mapping, several advanced mapping techniques help create even more realistic materials and surface effects.

Bump Mapping

Bump mapping is a technique that simulates small surface detail, such as wrinkles or bumps, by altering the normal vectors at each fragment based on a bump map (a grayscale image). This allows for the illusion of complex surface detail without modifying the actual geometry of the object.

Parallax Mapping

Parallax mapping is a more advanced technique that builds on bump mapping. It uses depth information stored in a texture to create the illusion of greater depth at the surface, simulating the appearance of detailed surfaces such as grooves and ridges. Parallax mapping accounts for the viewer's perspective and adjusts the texture coordinates based on the viewer's position to create more realistic depth effects.

Environment Mapping

Environment mapping is used to simulate reflections and environment-based lighting effects. This technique applies an environment texture (typically a cube map) to simulate reflections, such as reflections of the sky, water, or surrounding environment. It's commonly used for reflective surfaces like glass, water, and metal.

A typical environment mapping shader might look like this:

```glsl
uniform samplerCube envMap; // Cube map texture for environment
in vec3 viewDir; // View direction

void main() {
    vec4 reflectedColor = texture(envMap, reflect(viewDir,
    normal));
    FragColor = reflectedColor;
}
```

This shader samples the cube map based on the reflection vector, resulting in a realistic reflection of the environment on the surface.

Advanced shaders techniques such as **Phong**, **Blinn-Phong**, and **Lambertian** lighting models, as well as **texture mapping** (diffuse, specular, normal maps) and more sophisticated methods like **bump mapping, parallax**

mapping, and **environment mapping**, are essential tools for creating visually rich and realistic 3D graphics.

By combining these advanced techniques, you can build highly detailed and realistic scenes that respond dynamically to light, perspective, and user interaction. Mastering these techniques will enable you to create stunning visuals for games, simulations, virtual environments, and more. In the next chapters, we will continue exploring further aspects of shaders and how to optimize these advanced techniques for real-time applications.

3D Modeling and Scene Creation

Loading Complex 3D Models (Using Assimp or Custom Formats)

In the world of 3D graphics programming, working with complex 3D models is a critical skill. Whether you're building environments for games, creating interactive simulations, or rendering visual effects, the ability to load and manipulate detailed 3D models is essential. Models come in various formats, each tailored for specific needs, and understanding how to import them into OpenGL can be a challenging yet rewarding task. This chapter will focus on the techniques for **loading complex 3D models** from different formats using libraries like **Assimp (Open Asset Import Library)**, and discuss how to handle **custom formats** in OpenGL.

1. Introduction to 3D Model Loading

Before diving into the specific methods, it's important to understand what constitutes a **3D model** in the context of computer graphics. A 3D model is essentially a collection of geometric data that defines the structure of an object. This data typically includes the following:

- **Vertices**: Points in 3D space that form the shape of the object.
- **Normals**: Vectors at each vertex that define how light interacts with the surface.
- **Texture Coordinates**: 2D coordinates that map 3D objects to textures.
- **Materials**: Information that describes the surface properties of the model, such as color, texture, and reflectivity.
- **Bones and Skeletons**: For animated models, this data defines the

hierarchical structure that drives the motion of the model.

Models can also be **rigged** (skeleton-based for animation), and often, they include other features such as **vertex colors**, **lighting information**, and **animations**. For real-time rendering, OpenGL requires a specific format, but to get started, we need to load models from various file formats like **.obj**, **.fbx**, **.dae**, and **.3ds**, each of which has a different internal structure.

2. Using Assimp for Loading Models

One of the most powerful tools for loading 3D models in OpenGL is **Assimp**, an open-source library that simplifies the process of importing a wide variety of 3D model formats. Assimp abstracts the complexity of different file formats and provides a unified interface to load models, making it ideal for working with various 3D assets.

Why Use Assimp?

- **Multi-format support**: Assimp supports a large number of file formats, including but not limited to **.obj**, **.fbx**, **.dae**, **.3ds**, **.stl**, and more. This allows you to work with a variety of assets without worrying about the complexities of parsing each format manually.
- **Animation support**: Assimp provides functionality to load skeletons and animations, which can be used to animate 3D models in real-time.
- **Mesh and Material Data**: Assimp gives you access to vertex positions, normals, texture coordinates, and material properties, which are crucial for rendering models in OpenGL.

Setting Up Assimp in Your Project

To use Assimp in your OpenGL project, you first need to install it. The installation process can vary based on the operating system, but it typically involves downloading the Assimp library and linking it to your project.

Install Assimp: Assimp can be installed from the official Assimp website or through package managers like **vcpkg** (Windows), **brew** (macOS), or **apt-get** (Linux).

For example, on macOS you can use:

```bash
bash

brew install assimp
```

Link Assimp to Your Project: After installing Assimp, make sure to link the necessary libraries to your OpenGL project. Include the Assimp headers in your code to access its functions:

```cpp
cpp

#include <assimp/Importer.hpp>
#include <assimp/scene.h>
#include <assimp/postprocess.h>
```

Loading a Model Using Assimp

Here's an overview of the steps involved in loading a 3D model using Assimp:

Create an Importer Object: The Assimp::Importer object is responsible for loading the model data from the file.

```cpp
cpp

Assimp::Importer importer;
const aiScene* scene =
importer.ReadFile("path/to/your/model.obj",
aiProcess_Triangulate | aiProcess_FlipUVs);
if (!scene) {
    std::cerr << "Error loading model: " <<
    importer.GetErrorString() << std::endl;
    return;
}
```

In this code:

- **aiProcess_Triangulate**: Ensures that all polygons are converted into triangles, as OpenGL requires triangulated meshes.
- **aiProcess_FlipUVs**: Flips the texture coordinates to match OpenGL's coordinate system.

Extract Meshes: Assimp loads the 3D model into the aiScene structure. Each mesh in the scene is stored in the aiScene::mMeshes array.

cpp

```cpp
for (unsigned int i = 0; i < scene->mNumMeshes; ++i) {
    aiMesh* mesh = scene->mMeshes[i];
    // Process each mesh here
}
```

Extract Vertex Data: For each mesh, you need to extract the vertex positions, normals, texture coordinates, and any other necessary data (like colors).

cpp

```cpp
std::vector<glm::vec3> vertices;
std::vector<glm::vec3> normals;
std::vector<glm::vec2> texCoords;

for (unsigned int i = 0; i < mesh->mNumVertices; ++i) {
    vertices.push_back(glm::vec3(
        mesh->mVertices[i].x,
        mesh->mVertices[i].y,
        mesh->mVertices[i].z
    ));
    normals.push_back(glm::vec3(
        mesh->mNormals[i].x,
        mesh->mNormals[i].y,
        mesh->mNormals[i].z
    ));
    if (mesh->mTextureCoords[0]) {
```

```
        texCoords.push_back(glm::vec2(
            mesh->mTextureCoords[0][i].x,
            mesh->mTextureCoords[0][i].y
        ));
    }
}
```

Process Materials and Textures: Assimp also provides information about the materials used in the model. You can extract the texture paths and apply them to your OpenGL shaders.

cpp

```
aiMaterial* material = scene->mMaterials[mesh->mMaterialIndex];
aiString texPath;
if (material->GetTexture(aiTextureType_DIFFUSE, 0, &texPath) ==
AI_SUCCESS) {
    // Load texture using your preferred method
}
```

Render the Model: Once the model data has been loaded and stored in appropriate buffers, you can render it using OpenGL as you would with any other mesh.

Handling Animations

Assimp also provides support for **animations**. You can load the animation data from the model file and use it to animate the model in real-time. Assimp stores animations in the aiScene::mAnimations array, where each animation includes keyframes, bone transformations, and animation channels.

cpp

```
for (unsigned int i = 0; i < scene->mNumAnimations; ++i) {
    aiAnimation* animation = scene->mAnimations[i];
```

```
    // Process each animation here
}
```

You can then use this data to manipulate the model's bones and transform the vertices accordingly, enabling character animations and other motion effects.

3. Loading Custom Model Formats

While Assimp is an excellent tool for importing various file formats, there may be situations where you need to load models from custom or proprietary formats. In such cases, you'll need to parse the model data manually and create your own importer.

Steps for Loading Custom Models:

1. **File Parsing**: The first step is reading the model file. You'll need to parse the file format to extract the 3D geometry. This could involve reading binary data or parsing ASCII files.

2. Example for a custom format:

```cpp
std::ifstream modelFile("path/to/custom_model.myFormat",
std::ios::binary);
if (!modelFile.is_open()) {
    std::cerr << "Error: Could not open model file." <<
    std::endl;
    return;
}
```

1. **Extract Data**: Once the file is open, you can start reading the data in the format your model uses. This may involve reading vertex positions, normals, texture coordinates, and other data, and storing them in appropriate arrays or vectors.

2. **Store Data in Buffers**: After extracting the data, store it in OpenGL buffers for rendering. This involves creating vertex buffers and element buffers for efficient rendering.

3. **Handle Materials and Textures**: If your custom format includes material or texture data, ensure that these elements are loaded properly and mapped to the correct shaders.

4. **Animation**: If the custom model format includes animations, parse the relevant data and implement the logic for handling keyframes, bone transformations, and animation blending.

Understanding Vertex Attributes (Normals, Texture Coordinates, Colors)

When working with 3D models in OpenGL, it's essential to understand the role of **vertex attributes**—the data associated with each vertex in a 3D mesh. These attributes help define how a model is rendered, how light interacts with its surfaces, and how textures and colors are applied. In this section, we'll explore three critical vertex attributes: **normals**, **texture coordinates**, and **vertex colors**.

1. Normals

Normals are vectors that define the orientation of a surface at each vertex. In 3D graphics, normals play a crucial role in lighting calculations, such as determining how light interacts with a surface and how shadows are cast. Normals are essential for achieving realistic shading effects, particularly when using techniques like **Phong shading**, **Blinn-Phong shading**, or **normal mapping**.

Understanding Normals in OpenGL

- **Vertex normals**: A normal vector associated with each vertex represents the direction perpendicular to the surface at that point.
- **Face normals**: A normal associated with a polygon's face, often calculated by averaging the normals of the vertices forming that

polygon.

In OpenGL, each vertex can have its own normal, allowing the rendering of smooth, curved surfaces rather than flat polygonal faces. Here's how you define and use normals in OpenGL:

- **Storing normals**: Normals are typically stored in a separate attribute array from the vertex positions. In OpenGL, you store them in **vertex buffer objects (VBOs)**.
- **Using normals for lighting**: Shaders use normals to calculate how light interacts with the surface. The **normal vector** is compared to the direction of the light source to determine how much light hits a given point on the surface.

Example of Storing Normals

When creating a VBO for a model, you include the vertex positions and normals together. The following example shows how to store the normals alongside the vertices:

cpp

```cpp
std::vector<glm::vec3> vertices = {
    glm::vec3(0.0f, 0.5f, 0.0f),   // Vertex 1
    glm::vec3(-0.5f, -0.5f, 0.0f), // Vertex 2
    glm::vec3(0.5f, -0.5f, 0.0f)   // Vertex 3
};

std::vector<glm::vec3> normals = {
    glm::vec3(0.0f, 1.0f, 0.0f),   // Normal for Vertex 1
    glm::vec3(0.0f, 1.0f, 0.0f),   // Normal for Vertex 2
    glm::vec3(0.0f, 1.0f, 0.0f)    // Normal for Vertex 3
};
```

Once you have the normals, you use them in the vertex shader to calculate lighting and shading effects.

2. Texture Coordinates

Texture coordinates (also known as **UV coordinates**) define how a 2D texture is mapped onto a 3D surface. Essentially, they specify which part of the texture image should be applied to each vertex. Each vertex in a model can have corresponding 2D texture coordinates that map it to the texture.

Why Texture Coordinates Are Important

- **Mapping textures**: Texture coordinates are used to "unwrap" a 3D model into a 2D space. When a texture is applied to a 3D object, OpenGL needs to know how to map the 2D texture onto the 3D surface. This is done using the texture coordinates.
- **UV space**: Texture coordinates are typically defined in the range [0, 1] for both axes (u and v). The (0,0) coordinate corresponds to the bottom-left corner of the texture, while (1,1) corresponds to the top-right corner.

How Texture Coordinates Are Used in OpenGL

In OpenGL, texture coordinates are stored as a separate attribute in the vertex data. When rendering, the vertex shader will pass the texture coordinates to the fragment shader, where the texture is sampled to determine the final color of each fragment.

Example of Storing Texture Coordinates

Here's how you would store texture coordinates along with vertex positions and normals in a VBO:

cpp

```cpp
std::vector<glm::vec2> textureCoords = {
    glm::vec2(0.0f, 0.0f),  // Texture coordinate for Vertex 1
    glm::vec2(1.0f, 0.0f),  // Texture coordinate for Vertex 2
    glm::vec2(0.5f, 1.0f)   // Texture coordinate for Vertex 3
};
```

In this example, the texture coordinates indicate how the texture is applied to the triangle formed by the three vertices.

3. Vertex Colors

Vertex colors are a way of defining the color of each vertex, allowing you to directly influence the color of your 3D object. Vertex colors are often used for **flat shading, wireframe rendering**, or when textures are not required.

While textures provide detailed color information over a surface, vertex colors define a color at each vertex, which can be interpolated across the surface of the polygon. For example, if you have a triangle with three vertices, each with its own color, the color at each pixel (or fragment) of the triangle will be determined by interpolating the vertex colors.

Why Use Vertex Colors

- **Simplicity**: Vertex colors are simple to use and can be a good choice for low-complexity models or when you don't need detailed textures.
- **Performance**: For models that don't need complex textures, using vertex colors can save memory and processing time, as you don't need to load external texture maps.
- **Animation and effects**: Vertex colors can be used for effects like **vertex-based lighting, color transitions**, or **vertex-based animations**.

How Vertex Colors Are Used in OpenGL

Like normals and texture coordinates, vertex colors are stored in a separate attribute array. These colors are passed through the pipeline and interpolated in the fragment shader to produce the final color of each pixel.

Example of Storing Vertex Colors

You can store vertex colors alongside the position, normal, and texture coordinate data:

```cpp
std::vector<glm::vec3> vertexColors = {
    glm::vec3(1.0f, 0.0f, 0.0f),  // Red for Vertex 1
    glm::vec3(0.0f, 1.0f, 0.0f),  // Green for Vertex 2
    glm::vec3(0.0f, 0.0f, 1.0f)   // Blue for Vertex 3
};
```

In this case, each vertex has its own color (red, green, and blue), which will be interpolated across the face of the triangle.

4. Combining Vertex Attributes

In OpenGL, the vertex data is often stored together in a **vertex array object (VAO)**, which groups all the vertex attributes into a single object. A typical VAO might contain the following vertex attributes:

- **Position**: The location of the vertex in 3D space.
- **Normal**: The normal vector associated with the vertex for lighting calculations.
- **Texture Coordinates**: The UV coordinates used for texturing.
- **Color**: The color associated with the vertex.

Once these attributes are stored in buffers, they are passed to shaders for processing. The shaders then compute the final rendered output based on these attributes.

Example of Binding and Using Vertex Attributes

Here's an example of how to bind and use these vertex attributes in OpenGL:

```cpp
GLuint VAO, VBO, EBO;
glGenVertexArrays(1, &VAO);
glGenBuffers(1, &VBO);
```

```
glGenBuffers(1, &EBO);

glBindVertexArray(VAO);

// Position buffer
glBindBuffer(GL_ARRAY_BUFFER, VBO);
glBufferData(GL_ARRAY_BUFFER, sizeof(vertices), vertices.data(),
GL_STATIC_DRAW);
glVertexAttribPointer(0, 3, GL_FLOAT, GL_FALSE, 3 *
sizeof(GLfloat), (GLvoid*)0);
glEnableVertexAttribArray(0);

// Normal buffer
glBindBuffer(GL_ARRAY_BUFFER, VBO);
glBufferData(GL_ARRAY_BUFFER, sizeof(normals), normals.data(),
GL_STATIC_DRAW);
glVertexAttribPointer(1, 3, GL_FLOAT, GL_FALSE, 3 *
sizeof(GLfloat), (GLvoid*)0);
glEnableVertexAttribArray(1);

// Texture coordinate buffer
glBindBuffer(GL_ARRAY_BUFFER, VBO);
glBufferData(GL_ARRAY_BUFFER, sizeof(textureCoords),
textureCoords.data(), GL_STATIC_DRAW);
glVertexAttribPointer(2, 2, GL_FLOAT, GL_FALSE, 2 *
sizeof(GLfloat), (GLvoid*)0);
glEnableVertexAttribArray(2);

// Color buffer
glBindBuffer(GL_ARRAY_BUFFER, VBO);
glBufferData(GL_ARRAY_BUFFER, sizeof(vertexColors),
vertexColors.data(), GL_STATIC_DRAW);
glVertexAttribPointer(3, 3, GL_FLOAT, GL_FALSE, 3 *
sizeof(GLfloat), (GLvoid*)0);
glEnableVertexAttribArray(3);

glBindVertexArray(0);
```

In this example, the vertex data (positions, normals, texture coordinates, and colors) is loaded into OpenGL buffer objects and associated with the appropriate attribute locations in the vertex shader.

```
Summary
Normals define the orientation of surfaces and are critical for
lighting calculations.
Texture coordinates map 2D textures to 3D models, specifying how
textures are applied.
Vertex colors assign colors to vertices, which are interpolated
across a surface for simple color effects.
Each of these vertex attributes can be independently manipulated
in the shaders to produce a variety of visual effects. By
understanding how to use and combine these attributes, you can
achieve realistic rendering and visual effects in
OpenGL.Understanding Vertex Attributes (Normals, Texture
Coordinates, Colors)
```

When working with 3D models in OpenGL, it's essential to understand the role of **vertex attributes**—the data associated with each vertex in a 3D mesh. These attributes help define how a model is rendered, how light interacts with its surfaces, and how textures and colors are applied. In this section, we'll explore three critical vertex attributes: **normals**, **texture coordinates**, and **vertex colors**.

```
1. Normals
```

Normals are vectors that define the orientation of a surface at each vertex. In 3D graphics, normals play a crucial role in lighting calculations, such as determining how light interacts with a surface and how shadows are cast. Normals are essential for achieving realistic shading effects, particularly when using techniques like **Phong shading**, **Blinn-Phong shading**, or **normal mapping**.

```
Understanding Normals in OpenGL
Vertex normals: A normal vector associated with each vertex
represents the direction perpendicular to the surface at that
point.
```

137

```
Face normals: A normal associated with a polygon's face, often
calculated by averaging the normals of the vertices forming that
polygon.
```

In OpenGL, each vertex can have its own normal, allowing the rendering of smooth, curved surfaces rather than flat polygonal faces. Here's how you define and use normals in OpenGL:

```
Storing normals: Normals are typically stored in a separate
attribute array from the vertex positions. In OpenGL, you store
them in vertex buffer objects (VBOs).
Using normals for lighting: Shaders use normals to calculate how
light interacts with the surface. The normal vector is compared
to the direction of the light source to determine how much light
hits a given point on the surface.
```

Example of Storing Normals

When creating a VBO for a model, you include the vertex positions and normals together. The following example shows how to store the normals alongside the vertices:

```cpp
std::vector<glm::vec3> vertices = {
    glm::vec3(0.0f, 0.5f, 0.0f),  // Vertex 1
    glm::vec3(-0.5f, -0.5f, 0.0f), // Vertex 2
    glm::vec3(0.5f, -0.5f, 0.0f)  // Vertex 3
};

std::vector<glm::vec3> normals = {
    glm::vec3(0.0f, 1.0f, 0.0f),  // Normal for Vertex 1
    glm::vec3(0.0f, 1.0f, 0.0f),  // Normal for Vertex 2
    glm::vec3(0.0f, 1.0f, 0.0f)  // Normal for Vertex 3
};
```

Once you have the normals, you use them in the vertex shader to calculate lighting and shading effects.

```
2. Texture Coordinates
```

Texture coordinates (also known as **UV coordinates**) define how a 2D texture is mapped onto a 3D surface. Essentially, they specify which part of the texture image should be applied to each vertex. Each vertex in a model can have corresponding 2D texture coordinates that map it to the texture.

```
Why Texture Coordinates Are Important
Mapping textures: Texture coordinates are used to "unwrap" a 3D
model into a 2D space. When a texture is applied to a 3D object,
OpenGL needs to know how to map the 2D texture onto the 3D
surface. This is done using the texture coordinates.
UV space: Texture coordinates are typically defined in the range
[0, 1] for both axes (u and v). The (0,0) coordinate corresponds
to the bottom-left corner of the texture, while (1,1)
corresponds to the top-right corner.
```

How Texture Coordinates Are Used in OpenGL

In OpenGL, texture coordinates are stored as a separate attribute in the vertex data. When rendering, the vertex shader will pass the texture coordinates to the fragment shader, where the texture is sampled to determine the final color of each fragment.

Example of Storing Texture Coordinates

Here's how you would store texture coordinates along with vertex positions and normals in a VBO:

```
cpp
```

```cpp
std::vector<glm::vec2> textureCoords = {
    glm::vec2(0.0f, 0.0f),  // Texture coordinate for Vertex 1
    glm::vec2(1.0f, 0.0f),  // Texture coordinate for Vertex 2
    glm::vec2(0.5f, 1.0f)   // Texture coordinate for Vertex 3
};
```

139

In this example, the texture coordinates indicate how the texture is applied to the triangle formed by the three vertices.

```
3. Vertex Colors
```

Vertex colors are a way of defining the color of each vertex, allowing you to directly influence the color of your 3D object. Vertex colors are often used for **flat shading**, **wireframe rendering**, or when textures are not required.

While textures provide detailed color information over a surface, vertex colors define a color at each vertex, which can be interpolated across the surface of the polygon. For example, if you have a triangle with three vertices, each with its own color, the color at each pixel (or fragment) of the triangle will be determined by interpolating the vertex colors.

```
Why Use Vertex Colors
Simplicity: Vertex colors are simple to use and can be a good
choice for low-complexity models or when you don't need detailed
textures.
Performance: For models that don't need complex textures, using
vertex colors can save memory and processing time, as you don't
need to load external texture maps.
Animation and effects: Vertex colors can be used for effects
like vertex-based lighting, color transitions, or vertex-based
animations.
```

How Vertex Colors Are Used in OpenGL

Like normals and texture coordinates, vertex colors are stored in a separate attribute array. These colors are passed through the pipeline and interpolated in the fragment shader to produce the final color of each pixel.

Example of Storing Vertex Colors

You can store vertex colors alongside the position, normal, and texture coordinate data:

```cpp
std::vector<glm::vec3> vertexColors = {
    glm::vec3(1.0f, 0.0f, 0.0f),   // Red for Vertex 1
    glm::vec3(0.0f, 1.0f, 0.0f),   // Green for Vertex 2
    glm::vec3(0.0f, 0.0f, 1.0f)    // Blue for Vertex 3
};
```

In this case, each vertex has its own color (red, green, and blue), which will be interpolated across the face of the triangle.

```
4. Combining Vertex Attributes
```

In OpenGL, the vertex data is often stored together in a **vertex array object (VAO)**, which groups all the vertex attributes into a single object. A typical VAO might contain the following vertex attributes:

```
Position: The location of the vertex in 3D space.
Normal: The normal vector associated with the vertex for
lighting calculations.
Texture Coordinates: The UV coordinates used for texturing.
Color: The color associated with the vertex.
```

Once these attributes are stored in buffers, they are passed to shaders for processing. The shaders then compute the final rendered output based on these attributes.

Example of Binding and Using Vertex Attributes

Here's an example of how to bind and use these vertex attributes in OpenGL:

```cpp
GLuint VAO, VBO, EBO;
glGenVertexArrays(1, &VAO);
glGenBuffers(1, &VBO);
```

```
glGenBuffers(1, &EBO);

glBindVertexArray(VAO);

// Position buffer
glBindBuffer(GL_ARRAY_BUFFER, VBO);
glBufferData(GL_ARRAY_BUFFER, sizeof(vertices), vertices.data(),
GL_STATIC_DRAW);
glVertexAttribPointer(0, 3, GL_FLOAT, GL_FALSE, 3 *
sizeof(GLfloat), (GLvoid*)0);
glEnableVertexAttribArray(0);

// Normal buffer
glBindBuffer(GL_ARRAY_BUFFER, VBO);
glBufferData(GL_ARRAY_BUFFER, sizeof(normals), normals.data(),
GL_STATIC_DRAW);
glVertexAttribPointer(1, 3, GL_FLOAT, GL_FALSE, 3 *
sizeof(GLfloat), (GLvoid*)0);
glEnableVertexAttribArray(1);

// Texture coordinate buffer
glBindBuffer(GL_ARRAY_BUFFER, VBO);
glBufferData(GL_ARRAY_BUFFER, sizeof(textureCoords),
textureCoords.data(), GL_STATIC_DRAW);
glVertexAttribPointer(2, 2, GL_FLOAT, GL_FALSE, 2 *
sizeof(GLfloat), (GLvoid*)0);
glEnableVertexAttribArray(2);

// Color buffer
glBindBuffer(GL_ARRAY_BUFFER, VBO);
glBufferData(GL_ARRAY_BUFFER, sizeof(vertexColors),
vertexColors.data(), GL_STATIC_DRAW);
glVertexAttribPointer(3, 3, GL_FLOAT, GL_FALSE, 3 *
sizeof(GLfloat), (GLvoid*)0);
glEnableVertexAttribArray(3);

glBindVertexArray(0);
```

In this example, the vertex data (positions, normals, texture coordinates, and colors) is loaded into OpenGL buffer objects and associated with the appropriate attribute locations in the vertex shader.

Summary

- **Normals** define the orientation of surfaces and are critical for lighting calculations.
- **Texture coordinates** map 2D textures to 3D models, specifying how textures are applied.
- **Vertex colors** assign colors to vertices, which are interpolated across a surface for simple color effects.

Each of these vertex attributes can be independently manipulated in the shaders to produce a variety of visual effects. By understanding how to use and combine these attributes, you can achieve realistic rendering and visual effects in OpenGL.

Creating and Handling Materials: Diffuse, Specular, and Emission Maps

In the world of 3D graphics, **materials** define the visual properties of surfaces that determine how light interacts with objects in a scene. Unlike textures, which provide surface details (like patterns or colors), materials dictate the **shiny** or **rough** characteristics of an object, how light reflects off it, or whether it emits light. Understanding how to create and handle materials is essential for realistic rendering in OpenGL.

What are Materials in 3D Graphics?

A **material** is a set of properties that define how a surface interacts with light. These properties govern how the object will appear under various lighting conditions and contribute to the overall realism of the scene. Materials are typically represented by several maps (images) and values that determine surface characteristics like color, reflectivity, roughness, and emission.

Materials are usually composed of the following components:

1. **Diffuse**: The base color or texture of the surface, showing how light diffuses across it.
2. **Specular**: How shiny or reflective the surface is, and the color of specular reflections.
3. **Emission**: How much light the surface emits, making the object appear to glow.

These properties are most often controlled through maps (2D images) and shader parameters. Let's dive into each of these maps and how to use them in OpenGL.

1. Diffuse Map (Base Color)

The **diffuse map**, also called the **base color map**, is the most fundamental texture used in 3D graphics. It defines the basic color of the material without any reflections or lighting effects. The diffuse map tells the renderer how the material looks under normal lighting, displaying details like color patterns, surface texture (such as wood grain or fabric), and overall appearance.

Key Points:

- **Diffuse Reflection**: Diffuse reflection is the light that strikes a surface and is scattered in many directions. This scattering is what gives the object its basic color.
- **Color Information**: The diffuse map is often a standard texture image, where each pixel corresponds to the color that should be applied to that part of the model.

Usage in OpenGL

In OpenGL, the diffuse map is passed to the fragment shader, where it is sampled based on the texture coordinates of the vertices. The result is multiplied with the lighting calculations to produce the final pixel color.

Here's an example of how to load and use a diffuse texture in OpenGL:

```cpp
GLuint diffuseTexture;
glGenTextures(1, &diffuseTexture);
glBindTexture(GL_TEXTURE_2D, diffuseTexture);

// Load the texture from an image file (using an image loading
library like stb_image)
int width, height, nrChannels;
unsigned char *data = stbi_load("diffuse_map.jpg", &width,
&height, &nrChannels, 0);
if (data)
{
    glTexImage2D(GL_TEXTURE_2D, 0, GL_RGB, width, height, 0,
    GL_RGB, GL_UNSIGNED_BYTE, data);
    glGenerateMipmap(GL_TEXTURE_2D);
}
stbi_image_free(data);
```

In your fragment shader, you would sample this diffuse texture like so:

```glsl
uniform sampler2D diffuseTexture;
in vec2 TexCoord;

out vec4 FragColor;

void main()
{
    vec3 diffuseColor = texture(diffuseTexture, TexCoord).rgb;
    FragColor = vec4(diffuseColor, 1.0f);
}
```

2. Specular Map

A **specular map** controls the shininess and reflectivity of a material. It defines how much light is reflected off the surface in a specular fashion, which creates highlights and shiny spots on the object. A specular map

145

generally consists of grayscale values, where white areas represent highly reflective surfaces (like metal or glass) and black areas represent non-reflective surfaces (like rough stone or wood).

Key Points:

- **Specular Reflection**: This is the mirror-like reflection of light that creates sharp highlights on the surface. Specular reflections are more noticeable on smooth, shiny materials.
- **Control of Shininess**: The specular map not only defines the reflectivity but also influences the sharpness of the specular highlights. The sharper and more intense the highlight, the shinier the surface.

Usage in OpenGL

In OpenGL, the specular map is usually stored as a grayscale image (where white represents high reflectivity). This map is passed to the fragment shader, where it modulates the intensity of the specular reflection computed in the lighting model.

Here's an example of how to load and use a specular texture:

cpp

```cpp
GLuint specularTexture;
glGenTextures(1, &specularTexture);
glBindTexture(GL_TEXTURE_2D, specularTexture);

// Load the texture from an image file
unsigned char *data = stbi_load("specular_map.jpg", &width,
&height, &nrChannels, 0);
if (data)
{
    glTexImage2D(GL_TEXTURE_2D, 0, GL_RGB, width, height, 0,
    GL_RGB, GL_UNSIGNED_BYTE, data);
    glGenerateMipmap(GL_TEXTURE_2D);
}
stbi_image_free(data);
```

In your fragment shader, you would sample the specular map to modulate the reflection:

```glsl
uniform sampler2D specularTexture;
uniform float shininess;  // A parameter controlling the
sharpness of the specular reflection
in vec2 TexCoord;
in vec3 Normal;
in vec3 FragPos;
out vec4 FragColor;

void main()
{
    vec3 specularColor = texture(specularTexture, TexCoord).rgb;
    // Calculate the specular reflection based on the Phong model
    vec3 viewDir = normalize(cameraPos - FragPos);
    vec3 reflectDir = reflect(-lightDir, Normal);
    float spec = pow(max(dot(viewDir, reflectDir), 0.0),
    shininess);
    vec3 specular = spec * lightColor * specularColor;

    FragColor = vec4(specular, 1.0f);
}
```

3. Emission Map

An **emission map** makes a material emit light, simulating a glowing effect. Objects with emission maps will appear to glow, regardless of the surrounding lighting conditions. Emission maps are often used for creating effects like glowing signs, light sources (e.g., lamps, torches), or emissive elements in sci-fi or fantasy scenes.

Key Points:

- **Emission Reflection**: Emission is not a type of reflection. It represents light that is emitted from the surface, meaning it contributes to the scene's lighting, rather than reflecting incoming light.

- **Glow Effect**: When using an emission map, areas of the texture that are brighter (typically white or bright colors) will glow, making the object appear to radiate light.

Usage in OpenGL

The emission map is usually a grayscale image where the white areas represent the brightest points that emit light. This map is combined with the scene's lighting calculations to simulate light emission.

Here's how you could load and apply an emission map in OpenGL:

```cpp
GLuint emissionTexture;
glGenTextures(1, &emissionTexture);
glBindTexture(GL_TEXTURE_2D, emissionTexture);

// Load the emission texture
unsigned char *data = stbi_load("emission_map.jpg", &width,
&height, &nrChannels, 0);
if (data)
{
    glTexImage2D(GL_TEXTURE_2D, 0, GL_RGB, width, height, 0,
    GL_RGB, GL_UNSIGNED_BYTE, data);
    glGenerateMipmap(GL_TEXTURE_2D);
}
stbi_image_free(data);
```

In your fragment shader, you would add the emission effect like so:

```glsl
uniform sampler2D emissionTexture;
in vec2 TexCoord;
out vec4 FragColor;

void main()
```

```
{
    vec3 emissionColor = texture(emissionTexture, TexCoord).rgb;
    FragColor = vec4(emissionColor, 1.0f);
}
```

To simulate glowing objects, you can modify the final color output by adding the emission color to the overall fragment color:

glsl

```
FragColor = vec4(emissionColor + calculatedLighting, 1.0f);
```

4. Combining Material Maps

In a typical material, you may have **diffuse**, **specular**, and **emission maps** all used together. To combine them in OpenGL, you would sample each map and mix their effects in the fragment shader, like so:

glsl

```
uniform sampler2D diffuseTexture;
uniform sampler2D specularTexture;
uniform sampler2D emissionTexture;
in vec2 TexCoord;

out vec4 FragColor;

void main()
{
    vec3 diffuseColor = texture(diffuseTexture, TexCoord).rgb;
    vec3 specularColor = texture(specularTexture, TexCoord).rgb;
    vec3 emissionColor = texture(emissionTexture, TexCoord).rgb;

    vec3 finalColor = diffuseColor * lighting + specularColor *
    reflection + emissionColor;
    FragColor = vec4(finalColor, 1.0f);
}
```

This example shows how the material maps combine to produce the final color output, where each map contributes to the overall appearance of the surface.

- **Diffuse maps** define the base color of the material, affecting how light is scattered across the surface.
- **Specular maps** determine how reflective the material is, controlling the appearance of shiny spots and highlights.
- **Emission maps** simulate the glowing effect of a material, making objects appear to emit light.
- By combining these maps in the fragment shader, you can create realistic materials with a wide range of visual effects, from matte surfaces to glowing neon lights.

Materials play a key role in the realism and appearance of 3D scenes, and with a solid understanding of how to use these maps, you can achieve high-quality rendering results in OpenGL.

Building a 3D Scene and Adding Multiple Objects

Once you understand how to load and handle 3D models, textures, and materials, the next step is to combine multiple objects into a cohesive 3D scene. Building a 3D scene involves positioning, transforming, and organizing multiple objects in a way that allows you to create a rich, interactive environment. This can include static elements like terrain and buildings, as well as dynamic elements like moving objects, characters, and light sources.

In this section, we will go over the process of building a simple 3D scene in OpenGL, adding multiple objects, and transforming them using basic techniques like translation, rotation, and scaling. Additionally, we will also discuss organizing your scene and implementing a basic rendering pipeline for drawing multiple objects efficiently.

1. Organizing the Scene

A **3D scene** typically consists of multiple objects, and each object can have its own transformation, material, texture, and even animations. Organizing the scene properly helps you manage your objects, their transformations, and interactions with the camera, lights, and other objects.

Scene Graph

One way to organize a 3D scene is by using a **scene graph**, which is a tree-like structure where each node represents an object or group of objects in the scene. Nodes in the graph store information such as:

- **Transformations**: The position, rotation, and scale of objects.
- **Materials and Textures**: The appearance of objects.
- **Meshes**: The geometric data (vertices, indices, normals, etc.).
- **Lights**: The lighting sources in the scene.
- **Cameras**: The viewpoint or camera from which the scene is viewed.

While using a scene graph for complex scenes is a more advanced topic, for now, we'll keep things simple and focus on rendering multiple objects with transformations.

2. Setting Up the Scene in OpenGL

Before rendering objects, you need to set up your **view** and **projection matrices**, which define the camera's position and how the 3D scene is projected onto the 2D screen. Additionally, you'll need a transformation matrix for each object to handle its position, rotation, and scale in the world.

Let's go through the steps to set up the scene:

Camera Setup

First, you need to define a **view matrix** and a **projection matrix**. These matrices define how the camera interacts with the scene.

- **View Matrix**: Defines the camera's position and orientation relative to the world.

- **Projection Matrix**: Defines how 3D objects are projected onto the 2D screen, usually with a perspective or orthogonal projection.

Here's an example of how to set up these matrices using **GLM** (OpenGL Mathematics):

cpp

```cpp
glm::mat4 projection = glm::perspective(glm::radians(45.0f),
(float)windowWidth / (float)windowHeight, 0.1f, 100.0f);
glm::mat4 view = glm::lookAt(cameraPos, cameraPos + cameraFront,
cameraUp);
```

- glm::perspective: Creates a perspective projection matrix with a field of view of 45 degrees, an aspect ratio matching the window size, and a near and far plane.
- glm::lookAt: Creates a view matrix that simulates a camera looking at the world from cameraPos towards a target point.

Adding Objects to the Scene

Each object in your scene is defined by its **model matrix**, which defines the transformations to be applied to it. For example, you might have a cube, a sphere, and a textured object, each with different transformations.

Cube Example:

Here's how to set up and render a cube in the scene:

cpp

```cpp
glm::mat4 model = glm::mat4(1.0f);  // Identity matrix
model = glm::translate(model, glm::vec3(0.0f, 0.0f, -3.0f));  //
Move the cube 3 units back
model = glm::rotate(model, glm::radians(45.0f), glm::vec3(1.0f,
0.0f, 0.0f));  // Rotate along X-axis
```

```cpp
// Pass the model matrix to the shader
shader.setMat4("model", model);
glBindVertexArray(cubeVAO);
glDrawElements(GL_TRIANGLES, 36, GL_UNSIGNED_INT, 0);
```

- **Translation**: The cube is moved along the Z-axis to position it properly in the scene.
- **Rotation**: The cube is rotated by 45 degrees around the X-axis.

You can similarly apply transformations (like rotation, translation, and scaling) to other objects in the scene.

3. Adding Multiple Objects

Now that we have a basic setup, we can add multiple objects to the scene. Each object can have its own model matrix, material properties, textures, and lighting calculations. You can handle multiple objects in a loop or as individual render calls.

cpp

```cpp
// First object: Cube
glm::mat4 model1 = glm::mat4(1.0f);
model1 = glm::translate(model1, glm::vec3(-1.0f, 0.0f, -5.0f));
shader.setMat4("model", model1);
glBindVertexArray(cubeVAO);
glDrawElements(GL_TRIANGLES, 36, GL_UNSIGNED_INT, 0);

// Second object: Another Cube
glm::mat4 model2 = glm::mat4(1.0f);
model2 = glm::translate(model2, glm::vec3(1.0f, 0.0f, -5.0f));
shader.setMat4("model", model2);
glBindVertexArray(cubeVAO);
glDrawElements(GL_TRIANGLES, 36, GL_UNSIGNED_INT, 0);
```

In this example:

- The first cube is translated to the left (-1.0f) and positioned 5 units away on the Z-axis.
- The second cube is translated to the right (+1.0f) with a similar Z-axis position.

By adjusting the model matrices for each object, you can control their placement, rotation, and scale in the scene.

4. Handling Lighting for Multiple Objects

When you have multiple objects in the scene, you will need to account for how light interacts with each object. Typically, you would apply the same lighting model (like Phong or Blinn-Phong) to all objects in the scene. However, for more advanced scenes, you might want to apply different materials, shaders, or lighting effects to individual objects.

For simplicity, let's assume we have a **point light** in the scene that affects all objects. The point light's position and properties (color, intensity, etc.) are passed as uniforms to the fragment shaders of all objects.

```cpp
// Example point light position and color
glm::vec3 lightPos(1.2f, 1.0f, 2.0f);
glm::vec3 lightColor(1.0f, 1.0f, 1.0f);

// Pass light properties to the shader
shader.setVec3("light.position", lightPos);
shader.setVec3("light.color", lightColor);
```

In the fragment shader, you would calculate the diffuse and specular components based on the distance from the light source and the surface's normal.

```glsl
vec3 lightDir = normalize(light.position - fragPos);
float diff = max(dot(norm, lightDir), 0.0);
vec3 diffuse = diff * light.color * material.diffuse;
```

This process is repeated for each object in the scene, ensuring that the light interacts with every object accordingly.

5. Optimizing Rendering with Instancing

When dealing with many objects in the scene (such as trees, rocks, or any repetitive object), using **instancing** can drastically improve performance. Instancing allows you to render multiple copies of the same object using a single draw call, by passing a list of transformations for each instance.

Here's how you can render multiple instances of an object efficiently:

```cpp
glm::mat4 modelMatrices[10];  // Array to hold the model
matrices for each instance
for (int i = 0; i < 10; ++i) {
    modelMatrices[i] = glm::translate(glm::mat4(1.0f),
    glm::vec3(i * 2.0f, 0.0f, -5.0f));
}

// Pass all model matrices to the shader at once
glBindBuffer(GL_ARRAY_BUFFER, instanceVBO);
glBufferData(GL_ARRAY_BUFFER, sizeof(modelMatrices),
&modelMatrices[0], GL_STATIC_DRAW);

// Enable instancing in the vertex shader
shader.setMat4("model", modelMatrices[0]);  // Pass the first
instance matrix
glDrawArraysInstanced(GL_TRIANGLES, 0, 36, 10);  // Draw 10
instances of the object
```

This technique reduces the number of draw calls, improving performance when rendering a large number of identical objects.

Building a 3D scene and adding multiple objects in OpenGL involves a number of key steps:

- Setting up the **view** and **projection matrices** to define the camera and perspective.
- Adding objects to the scene and applying transformations (translation, rotation, scaling) using **model matrices**.
- Handling lighting and materials to ensure that all objects in the scene interact correctly with the light.
- Optimizing performance by using techniques like **instancing** for rendering large numbers of objects.

Once you're comfortable with these basic principles, you can expand your scenes with more complex objects, camera movements, dynamic lighting, shadows, and more advanced techniques like particle systems and physics simulations. The flexibility of OpenGL combined with efficient scene management will allow you to create stunning and interactive 3D environments.

Optimizing Geometry and Reducing Draw Calls

When building a complex 3D scene with many objects, one of the primary challenges is performance. Rendering many objects can quickly become computationally expensive if you don't optimize the way you handle geometry and manage draw calls. Reducing the number of draw calls and optimizing the geometry itself are two essential techniques for improving the performance of your OpenGL application, especially for large and complex scenes.

In this section, we'll dive into methods for optimizing geometry, reducing draw calls, and efficiently handling large numbers of objects in OpenGL.

1. What Are Draw Calls and Why Do They Matter?

A **draw call** is a command issued to the GPU to render an object. Each draw call involves a set of commands that tells OpenGL what data to use (e.g., which vertex buffers, index buffers, or textures) and how to render that data (e.g., the shape, color, or texture). In a basic OpenGL program, each object might require a separate draw call, which means that for each object in your scene, OpenGL has to bind buffers, configure shaders, and send commands to the GPU.

Draw calls are expensive because:

- **State Changes**: Every time a new draw call is made, OpenGL may need to change state (e.g., binding different textures or shaders). This involves overhead in CPU processing.
- **CPU-GPU Communication**: Each draw call involves communication between the CPU (which issues the draw calls) and the GPU (which performs the rendering). Too many draw calls can create a bottleneck.
- **Pipeline Stalls**: Excessive draw calls can slow down the GPU by causing pipeline stalls, where the GPU waits for data from the CPU.

To maintain high performance, it's crucial to reduce the number of draw calls and minimize the overhead involved in rendering large numbers of objects.

2. Reducing Draw Calls with Instancing

As mentioned earlier, **instancing** is one of the most powerful techniques for reducing draw calls when rendering large numbers of identical objects. With instancing, you can draw many objects using a single draw call by passing multiple transformation matrices to the GPU. The GPU then renders each instance of the object with its corresponding transformation.

For example, imagine you want to render a forest of trees. Instead of creating a separate draw call for each tree, you can use instancing to render all the trees with a single draw call, and vary their positions, rotations, and scales by passing a list of transformation matrices.

157

Here's an example of how you can implement instancing:

cpp

```cpp
// Prepare an array of transformation matrices for the instances
glm::mat4 modelMatrices[100];
for (int i = 0; i < 100; ++i) {
    modelMatrices[i] = glm::translate(glm::mat4(1.0f),
    glm::vec3(i * 2.0f, 0.0f, -5.0f));  // Varying the position
}

// Pass the model matrices to the GPU in a single buffer
glBindBuffer(GL_ARRAY_BUFFER, instanceVBO);
glBufferData(GL_ARRAY_BUFFER, sizeof(modelMatrices),
&modelMatrices[0], GL_STATIC_DRAW);

// Draw all instances with a single draw call
glDrawArraysInstanced(GL_TRIANGLES, 0, 36, 100);  // 100
instances of the object
```

In this example:

- The **model matrices** for each tree are calculated and stored in an array.
- These matrices are uploaded to the GPU via the instanceVBO buffer.
- The glDrawArraysInstanced function then renders 100 trees with a single draw call.

This technique significantly reduces the number of draw calls and improves performance, particularly when rendering a large number of objects with the same geometry.

3. Combining Geometry with Vertex Buffers

In addition to instancing, you can also **combine** the geometry of multiple objects into a single vertex buffer. This technique, known as **batching**, involves grouping several objects with the same material or texture into a single mesh. Instead of issuing multiple draw calls for each object, you can draw all objects in a single draw call by merging their vertex data into one large buffer.

Batching Example

Suppose you have a scene with many cubes. Instead of rendering each cube separately, you can merge their geometry into a single vertex buffer and draw them all at once:

1. Create a large **vertex buffer** that contains the vertices of all cubes in the scene.
2. Use **index buffers** to specify how the vertices are connected to form triangles.
3. Apply a single transformation to each cube (using instancing) to position it correctly in the scene.

Here's a simplified process of combining multiple objects:

cpp

```cpp
// Combine the vertices of multiple cubes into a single buffer
std::vector<float> combinedVertices;
for (int i = 0; i < numCubes; ++i) {
    glm::mat4 model = glm::translate(glm::mat4(1.0f),
    glm::vec3(i * 2.0f, 0.0f, -5.0f));  // Position each cube
    addCubeVertices(combinedVertices, model);  // Add vertices
    to combined buffer
}

// Upload the combined vertex buffer
glBindBuffer(GL_ARRAY_BUFFER, combinedVBO);
glBufferData(GL_ARRAY_BUFFER, combinedVertices.size() *
sizeof(float), &combinedVertices[0], GL_STATIC_DRAW);

// Draw all cubes in a single draw call
glDrawArrays(GL_TRIANGLES, 0, combinedVertices.size() / 3);  //
Adjust size for total number of vertices
```

By merging the geometry and using **index buffers** to define how the vertices are connected, you reduce the number of draw calls and increase efficiency.

4. Using Level of Detail (LOD) for Complex Geometry

In large 3D scenes, you often have objects that are distant from the camera and occupy a small portion of the screen. Rendering these objects with high-detail geometry is unnecessary, and can hurt performance. This is where **Level of Detail (LOD)** comes into play.

LOD is a technique where objects are rendered with different levels of detail based on their distance from the camera. The further away an object is, the simpler its geometry can be. For example, distant terrain might be rendered using a low-poly version, while objects close to the camera will have high-polygon models.

In OpenGL, implementing LOD typically involves:

1. **Creating multiple versions** of the object with varying levels of detail.
2. **Selecting the appropriate version** based on the distance from the camera.
3. **Switching between models** dynamically during the rendering process.

This can drastically reduce the number of polygons that need to be processed, improving rendering speed without sacrificing visual quality.

5. Using Occlusion Culling to Remove Invisible Objects

Another technique for optimizing performance is **occlusion culling**, which involves determining which objects are visible to the camera and which are hidden behind other objects. Objects that are not visible (i.e., those blocked by other objects) don't need to be rendered, so culling them can save a lot of computation.

There are several ways to implement occlusion culling:

- **Frustum Culling**: This method involves checking whether objects are inside the camera's viewing frustum (the pyramid-shaped volume that defines the visible area). Objects outside the frustum can be skipped.
- **Bounding Volumes**: You can encapsulate each object in a simple shape, such as a bounding box or sphere, and check if that volume intersects the camera's frustum. If the bounding volume is outside the frustum, the object is not rendered.
- **Hardware Occlusion Queries**: OpenGL provides occlusion queries, which can be used to determine whether a specific object is visible or blocked by others. This can be more computationally expensive, but it's useful in more complex scenarios.

Using **frustum culling** and **bounding volumes** is often sufficient for most scenes, but hardware occlusion queries can be helpful when dealing with highly complex or dense environments.

6. Optimizing Textures and Materials

Textures are another area where optimization can have a significant impact on performance. A few ways to optimize textures include:

- **Texture Atlases**: Rather than using multiple texture maps for different objects, combine several textures into a single large texture atlas. This reduces the number of texture bindings and draw calls, improving performance.
- **Mipmapping**: Mipmaps are precomputed textures at various levels of detail, used to optimize texture sampling. When an object is far away, OpenGL can sample from a lower-resolution mipmap, reducing memory usage and improving performance.
- **Compressed Textures**: OpenGL supports compressed texture formats (such as DXT1/5, etc.), which reduce the amount of memory required for textures, leading to faster loading times and lower memory usage.

Optimizing geometry and reducing draw calls are crucial for creating high-performance 3D applications in OpenGL. By using techniques like **instancing**, **batching**, **level of detail (LOD)**, **occlusion culling**, and **texture optimization**, you can significantly reduce the workload on the GPU and improve frame rates, even in complex scenes.

With the right optimizations, your OpenGL application can handle large, dynamic environments efficiently, ensuring smooth rendering and interactivity. Understanding and applying these techniques will allow you to create professional-grade 3D graphics that run smoothly on a variety of hardware configurations.

Lighting and Shadows in 3D Environments

Lighting is one of the most important elements in 3D graphics. It can define the mood, add depth, highlight key features, and make objects appear more realistic or stylized. In this chapter, we will focus on understanding the different types of lighting used in 3D environments: **Point Lights**, **Directional Lights**, and **Spotlights**. Each type has unique properties that can be utilized to achieve specific effects, and understanding how to work with them will elevate the realism and functionality of your 3D scenes.

1. What is Lighting in 3D Graphics?

Lighting in 3D graphics refers to the use of light sources to illuminate objects in a scene. The way light interacts with surfaces affects how objects appear to the viewer, influencing the perception of depth, material properties, and the overall atmosphere of the scene. In OpenGL, lighting calculations are typically done using the **Phong Reflection Model** or other more advanced models, which consider multiple types of light and how they interact with the objects' surfaces.

Understanding the different types of lighting sources is crucial to creating realistic or artistic lighting effects. The three most commonly used light types in 3D graphics are:

- **Point Lights**
- **Directional Lights**

- **Spotlights**

Each light type behaves differently and serves specific purposes depending on the scene's needs.

2. Point Lights

A **point light** is a light source that emits light in all directions from a single point in space. This type of light mimics real-world sources like light bulbs, fireflies, or candles. The key characteristic of a point light is that it radiates light in every direction, creating a spherical illumination radius.

Characteristics of Point Lights:

- **Position-based**: The light source has a specific position in 3D space, and its intensity decreases as the distance from the light increases.
- **Attenuation**: Point lights typically have a falloff or attenuation over distance. The light intensity decreases with distance from the light source, and this can be controlled via attenuation coefficients.
- **Constant Attenuation**: The light's intensity remains constant, regardless of distance.
- **Linear Attenuation**: The intensity decreases linearly with distance.
- **Quadratic Attenuation**: The intensity decreases quadratically, meaning it gets weaker more quickly as the distance increases.

Use Case for Point Lights:

Point lights are great for simulating small, localized light sources. They are commonly used to represent:

- Light bulbs
- Lanterns or torches
- Street lamps
- Fireplace lighting

In OpenGL, a simple point light calculation would involve computing the distance between the point light and the surface point, and then applying an attenuation function to determine the final intensity.

cpp

```
float distance = glm::length(lightPos - fragPos);
float attenuation = 1.0f / (1.0f + 0.1f * distance + 0.01f *
(distance * distance));
vec3 lightColor = pointLightColor * attenuation;
```

This formula calculates the attenuation of light based on its distance from the point being illuminated.

3. Directional Lights

A **directional light** simulates a light source that is infinitely far away, meaning it has parallel rays that do not diminish with distance. It is typically used to represent sunlight or other distant light sources. Unlike point lights, directional lights do not have a specific position; instead, they are defined by a direction vector.

Characteristics of Directional Lights:

- **Parallel light rays**: The light comes from a single direction, and its rays are parallel. There is no attenuation based on distance, meaning it illuminates every object in the scene with equal intensity, regardless of how far the object is from the light source.
- **Global Influence**: Since it does not have a position, a directional light affects the entire scene evenly. Every object illuminated by this light will experience the same intensity, which makes it ideal for simulating environmental lighting conditions like sunlight.

Use Case for Directional Lights:

Directional lights are commonly used for simulating:

- **Sunlight**: The sun is so far away that the light rays can be treated as parallel.
- **Moonlight**: Similar to sunlight, moonlight is treated as a directional light.
- **Street lights at night**: When simulating cityscapes with ambient light.

In OpenGL, the lighting calculation for a directional light is simpler since the distance doesn't affect the light's intensity. Instead, it focuses on the angle between the surface normal and the direction of the light:

cpp

```
vec3 lightDir = normalize(-lightDir); // Direction of light,
e.g., from the sun
float diff = max(dot(normal, lightDir), 0.0);
vec3 diffuse = diff * lightColor;
```

This formula uses the **dot product** to calculate how much of the light hits a surface, with the result being 1 when the surface is directly facing the light and 0 when it's perpendicular to the light.

4. Spotlights

A **spotlight** is a light source that emits light in a cone shape, with its intensity decreasing as the light spreads out. Spotlights are commonly used for simulating effects such as flashlights, theater lights, or car headlights. A spotlight is defined by three parameters:

- **Position**: Where the light is located in the scene.
- **Direction**: The direction in which the light is pointing.
- **Cone Angle**: The angle that defines the spread of the light.

Characteristics of Spotlights:

- **Cone of influence**: The spotlight affects objects only within a specific cone. The light is strongest at the center of the cone and fades as the distance from the cone's center increases.

- **Attenuation**: Like point lights, spotlights also experience attenuation, but their intensity is also influenced by the angle of the surface relative to the light's direction.
- **Spotlight Falloff**: The intensity of the light decreases as you move further from the center of the cone, and this is often controlled by a factor called the **spotlight exponent**.

Use Case for Spotlights:
Spotlights are useful for focused lighting effects, such as:

- **Flashlights**: Used in games to simulate handheld lights.
- **Theater lighting**: Spotlights highlighting actors or specific areas on stage.
- **Vehicle headlights**: Simulating the headlights of cars or other vehicles.

In OpenGL, the calculation for a spotlight is more complex than a point light or directional light. It takes into account both the **distance** from the light and the **cone angle** of the spotlight, as well as the **spotlight exponent**, which controls how quickly the light intensity decreases:

cpp

```
vec3 lightDir = normalize(lightPos - fragPos);
float theta = dot(lightDir, normalize(-lightDirection)); //
Angle of light
float epsilon = (cos(innerCutOff) - cos(outerCutOff));
float intensity = clamp((theta - cos(outerCutOff)) / epsilon,
0.0, 1.0);
float attenuation = 1.0f / (1.0f + 0.1f * distance + 0.01f *
(distance * distance));
vec3 spotlightColor = lightColor * intensity * attenuation;
```

This code calculates both the attenuation based on distance and the intensity of the spotlight depending on the angle between the surface and the light's direction.

5. Combining Multiple Light Sources in a Scene

In most 3D scenes, multiple light sources are often combined to create the desired visual effects. OpenGL allows you to combine multiple lights by performing the necessary calculations for each light type and summing their contributions to a fragment's final color.

For instance, a scene might have one directional light (sunlight) and several point lights (light bulbs) scattered around the scene. You would compute the contribution of each light type and then combine their effects.

In an OpenGL program, this could look something like this:

```cpp
vec3 result = ambientLight + pointLight + directionalLight +
spotlight;
```

Where ambientLight, pointLight, directionalLight, and spotlight represent the light contribution from each light source.

Lighting is a powerful tool in 3D graphics, and understanding the different types of lights and how they behave can vastly improve the realism and immersion of your scenes. **Point lights**, **directional lights**, and **spotlights** each serve a unique purpose, from simulating distant sunlight to localized, focused lighting effects. By mastering these light types and combining them effectively, you can create a range of visual effects that bring your 3D environments to life.

As you continue to experiment with these light sources, consider how each type can be used creatively in your projects. Whether you're aiming for a realistic simulation or a stylized artistic effect, lighting will play a crucial role in the success of your scene.

Implementing Shadow Mapping for Realistic Depth

Shadows are essential for creating a realistic 3D environment. They add depth, provide a sense of spatial relationships between objects, and contribute to the overall atmosphere of a scene. One of the most widely used techniques for simulating shadows in real-time 3D graphics is **shadow mapping**.

Shadow mapping is a technique that generates a depth map from the perspective of the light source, which can then be used to determine whether a fragment (or pixel) is in shadow or illuminated by the light source. The shadow map stores the distance from the light to the nearest surface for each pixel in the light's view. This data is later used during the rendering process to compare the depth of fragments to the depth stored in the shadow map, thereby determining if a pixel is in shadow or lit.

In this section, we'll go over the following steps to implement shadow mapping in OpenGL:
- **Understanding the basics of shadow mapping**
- **Setting up the shadow map framebuffer**
- **Rendering the scene from the light's perspective**
- **Using the shadow map for shading**
- **Optimizing shadow mapping**

1. Understanding the Basics of Shadow Mapping

Shadow mapping works by creating a depth map, or a **shadow map**, that represents the distances from the light to the surfaces in the scene. When a scene is rendered, the depth of each pixel is stored in this map from the point of view of the light source.

When rendering the scene from the camera's perspective, the depth at each pixel is compared to the depth stored in the shadow map. If the pixel is further away from the light than the value in the shadow map, the pixel is considered to be in shadow. If the pixel is closer to the light, it is illuminated.

Key Steps in Shadow Mapping:

1. **Render the scene from the light's perspective** and capture the depth information. This depth information is stored in the shadow map.
2. **Render the scene from the camera's perspective** using the shadow map to determine whether each fragment is in shadow or lit.

2. Setting Up the Shadow Map Framebuffer

The first step in shadow mapping is creating a framebuffer that will hold the shadow map. This framebuffer stores the depth information of the scene as seen from the light's perspective. To set it up, we will need a **depth texture** that will hold the depth values.

Here's how to set up the shadow map framebuffer:

cpp

```
GLuint depthMapFBO;
GLuint depthMap;

glGenFramebuffers(1, &depthMapFBO);

// Create depth texture for the shadow map
glGenTextures(1, &depthMap);
glBindTexture(GL_TEXTURE_2D, depthMap);
glTexImage2D(GL_TEXTURE_2D, 0, GL_DEPTH_COMPONENT, SHADOW_WIDTH,
SHADOW_HEIGHT, 0, GL_DEPTH_COMPONENT, GL_FLOAT, NULL);
glTexParameteri(GL_TEXTURE_2D, GL_TEXTURE_MIN_FILTER,
GL_NEAREST);
glTexParameteri(GL_TEXTURE_2D, GL_TEXTURE_MAG_FILTER,
GL_NEAREST);
glTexParameteri(GL_TEXTURE_2D, GL_TEXTURE_WRAP_S,
GL_CLAMP_TO_BORDER);
glTexParameteri(GL_TEXTURE_2D, GL_TEXTURE_WRAP_T,
GL_CLAMP_TO_BORDER);
float borderColor[] = {1.0f, 1.0f, 1.0f, 1.0f};
```

```
glTexParameterfv(GL_TEXTURE_2D, GL_TEXTURE_BORDER_COLOR,
borderColor);

// Bind the texture to the framebuffer
glBindFramebuffer(GL_FRAMEBUFFER, depthMapFBO);
glFramebufferTexture2D(GL_FRAMEBUFFER, GL_DEPTH_ATTACHMENT,
GL_TEXTURE_2D, depthMap, 0);
glDrawBuffer(GL_NONE); // No color buffer is needed
glReadBuffer(GL_NONE); // No color buffer is needed

// Check if the framebuffer is complete
if (glCheckFramebufferStatus(GL_FRAMEBUFFER) !=
GL_FRAMEBUFFER_COMPLETE)
    std::cout << "ERROR::SHADOW::FRAMEBUFFER:: Framebuffer is
    not complete!" << std::endl;
glBindFramebuffer(GL_FRAMEBUFFER, 0);
```

Here, we've created a framebuffer and attached a depth texture to it. This texture will store the depth information from the light's point of view. The texture is configured with the GL_DEPTH_COMPONENT format, meaning it will store only depth data, and it uses a filtering method (GL_NEAREST) that works well for shadow maps.

3. Rendering the Scene from the Light's Perspective

Once the shadow map framebuffer is set up, we can render the scene from the light's perspective to populate the shadow map. This is done by setting the camera to be at the light's position and looking at the scene from that viewpoint.

You'll need a **light's view matrix** and **projection matrix** to properly set the camera for rendering from the light's point of view. For example:

cpp

```
glm::mat4 lightProjection = glm::ortho(-10.0f, 10.0f, -10.0f,
10.0f, 0.1f, 100.0f);  // Or perspective projection for
spotlights
```

171

```
glm::mat4 lightView = glm::lookAt(lightPos, lightTarget,
lightUp);
glm::mat4 lightSpaceMatrix = lightProjection * lightView;
```

Here, lightProjection is the projection matrix used for rendering from the light's perspective. If using a **point light**, you may use a perspective projection, while for a **directional light** or **spotlight**, you may use an orthographic projection.

Once the light's camera is set up, you can begin rendering the scene from its perspective:

cpp

```
glBindFramebuffer(GL_FRAMEBUFFER, depthMapFBO);
glClear(GL_DEPTH_BUFFER_BIT);
glViewport(0, 0, SHADOW_WIDTH, SHADOW_HEIGHT);

// Set the shader for depth rendering
shadowShader.use();
shadowShader.setMat4("lightSpaceMatrix", lightSpaceMatrix);

// Render the scene objects from the light's perspective
renderScene(shadowShader);
glBindFramebuffer(GL_FRAMEBUFFER, 0);
```

In this code, the scene is rendered from the light's point of view, and the depth information is written to the shadow map.

4. Using the Shadow Map for Shading

After rendering the scene from the light's perspective, you can use the shadow map to calculate shadows when rendering the scene from the camera's perspective. The shadow map is sampled during the fragment shading stage.

In your fragment shader, you need to compare the depth of each fragment with the depth stored in the shadow map to determine if it is in shadow.

Here is an example of how to implement shadow comparison in the fragment shader:

```cpp
float shadowCalculation(vec4 fragPosLightSpace)
{
    // Transform the fragment position to light space
    vec3 projCoords = fragPosLightSpace.xyz /
    fragPosLightSpace.w;
    projCoords = projCoords * 0.5 + 0.5; // Map to [0, 1]

    // Sample depth from the shadow map
    float closestDepth = texture(depthMap, projCoords.xy).r;
    float currentDepth = projCoords.z;

    // Perform the shadow comparison
    float shadow = currentDepth > closestDepth + bias ? 1.0 :
    0.0;
    return shadow;
}
```

In this shader, fragPosLightSpace is the fragment's position in the light's view space, and we compare its depth to the closest depth stored in the shadow map. If the current depth is greater than the depth stored in the shadow map (with some bias to avoid shadow acne), we consider the fragment to be in shadow.

5. Optimizing Shadow Mapping

Shadow mapping can be computationally expensive, especially with large scenes or many light sources. Here are a few techniques to optimize shadow mapping:

1. Shadow Map Resolution:

Reducing the resolution of the shadow map can significantly speed up the rendering process. However, this may result in low-quality shadows. You should balance performance and quality based on your specific use case.

2. Biasing the Depth Comparison:

To prevent **shadow acne** (unwanted self-shadowing artifacts), apply a small bias when comparing depths in the fragment shader. However, too large a bias will create **Peter Panning** (where objects appear to float off the ground), so it's essential to find the right balance.

```cpp
float bias = 0.005f;
float shadow = currentDepth > closestDepth + bias ? 1.0 : 0.0;
```

3. Cascaded Shadow Maps (CSM):

For scenes with large view distances (e.g., outdoors), you may use **Cascaded Shadow Maps**, where multiple shadow maps are used at different levels of detail, depending on the camera's distance from the light.

4. Soft Shadows:

To make shadows look less harsh and more natural, consider implementing **soft shadows** using techniques such as **Percentage-Closer Filtering (PCF)** or **Variance Shadow Maps**.

Shadow mapping is an essential technique for adding realism to 3D scenes. By generating a shadow map that stores depth information from the light's perspective, and comparing that information to the scene during rendering, you can simulate realistic shadows. This method allows you to control the presence and quality of shadows in your 3D scenes, from simple point lights to complex spotlights.

With the proper implementation of shadow mapping, along with optimization techniques such as biasing and Cascaded Shadow Maps, you can create realistic, dynamic lighting in your OpenGL applications. This not only enhances the visual fidelity of your scenes but also adds a layer of immersion, depth, and realism to your 3D world.

Advanced Lighting Effects: Global Illumination, HDR (High Dynamic Range)

While basic lighting techniques such as ambient, diffuse, and specular lighting can create visually appealing 3D scenes, more advanced lighting effects are needed to achieve greater realism and depth. Two of the most important techniques in advanced lighting are **Global Illumination (GI)** and **High Dynamic Range (HDR)** rendering. These techniques help simulate more lifelike lighting interactions and improve the visual richness of scenes.

In this section, we will dive into the concepts behind **Global Illumination (GI)** and **HDR**, how they enhance the realism of 3D environments, and how to implement them in OpenGL.

1. Global Illumination (GI)

Global Illumination (GI) refers to a set of algorithms used in 3D graphics to simulate the way light bounces off surfaces and interacts with other objects in a scene. Traditional lighting models, such as the Phong shading model, consider only direct light sources (light directly reaching the surface from the light source). However, in the real world, light doesn't just travel directly from a source to a surface—it also bounces off other surfaces, influencing how light interacts with the environment.

In real life, when light hits an object, it not only reflects off that object but also illuminates nearby objects. This phenomenon, known as **indirect lighting**, is a major contributor to the overall lighting of a scene. GI algorithms attempt to model this behavior by simulating the effects of light bouncing multiple times throughout a scene.

Types of Global Illumination Methods:

- **Ray Tracing**: Simulates light paths through the scene by casting rays from the camera, then tracing their interactions with objects, light sources, and surfaces. While ray tracing can produce very realistic images, it is computationally expensive.

- **Radiosity**: Focuses on the exchange of light energy between diffuse surfaces. Radiosity methods are suitable for scenes with primarily diffuse materials (e.g., matte surfaces).

- **Photon Mapping**: A two-pass technique where photons (light particles) are shot from the light sources, and their interactions with surfaces are stored. In the second pass, the stored photon data is used to estimate the indirect lighting.
- **Screen Space Global Illumination (SSGI)**: A real-time approximation technique that computes GI effects in screen space, suitable for real-time applications, such as video games.

Implementing Basic Global Illumination in OpenGL

For real-time applications such as video games, implementing GI is challenging due to the heavy computational load. One efficient way to simulate GI is by using **Screen-Space Ambient Occlusion (SSAO)** and approximations based on depth and normal data.

- **SSAO (Screen-Space Ambient Occlusion)**: A technique that approximates how light interacts with the geometry of a scene by darkening areas that are more occluded by other geometry, simulating the way indirect light behaves in tight spaces or corners.

Basic SSAO implementation steps:

1. **Render depth and normal information**: Render the scene to a framebuffer with depth and normal buffers. These will be used to estimate how much light is blocked in a given area.
2. **Generate random sample points**: For each fragment in screen space, generate random sample points in a spherical distribution around the fragment. These points will be used to sample occlusion values.
3. **Calculate occlusion**: For each sample point, check if the sample point lies within the geometry in the scene. If it does, it is considered occluded, and its contribution to the lighting is reduced.
4. **Apply SSAO effect**: Combine the occlusion information with the ambient light to darken areas that are more occluded, creating the

illusion of indirect lighting.

2. High Dynamic Range (HDR) Rendering

High Dynamic Range (HDR) is a rendering technique that aims to represent a broader range of light intensities than traditional rendering methods. In standard rendering, the range of light values is typically limited to a small subset (from black to white). This range is not capable of capturing the true intensity of light found in real-world scenes, especially in bright areas or dark shadows. HDR rendering addresses this by capturing and displaying a wider range of luminance values, resulting in more realistic lighting and brighter, more vivid scenes.

Key Concepts of HDR:

- **HDR Images**: HDR images store higher precision color and brightness values, often using floating-point formats for each color channel (RGB). This allows for more detailed color gradients and the ability to capture extreme lighting conditions (bright light sources, reflections, etc.).
- **Tone Mapping**: Since most display devices (monitors, TVs, etc.) cannot display the full range of HDR intensities, tone mapping is applied to convert the HDR image into a format that fits the display's capabilities (usually in the range of 0–1 for each color channel).
- **Exposure**: HDR rendering allows for the simulation of varying exposure settings, just like a camera sensor. By adjusting exposure, you can simulate how different light levels are captured, allowing bright areas to shine while keeping darker regions visible.
- **Bloom Effects**: Bloom is a visual effect that simulates the scattering of light when it hits a bright surface, creating a halo-like glow around bright objects. This is particularly useful for simulating light sources like the sun, street lamps, or computer screens.

Implementing HDR in OpenGL:

To implement HDR in OpenGL, you will typically follow these steps:

1. **Render the Scene to a Floating-Point Buffer**: First, render the scene using floating-point textures to store the color and intensity of each pixel.

cpp

```cpp
GLuint hdrFBO;
GLuint colorBuffers[2];
glGenFramebuffers(1, &hdrFBO);
glBindFramebuffer(GL_FRAMEBUFFER, hdrFBO);

glGenTextures(2, colorBuffers);
for (int i = 0; i < 2; i++) {
    glBindTexture(GL_TEXTURE_2D, colorBuffers[i]);
    glTexImage2D(GL_TEXTURE_2D, 0, GL_RGB16F, SCR_WIDTH,
    SCR_HEIGHT, 0, GL_RGB, GL_FLOAT, NULL);
    glTexParameteri(GL_TEXTURE_2D, GL_TEXTURE_MIN_FILTER,
    GL_LINEAR);
    glTexParameteri(GL_TEXTURE_2D, GL_TEXTURE_MAG_FILTER,
    GL_LINEAR);
    glFramebufferTexture2D(GL_FRAMEBUFFER, GL_COLOR_ATTACHMENT0
    + i, GL_TEXTURE_2D, colorBuffers[i], 0);
}

GLuint attachments[2] = {GL_COLOR_ATTACHMENT0,
GL_COLOR_ATTACHMENT1};
glDrawBuffers(2, attachments);
glBindFramebuffer(GL_FRAMEBUFFER, 0);
```

Tone Mapping: Once the scene is rendered to an HDR framebuffer, the next step is tone mapping. A simple tone mapping operator is **Reinhard** which scales down the HDR color values to fit into a standard dynamic range (SDR).

Here's an example of how to implement Reinhard tone mapping in your fragment shader:

```cpp
vec3 toneMapping(vec3 color)
{
    return color / (color + vec3(1.0));
}
```

In this shader, the color is divided by itself plus one, reducing the intensity of bright areas and bringing them into a more viewable range.

Apply Bloom (Optional): Bloom is implemented by blurring the brightest parts of the scene and adding them back to the final image, creating a glowing effect.

A common approach to creating a bloom effect in HDR is as follows:

- **Extract Bright Areas**: Use a threshold to extract the bright areas from the HDR image.
- **Blur the Extracted Areas**: Apply a Gaussian blur to these bright areas to simulate light scattering.
- **Combine the Bright Areas with the Original Image**: Finally, add the blurred bright areas back to the original HDR image.

Render the Final Image: After tone mapping and optional effects like bloom, render the final image to the screen.

3. Combining Global Illumination and HDR for Realism

To achieve truly realistic lighting in modern 3D graphics, combining **Global Illumination** with **HDR** is essential. GI models the natural scattering of light, creating more accurate light behavior, while HDR allows those light interactions to be displayed with much greater dynamic range.

A typical real-time rendering pipeline that uses both GI and HDR might follow these steps:

1. **Compute indirect lighting (Global Illumination)** using methods

like SSAO, Radiosity, or Ray Tracing.

2. **Render the scene to an HDR framebuffer**, capturing a wide range of light intensities.

3. **Apply tone mapping** to bring the HDR image into the displayable range.

4. **Apply post-processing effects** like bloom or lens flares to further enhance the realism.

By combining these techniques, OpenGL allows you to render stunning, lifelike scenes that closely resemble the natural world.

Implementing **Global Illumination** and **High Dynamic Range (HDR)** rendering in OpenGL takes your 3D scenes to the next level by simulating realistic lighting effects. While GI improves the interaction of light with the environment, HDR enables the display of high-fidelity light intensities, adding vibrancy and realism.

Although these techniques can be computationally intensive, using optimized algorithms and smart resource management makes it possible to use these techniques in real-time applications like video games and simulations. Mastering both GI and HDR will significantly elevate the visual quality of your OpenGL projects, making your scenes more immersive and realistic.

Special Effects: Reflections, Refractions, and Transparency

Special effects such as **reflections**, **refractions**, and **transparency** are crucial for creating visually rich and immersive 3D environments. These effects mimic how light interacts with surfaces in the real world, and they play a significant role in enhancing realism in 3D graphics. In OpenGL, these effects are achievable through various techniques, each requiring a different approach for rendering and optimizing. This section will provide an in-depth look into these special effects and how they can be implemented in OpenGL.

1. Reflections

Reflections occur when light bounces off a surface and is redirected to the viewer's eye. In computer graphics, simulating reflections is important for adding depth and realism to objects in a scene, particularly when objects are near reflective surfaces like water, glass, or mirrors. OpenGL offers several techniques for implementing reflections, with **cube mapping** and **planar reflections** being the most common.

Cube Mapping for Reflections

Cube mapping is a technique used to simulate reflections on objects by mapping the environment onto a cube surrounding the object. This cube acts as a virtual reflection map, providing the illusion of the environment being reflected on surfaces like mirrors or metallic objects.

To implement cube mapping for reflections in OpenGL, the following steps are involved:

Create a Cube Map: A cube map consists of six textures representing the six faces of a cube. Each face corresponds to a view of the environment from a specific direction (positive X, negative X, positive Y, negative Y, positive Z, negative Z).

```cpp
GLuint cubemapTexture = loadCubemap(faces);
```

Render the Scene to the Cube Map: The cube map is created by rendering the scene from the viewpoint of the reflective object. In this process, the camera is placed at the object's location, and the scene is rendered from six directions. Each direction corresponds to one face of the cube map.

Apply the Cube Map as a Reflection Texture: Once the cube map is generated, you can sample it in a fragment shader to reflect the environment based on the surface's normal vector.

```cpp
vec3 reflectDir = reflect(normalize(cameraPos - FragPos),
normalize(Normal));
vec3 reflectedColor = texture(cubemap, reflectDir).rgb;
```

In the shader, reflectDir is the reflection direction, computed using the camera position and the surface normal. By sampling the cube map along the reflection direction, we can get the appropriate reflection color.

Planar Reflections

Planar reflections are used to simulate reflections on flat surfaces such as water, mirrors, or windows. The basic principle involves rendering the scene as if seen through the reflected surface, followed by flipping the geometry to create the mirrored effect.

The steps for implementing planar reflections in OpenGL are as follows:

Render the Scene Normally: First, render the scene from the camera's viewpoint without any reflection.

Reflect the Geometry Across the Reflective Surface: The geometry of the scene is reflected by flipping the geometry's coordinates along the plane of reflection (e.g., for water, this would be along the XY plane).

```cpp
glm::mat4 reflectionMatrix = glm::scale(glm::mat4(1.0f),
glm::vec3(1.0f, -1.0f, 1.0f)); // Reflect across XY plane
```

Render Reflected Scene to a Texture: The reflected scene is rendered to a texture (often a framebuffer object). This texture is then used as a reflection map when rendering the reflective surface.

Combine Reflections with the Original Scene: After rendering the reflection, combine the reflected image with the original scene to create a seamless reflection effect.

2. Refractions

Refraction is the bending of light as it passes through different media, such as from air to water or through glass. Simulating refraction in 3D graphics is crucial for rendering transparent objects like glass, water, and lenses. OpenGL offers several ways to achieve refraction, and one of the most common methods involves ray tracing or refraction maps.

Simulating Refraction Using the Fresnel Effect

The **Fresnel effect** describes how light reflects and refracts at the surface of a material. At shallow angles, most of the light is reflected, while at steeper angles, more light refracts into the material. This effect is often used in conjunction with refraction to create realistic glass and water surfaces.

To simulate refraction using the Fresnel effect:

Calculate the Fresnel Term: This is the amount of reflection at the surface, which varies based on the angle of incidence. The basic Fresnel equation is:

```cpp
float fresnel = pow(1.0f - dot(normal, viewDir), 5.0f);
```

Where normal is the surface normal, and viewDir is the direction from the fragment to the camera. This term will control how much light is reflected versus refracted.

Compute the Refraction Direction: The refraction direction can be calculated using **Snell's Law**, which defines the angle of refraction based on the angle of incidence and the refractive indices of the two media.

cpp

```
vec3 refractDir = refract(normalize(viewDir), normalize(normal),
refractionIndex);
```

The refractionIndex refers to the relative indices of refraction between two media (e.g., 1.0 for air, 1.33 for water).

Sample the Refraction Map: Once you have the refraction direction, you can sample a refraction texture (or use a ray tracing technique) to simulate the bending of light as it passes through the transparent material.

cpp

```
vec3 refractedColor = texture(refractionMap, refractDir).rgb;
```

3. Transparency

Transparency allows light to pass through an object, making it partially or fully see-through. In 3D graphics, transparency is often used to simulate materials like glass, water, and certain types of plastic. OpenGL provides a way to handle transparency through alpha blending, where each pixel is assigned an alpha value that determines its opacity.

Alpha Blending

Alpha blending is the process of combining a transparent object with the background based on the object's alpha channel. The alpha channel represents the opacity of the object, where 1.0 means fully opaque and 0.0 means fully transparent.

To implement alpha blending in OpenGL:

Enable Alpha Blending: Set up blending in OpenGL by enabling the GL_BLEND mode and configuring the blend function.

cpp

```
glEnable(GL_BLEND);
glBlendFunc(GL_SRC_ALPHA, GL_ONE_MINUS_SRC_ALPHA);
```

This blend function ensures that transparent objects are blended with the background based on their alpha values.

Render Transparent Objects: When rendering transparent objects, sort them by distance from the camera. Render the opaque objects first, then render the transparent objects in back-to-front order to ensure correct blending.

Handling Transparency with Textures: To achieve realistic transparency, you can use texture maps with alpha channels. A texture's alpha channel controls the transparency of the object at each pixel.

4. Combining Reflections, Refractions, and Transparency

In many 3D scenes, you might need to combine reflections, refractions, and transparency to create complex materials like water, glass, or liquids. OpenGL provides the necessary tools to combine these effects to create convincing materials.

For example, a glass object might involve the following effects:

1. **Reflections**: Glass often reflects its surroundings, so you would map the environment onto the glass using cube mapping (or planar reflections for flat surfaces).
2. **Refraction**: Light passing through the glass would bend based on the object's refractive index, simulating the transparent nature of the material.
3. **Transparency**: The glass material would be partially transparent, allowing the scene behind the glass to be visible.

You can blend these effects by adjusting the weight of the reflection, refraction, and transparency in the final fragment shader.

Example of combining effects in a fragment shader:

cpp

```cpp
vec3 finalColor = mix(reflectedColor, refractedColor, fresnel);
finalColor = mix(finalColor, backgroundColor, transparency);
```

In this shader, the final color is a mix of the reflected and refracted colors, with transparency applied as a blend factor.

Reflections, refractions, and transparency are vital special effects in 3D graphics, adding realism to materials such as glass, water, mirrors, and more. In OpenGL, these effects can be achieved through techniques such as **cube mapping**, **planar reflections**, **Snell's law for refraction**, and **alpha blending** for transparency.

By combining these effects, you can simulate realistic materials and lighting interactions in 3D environments, enhancing the overall realism of your scene. While these techniques can be computationally demanding, optimizations like using environment maps, reducing overdraw, and managing scene complexity can help achieve real-time performance even with these advanced effects.

Basic 3D Animation Techniques

Animation is one of the most powerful aspects of 3D graphics, bringing models and environments to life. It allows you to create motion, transform objects over time, and create engaging visual experiences. While advanced animation techniques such as skeletal animation or physics-based simulations are essential for complex movements, **keyframe animation** is the foundational technique that underpins much of 3D animation, especially in games, films, and interactive media.

In this chapter, we will introduce you to **keyframe animation** and the concept of **interpolation**. These two concepts are essential for creating smooth, visually appealing animations and are the building blocks for more complex animation systems. By the end of this chapter, you will have a solid understanding of how to animate objects in OpenGL using keyframes and interpolation, as well as how to apply these techniques to create effective animations.

1. What is Keyframe Animation?

Keyframe animation is a technique where specific, important points (called keyframes) are defined at certain points in time, and the in-between frames (or "in-betweens") are automatically calculated to create a smooth transition between them. These keyframes define the state of an object (such as position, rotation, scale, or other properties) at specific moments, while interpolation methods are used to generate intermediate frames to ensure the motion appears smooth and continuous.

In the context of 3D graphics, keyframe animation often involves transforming an object's position, rotation, and scale over time. These transformations are represented mathematically, and the computer uses algorithms to smoothly transition between keyframes.

How Keyframe Animation Works:

- **Keyframes**: These are the specific, fixed points in time that define the desired properties of an object at that moment. For example, you may define a keyframe for an object's position at t=0 (the start of the animation) and another keyframe at t=1 (one second later).
- **Interpolation**: This process is what happens between the keyframes. Interpolation calculates the values (such as position, rotation, or scale) of the object at intermediate points in time, effectively "filling in the gaps" between the keyframes. This smooth transition between keyframes is what makes the animation fluid.
- **Ease In and Ease Out**: These techniques are often used in keyframe animation to make the animation appear more natural. "Ease in" means starting slowly and accelerating over time, while "ease out" means starting quickly and decelerating. These techniques can be applied to motion, rotation, and other properties.

Keyframe animation is particularly useful for tasks like:

- Animating an object's movement along a path
- Rotating an object over time
- Scaling an object for a zoom effect
- Moving cameras or lights

By defining only a few keyframes, complex animations can be created with relatively minimal effort.

2. Understanding Interpolation in Animation

Interpolation in animation refers to the mathematical process of calculating intermediate values between two keyframes. While keyframes define the major milestones of an animation, interpolation fills in the details between those milestones. The type of interpolation used determines how the transitions between keyframes are handled, whether they are linear, smooth, or more complex (e.g., easing functions).

Types of Interpolation:

Linear Interpolation (Lerp)

Linear interpolation (often abbreviated as "lerp") is the simplest and most common interpolation technique. In linear interpolation, the transition between two keyframes happens at a constant rate, meaning the object moves from one keyframe to the next at a uniform speed. This technique is easy to implement, but it can result in unnatural-looking movements because real-world motions are rarely uniform.

- **Formula**: The general formula for linear interpolation is: Interpolated Value=$(1-t)$·Value0+t·Value1 $\text{Interpolated Value} = (1 - t) \cdot \text{Value}_0 + t \cdot \text{Value}_1$ Interpolated Value=$(1-t)$·Value0+t·Value1 where:
- t is the interpolation factor, usually between 0 and 1.
- Value_0 and Value_1 are the start and end values, respectively.
- t represents the time, with t=0 being the starting keyframe and t=1 being the ending keyframe.

For example, if you are animating the position of an object from (0, 0) to (10, 0) over 1 second, linear interpolation would move the object at a constant speed from the starting point to the destination.

Spherical Linear Interpolation (SLERP)

SLERP is used for smoothly interpolating rotations between two quaternions, which are often used for rotating 3D objects. While linear interpolation works for translations and scales, SLERP is better suited for rotating objects because it interpolates the angles along the shortest path on a unit sphere.

SLERP is typically used to avoid the problems of gimbal lock and to produce smoother, more natural-looking rotations.

Bezier Curves and Ease Functions

For more natural animations, ease-in and ease-out effects are often used. These effects are typically implemented using **Bezier curves**, which allow for gradual acceleration and deceleration of an object's motion. By defining a curve, you can control how the speed of the transition changes over time.

- **Ease In**: The motion starts slowly and then accelerates.
- **Ease Out**: The motion starts quickly and then decelerates.
- **Ease In/Out**: The motion starts slowly, accelerates in the middle, and then decelerates at the end.

These easing functions can be implemented using cubic Bezier curves, where the transition between two keyframes is influenced by a set of control points. This provides greater flexibility and can be used to simulate more natural behaviors, like the slow start and stop of a car.

3. Implementing Keyframe Animation in OpenGL

In OpenGL, keyframe animation is typically handled by updating an object's transformation matrices (position, rotation, and scale) over time based on keyframes and interpolating between those keyframes. Below are the general steps to implement keyframe animation:

1. Define Keyframes:

Keyframes define the object's properties at specific times. Each keyframe contains the following information:

- **Time**: The time at which the keyframe occurs.
- **Transformation**: The object's position, rotation, and scale values at that time.

For example, you might have keyframes for the object's position at t=0 (start) and t=1 (end), as well as keyframes for rotation and scaling.

cpp

```cpp
struct Keyframe {
    float time;          // Time at which the keyframe occurs
    glm::vec3 position;  // Position at that time
    glm::quat rotation;  // Rotation quaternion
    glm::vec3 scale;     // Scale at that time
};
```

2. Interpolate Between Keyframes:

To calculate intermediate transformations between keyframes, you can use linear interpolation (for position and scale) or spherical linear interpolation (for rotation).

cpp

```cpp
// Interpolate position using linear interpolation
glm::vec3 interpolatePosition(const Keyframe& kf0, const
Keyframe& kf1, float t) {
    return glm::mix(kf0.position, kf1.position, t);
}

// Interpolate rotation using spherical linear interpolation
(SLERP)
glm::quat interpolateRotation(const Keyframe& kf0, const
Keyframe& kf1, float t) {
    return glm::slerp(kf0.rotation, kf1.rotation, t);
}

// Interpolate scale using linear interpolation
glm::vec3 interpolateScale(const Keyframe& kf0, const Keyframe&
kf1, float t) {
    return glm::mix(kf0.scale, kf1.scale, t);
}
```

3. Update the Object Transformation:

Once the interpolated position, rotation, and scale values are computed, these can be applied to the object's transformation matrix.

cpp

```
glm::mat4 modelMatrix = glm::translate(glm::mat4(1.0f),
interpolatePosition(kf0, kf1, t));
modelMatrix *= glm::mat4_cast(interpolateRotation(kf0, kf1, t));
modelMatrix *= glm::scale(glm::mat4(1.0f), interpolateScale(kf0,
kf1, t));
```

4. Render the Scene:

Finally, you update the object's transformation matrix on each frame based on the current time and keyframe progression, and render the scene.

Keyframe animation and interpolation form the backbone of 3D animation, allowing developers to create smooth and realistic motion over time. Whether animating an object's movement, rotation, or scale, keyframes define the milestones, while interpolation ensures a smooth transition between those points. By mastering these concepts, you will be able to create more dynamic, engaging, and visually compelling 3D scenes.

Applying Transformations Over Time: Moving, Rotating, and Scaling Objects

In keyframe animation, transformations such as **translation (movement)**, **rotation**, and **scaling** are the core manipulations applied to objects in the 3D space over time. These transformations allow objects to change their position, orientation, and size as the animation progresses. In this section, we will explore how to apply these transformations and animate them over time using keyframes and interpolation, enabling dynamic and visually appealing animations in OpenGL.

1. Translating (Moving) Objects Over Time

Translation refers to the movement of an object from one position to another in 3D space. This is one of the most basic and essential transformations in animation. To animate an object's translation, we define keyframes at specific times, each specifying a different position in space. Interpolation between those keyframes allows the object to move smoothly from one position to the next.

Animating Translation:

When animating the translation of an object, you need to define two keyframes: the start and end positions. Using linear interpolation (lerp) or more advanced interpolation techniques like ease-in or ease-out, you can calculate the intermediate positions and apply them to the object at each frame.

Linear Interpolation for Translation:
- **Start Keyframe**: Define the initial position of the object at time t0.
- **End Keyframe**: Define the final position of the object at time t1.

For a linear interpolation between two positions P0 and P1 at times t0 and t1, the formula is:

$$\text{Position}(t) = (1 - t) \cdot P_0 + t \cdot P_1$$

Where:

- P0 and P1 are the initial and final positions of the object.
- t is the time factor between 0 and 1 that controls the transition.

As the animation progresses, t gradually increases from 0 (at the start of the animation) to 1 (at the end), causing the object to move smoothly from P0 to P1.

Example:

Let's assume we want to move an object from position (0, 0, 0) to (10, 0, 0) over 3 seconds. Using a linear interpolation, the position of the object at any point in time t can be calculated as follows:

```cpp
glm::vec3 positionStart(0.0f, 0.0f, 0.0f);
glm::vec3 positionEnd(10.0f, 0.0f, 0.0f);

// Interpolate between start and end positions
glm::vec3 currentPosition = glm::lerp(positionStart,
positionEnd, currentTime / totalAnimationTime);
```

The object's position will gradually move from (0, 0, 0) to (10, 0, 0) as currentTime progresses from 0 to totalAnimationTime (3 seconds in this case).

2. Rotating Objects Over Time

Rotation is another key transformation that is commonly animated. It allows objects to change their orientation over time. The rotation can occur around one or more axes (X, Y, or Z), and just like translation, keyframes define the start and end orientations of the object.

Animating Rotation:

In OpenGL, rotations are typically represented using **quaternions** or **rotation matrices**, both of which are more efficient and less prone to issues like gimbal lock compared to Euler angles. However, for simplicity, let's start by discussing Euler angles and how to animate rotations between keyframes using linear interpolation.

To interpolate between two rotations, we can use a technique called **spherical linear interpolation (SLERP)**, which provides a smooth rotation between two orientations.

SLERP for Rotation Interpolation:

For rotation, we use quaternions to interpolate between two rotation keyframes. The formula for SLERP is:

$$Slerp(\mathbf{q_0}, \mathbf{q_1}, t) = \frac{\sin((1-t)\cdot\theta)}{\sin(\theta)}\cdot\mathbf{q_0} + \frac{\sin(t\cdot\theta)}{\sin(\theta)}\cdot\mathbf{q_1}$$

Where:

- q0 and q1 are the initial and final quaternions representing the start and end rotations.
- t is the time factor between 0 and 1.
- θ is the angle between q0 and q1.

By applying SLERP, you can smoothly interpolate between two rotations, ensuring that the object rotates smoothly from one orientation to the next.

Example:

Let's say we want to rotate an object from its initial orientation to a 90-degree rotation around the Y-axis.

cpp

```cpp
glm::quat startRotation = glm::quat(glm::vec3(0.0f, 0.0f,
0.0f));  // No initial rotation
glm::quat endRotation = glm::quat(glm::vec3(0.0f,
glm::radians(90.0f), 0.0f)); // 90 degree rotation

// Interpolate between the rotations
glm::quat currentRotation = glm::slerp(startRotation,
endRotation, currentTime / totalAnimationTime);
```

This will smoothly rotate the object from the starting orientation to a 90-degree rotation around the Y-axis as the animation progresses.

3. Scaling Objects Over Time

Scaling refers to the process of changing the size of an object. Like translation and rotation, scaling can be animated by defining keyframes for the object's scale and interpolating between them over time. Scaling

195

is often used for effects like zooming, object deformation, or showing the growth or shrinking of an object.

Animating Scaling:

To animate scaling, we define keyframes for the start and end scale vectors. These keyframes will typically contain a glm::vec3 scale factor representing the scaling in the X, Y, and Z axes. Interpolation is applied between these keyframes to transition smoothly from one scale to another.

Example:

Let's animate an object that grows from a scale of (1.0f, 1.0f, 1.0f) to (2.0f, 2.0f, 2.0f) over 4 seconds.

```cpp
glm::vec3 scaleStart(1.0f, 1.0f, 1.0f);
glm::vec3 scaleEnd(2.0f, 2.0f, 2.0f);

// Interpolate between start and end scale
glm::vec3 currentScale = glm::lerp(scaleStart, scaleEnd,
currentTime / totalAnimationTime);
```

This will gradually increase the scale of the object from its original size to twice as large over the animation duration.

4. Combining Multiple Transformations

In a typical animation, an object will undergo multiple transformations simultaneously, such as moving, rotating, and scaling. These transformations are applied in a specific order, with translation, rotation, and scaling typically being applied in that order. The **transformation matrix** for an object is computed by multiplying its individual transformation matrices together.

For example:

- Apply scaling first
- Then apply rotation
- Finally, apply translation

This combined transformation matrix is then used to position, orient, and size the object during rendering.

cpp

```cpp
glm::mat4 model = glm::mat4(1.0f); // Identity matrix
model = glm::scale(model, currentScale); // Apply scaling
model = glm::rotate(model, glm::radians(currentRotation),
glm::vec3(0.0f, 1.0f, 0.0f)); // Apply rotation
model = glm::translate(model, currentPosition); // Apply
translation

// Pass the model matrix to the shader
shader.setMat4("model", model);
```

Animating objects in 3D space through keyframe animation is a powerful way to create dynamic and engaging scenes. By applying transformations over time—such as translation, rotation, and scaling—and using interpolation techniques, you can create smooth, fluid animations. These animations serve as the foundation for more complex animations in 3D graphics, and with the skills you've learned in this chapter, you are well on your way to animating objects and building rich, dynamic 3D worlds.

Creating Smooth Animations with Easing Functions

While basic linear interpolation works for simple animations, it can often result in mechanical or unnatural movements. Real-world motions—such as those involving people, vehicles, or natural phenomena—typically begin and end more slowly, with a gradual acceleration or deceleration in between. This is where **easing functions** come into play. Easing functions allow you to create smooth, natural-looking animations by controlling how an object accelerates or decelerates between keyframes.

In this section, we'll discuss how to apply easing functions in OpenGL

197

to create smooth transitions between keyframes and improve the overall fluidity of animations.

1. What Are Easing Functions?

Easing functions are mathematical functions that control the rate of change of a property over time, such as position, rotation, or scale. Rather than interpolating in a linear fashion, easing functions modify the interpolation curve to make the transition more organic. They allow an object to start moving slowly, accelerate in the middle of the animation, and then slow down again as it approaches the end keyframe.

In essence, easing functions provide more control over the animation timing, which is essential for creating natural, believable motion.

There are several types of easing functions, each producing a different type of motion. The most common easing functions are:

- **Ease-In**: Starts slowly and gradually speeds up.
- **Ease-Out**: Starts quickly and gradually slows down.
- **Ease-In-Out**: Combines both ease-in and ease-out, with a slow start, fast middle, and slow end.
- **Bounce**: Creates a bouncing effect at the end of the animation, making the object appear to "bounce" as it slows down.
- **Elastic**: Similar to bounce, but with a more elastic, spring-like motion.

These easing functions allow for more expressive and visually appealing animations, as opposed to the linear "one-speed" approach used by simple interpolation.

2. Types of Easing Functions

Here are some of the most popular easing functions used in animation:

Ease-In

An **ease-in** function makes an object start moving slowly and then accelerate over time. This type of easing is often used when animating objects that begin with a gentle motion and then gain speed.

The mathematical formula for ease-in is typically represented as:

$$f(t) = t^n$$

where n is greater than 1 (commonly 2, 3, or higher), and t is the time factor (between 0 and 1).

For example, using $n = 3$ (which gives a cubic ease-in):

$$f(t) = t^3$$

This means that at the start of the animation ($t=0$), the speed is zero, and it gradually speeds up. By the end of the animation ($t=1$), the object reaches its full speed.

This means that at the start of the animation (t=0), the speed is zero, and it gradually speeds up. By the end of the animation (t=1), the object reaches its full speed.

Ease-Out

An **ease-out** function starts with fast movement and then slows down as it reaches the end of the animation. This type of easing is useful when you want an object to come to a smooth stop, such as when an object reaches its final position after a fast movement.

The mathematical formula for ease-out is typically:

$$f(t) = 1 - (1 - t)^n$$

where n is typically a value greater than 1.

For instance, with $n = 3$ (cubic ease-out):

$$f(t) = 1 - (1 - t)^3$$

With ease-out, the motion begins quickly and decelerates smoothly, providing a natural deceleration at the end of the animation.

Ease-In-Out

199

An **ease-in-out** function is a combination of both ease-in and ease-out. It starts slowly, accelerates in the middle, and slows down again at the end. This is one of the most commonly used easing functions because it produces the most natural-looking animations.

The formula for ease-in-out is usually:

$$f(t) = \begin{cases} 2t^2 & \text{if } t < 0.5 \\ 1 - (-2t + 2)^2/2 & \text{if } t \geq 0.5 \end{cases}$$

In this formula:

- For values of t less than 0.5, the function behaves like ease-in.
- For values greater than or equal to 0.5, the function behaves like ease-out.

This creates a smooth transition, where the object gradually accelerates to a mid-speed before decelerating smoothly toward the target.

Bounce

A **bounce** easing function creates the illusion of an object bouncing as it decelerates, similar to a ball falling and then bouncing off a surface. The formula for bounce easing is more complex, involving multiple phases of bouncing:

$$f(t) = \begin{cases} 7.5625t^2 & \text{if } t < \frac{1}{2.75} \\ 7.5625(t - \frac{1.5}{2.75})^2 + 0.75 & \text{if } t < \frac{2}{2.75} \\ 7.5625(t - \frac{2.25}{2.75})^2 + 0.9375 & \text{if } t < \frac{2.5}{2.75} \\ 7.5625(t - \frac{2.625}{2.75})^2 + 0.984375 & \text{if } t \geq \frac{2.5}{2.75} \end{cases}$$

The effect produces a series of small "bounces" as the object slows down,

200

giving it a lively, dynamic appearance.

Elastic

The **elastic** easing function simulates a spring-like effect where the object overshoots its target and then oscillates back and forth before settling. This type of easing is often used for dramatic movements, such as when an object "snaps" into place or when simulating elastic materials.

The formula for elastic easing can vary, but a general form is:

$$f(t) = \sin(t * \pi * (0.5 + 2 * \tfrac{t}{2})) \times e^{-3t}$$

This results in a spring-like oscillation that gives a dramatic, exaggerated motion.

3. Implementing Easing Functions in OpenGL

To implement easing functions in OpenGL, we typically integrate them into the animation system's update function. As the animation progresses, we apply the easing function to modify the interpolation factor t. The new t value is used to calculate the intermediate transformation at each frame, whether it's for translation, rotation, or scaling.

Here is an example of how to apply easing to the position of an object:

cpp

```cpp
// Define easing function (ease-in-out)
float easeInOut(float t) {
    if (t < 0.5f) {
        return 2 * t * t; // Ease-in part
    } else {
        return 1 - pow(-2 * t + 2, 2) / 2; // Ease-out part
    }
}
```

```
// Apply easing to position interpolation
glm::vec3 startPosition(0.0f, 0.0f, 0.0f);
glm::vec3 endPosition(10.0f, 0.0f, 0.0f);

float easedT = easeInOut(currentTime / totalAnimationTime);
glm::vec3 currentPosition = glm::lerp(startPosition,
endPosition, easedT);
```

In this example:

- The easing function easeInOut() is used to modify the interpolation factor t between keyframes.
- The position of the object is then calculated by applying linear interpolation using the eased t.

This process can be applied to other properties, such as rotation or scaling, using similar easing functions to create more natural, fluid animations.

Easing functions are a powerful tool for creating smooth and natural animations in OpenGL. By controlling how objects move, accelerate, and decelerate over time, easing functions help make animations appear more lifelike and engaging. Whether you're animating simple object translations, camera movements, or complex interactions, applying easing functions is a great way to improve the quality of your animations.

Using Time-Based Animation Loops and Frame Rates

When creating animations, the timing and smoothness of the animation are crucial for providing a visually appealing experience. One of the fundamental challenges of 3D animation is ensuring that objects move smoothly over time, regardless of the frame rate at which the application is running. This is where **time-based animation** comes into play.

In this section, we will explore how to create time-based animation loops that are independent of the frame rate and how to manage frame rates to maintain a consistent and smooth animation experience.

1. Time-Based Animation vs. Frame-Based Animation

There are two primary types of animation approaches in computer graphics: **time-based animation** and **frame-based animation**.

- **Frame-based animation** relies on a fixed number of frames per second (FPS). For example, an animation might be designed to progress a fixed amount per frame, and if the FPS drops, the animation will appear slower or choppier.
- **Time-based animation**, on the other hand, uses the actual time elapsed between frames (often measured in seconds) to control how the animation progresses. This method ensures that the animation moves at a consistent speed, regardless of the frame rate.

For example, if an animation is supposed to take 2 seconds, a time-based animation will ensure that the object reaches its final position in exactly 2 seconds, even if the FPS fluctuates. This is because the animation is calculated based on time, not the number of frames rendered.

Using time-based animation is particularly important when developing interactive applications like games, where the frame rate may vary depending on hardware performance.

2. Implementing Time-Based Animation Loops

Time-based animation requires tracking how much time has passed since the last frame (delta time) and using this value to control the animation. This approach decouples the animation from the frame rate, making it more consistent across different hardware and rendering conditions.

Delta Time (Δt)

Delta time (often referred to as dt) represents the time difference between the current frame and the previous frame. This value is essential for calculating how much an object should move or change over time.

Delta time can be obtained by querying the system's clock or timer, often using functions such as glfwGetTime() in OpenGL, or platform-specific APIs like std::chrono in C++.

Example: Using Delta Time for Movement

To animate an object moving across the screen, we can use the delta time to move the object by a certain distance each second, ensuring that the object moves at the same speed regardless of the frame rate.

Here's how this can be implemented in C++ with OpenGL:

```cpp
float lastTime = 0.0f;
float deltaTime = 0.0f;
float speed = 5.0f; // Movement speed in units per second

void update(float currentTime) {
    // Calculate deltaTime (time elapsed since the last frame)
    deltaTime = currentTime - lastTime;
    lastTime = currentTime;

    // Move the object based on speed and deltaTime
    float distance = speed * deltaTime;  // Distance moved in
    this frame
    objectPosition += glm::vec3(distance, 0.0f, 0.0f);  // Move
    the object along X-axis

    // Update any other object properties (e.g., rotation or
    scaling) here
}
```

In this example:

- currentTime represents the current time in seconds (e.g., obtained from glfwGetTime()).
- deltaTime is the time difference between the current and the previous frame.

- The speed variable controls how fast the object moves, and multiplying it by deltaTime ensures that the object moves the correct distance regardless of the frame rate.

By using delta time, the movement is frame rate-independent, meaning that the object will always move at the same speed, whether the frame rate is 30 FPS or 120 FPS.

3. Frame Rate and Frame Limiting

While time-based animation ensures consistent movement, managing the frame rate is still important for performance reasons. If the frame rate is too high, it may result in unnecessary computational load and energy consumption. On the other hand, too low a frame rate can cause stuttering and performance issues.

Frame rate limiting can be used to cap the number of frames per second that the game or application will render. Common frame rate caps are 30 FPS or 60 FPS, as these are generally sufficient for most applications, particularly in games or 3D environments.

Limiting Frame Rate in OpenGL

In OpenGL, you can use tools like **GLFW** to limit the frame rate. Here's how to set a fixed frame rate cap in GLFW:

cpp

```
glfwSwapInterval(1);  // Limits the frame rate to the refresh
rate of the display (vsync)
```

Alternatively, you can implement manual frame rate capping by controlling how often the game loop is allowed to update:

cpp

```
const float maxFPS = 60.0f;
const float maxFrameTime = 1.0f / maxFPS;
```

```cpp
float lastFrameTime = glfwGetTime();

while (!glfwWindowShouldClose(window)) {
    float currentTime = glfwGetTime();
    float deltaTime = currentTime - lastFrameTime;

    if (deltaTime >= maxFrameTime) {
        lastFrameTime = currentTime;

        // Process input, update objects, and render the scene
        update(currentTime);
        render();
    }
}
```

In this example, the game loop checks if enough time has passed before allowing the next frame to update. If the frame time is less than the desired frame time (maxFrameTime), the loop simply waits until the time threshold is reached. This ensures that the application doesn't render more than the specified frame rate.

4. Using Time-Based Animation for Smooth Transitions

In addition to animating object properties like position and rotation, time-based animation is also essential for creating smooth transitions between keyframes. For example, when animating a character's walk cycle, you might want the animation to proceed at a constant speed regardless of the frame rate, ensuring that the character's movement looks smooth and consistent across different machines.

To achieve this, you can use time-based interpolation for each keyframe. This ensures that, for example, a character's walk cycle completes in exactly 3 seconds, whether the frame rate is high or low.

cpp

```
float animationDuration = 3.0f; // Duration of animation in
seconds
float currentTime = glfwGetTime();
float normalizedTime = fmod(currentTime, animationDuration) /
animationDuration; // Loop animation over time

// Interpolate between keyframe positions based on normalized
time
glm::vec3 currentPos = glm::lerp(keyframeStartPos,
keyframeEndPos, normalizedTime);
```

In this case, normalizedTime is used to determine the position of the animation relative to the total duration. The lerp function interpolates between two keyframe positions based on the normalized time, ensuring the object moves smoothly from one keyframe to the next over the animation duration.

Time-based animation is a crucial concept for ensuring that animations run smoothly and consistently across different frame rates. By using **delta time** and time-based loops, you can decouple your animations from the frame rate, providing a more natural and fluid experience for users. Additionally, managing frame rates and using **easing functions** allows for greater control over the feel and smoothness of your animations.

By mastering time-based animation techniques in OpenGL, you can create professional, smooth, and dynamic animations that add depth and life to your 3D graphics projects.

Advanced Animation and Skeletal Animation

Animation is a fundamental part of creating dynamic and lifelike 3D models. While keyframe animation is an essential tool for animating transformations over time, more advanced animation systems are required to create realistic character movements, such as **skeletal animation**. **Skeletal animation** is the process of animating 3D models using a "skeleton" of bones, which are rigged to control the mesh of the character or object. This method is especially effective for creating organic movements, such as walking, running, or bending, which are difficult to achieve with simpler keyframe techniques.

In this chapter, we will dive into the process of **rigging 3D models** for skeletal animation. We will cover the basics of how skeletal animation works, explain the steps involved in rigging a model, and discuss how bones and skeletons are applied to create realistic animations. By the end of this chapter, you will have a solid understanding of how to set up, rig, and animate characters in OpenGL, as well as how to manage bones, meshes, and joint transformations.

1. What is Skeletal Animation?

Skeletal animation is a technique used to animate characters and objects by moving and rotating a skeleton (a hierarchy of bones or joints) that influences the geometry of a 3D mesh. The mesh is usually made up of vertices, which are attached to bones in a way that allows them to move and deform according to the skeleton's transformation. This approach allows for efficient animation of complex characters without having to manipulate every vertex individually.

Skeletal animation has several advantages over other animation techniques:

- **Efficiency**: Animating bones instead of directly manipulating vertices is computationally cheaper. Rather than updating every vertex in the mesh, the bone positions are updated, and the mesh deforms according to the bones' transformations.
- **Reusability**: Once a skeleton is created, it can be reused for different characters that share similar body structures, saving time and effort.
- **Flexibility**: With skeletal animation, you can animate complex movements like bending, twisting, and posing, which would be much more difficult to achieve using simple keyframe animation.

How Skeletal Animation Works

At the core of skeletal animation is the idea of a **skeleton** (a hierarchical structure made of bones) and a **mesh** (the 3D model that is deformed by the bones).

- **Bones**: Bones are individual objects or nodes in a hierarchical structure that define the skeleton. Each bone represents a part of the body or object, such as an arm, leg, or head. The bones are connected to each other in a parent-child relationship, where each bone can have one or more child bones (for example, an upper arm bone has a child lower arm bone).
- **Joints**: Joints are the points where two bones are connected. These points allow for rotation and other transformations to occur. Joints are typically defined as the points around which the bones can rotate and bend.
- **Mesh**: The mesh is the 3D model that is deformed by the bones. Each vertex of the mesh is associated with one or more bones, and these

vertices will move according to the transformations applied to the bones. This process is known as **skinning**.

Skinning is the technique used to attach the mesh to the bones of the skeleton. There are two primary types of skinning:

- **Rigid Skinning**: Each vertex in the mesh is influenced by a single bone. This is useful for hard, rigid objects (e.g., robots or mechanical objects), but it doesn't work well for soft, organic objects like characters.
- **Smooth (or Linear) Skinning**: Each vertex in the mesh is influenced by multiple bones. This is much more common for organic characters (like humans or animals), as it allows for more natural bending and deformation of the mesh.

2. Steps to Rigging a 3D Model for Skeletal Animation

Rigging is the process of setting up a skeleton for a 3D model and assigning bones to the model's mesh. It typically involves the following steps:

Creating the Skeleton (Bones and Joints)

The first step in rigging is to create the skeleton, which consists of bones and joints that define the structure and movement of the model. A skeleton might be made up of a few bones (such as a spine, arms, and legs) for simple objects, or a more complex set of bones for detailed models like characters.

- **Spine**: The spine is typically the central bone structure for a character. All other bones (such as arms, legs, head, etc.) are attached to the spine.
- **Limbs**: Each limb (arms, legs, etc.) will have multiple bones to define its parts (upper arm, lower arm, hand, etc.).
- **Head**: The head is usually connected to the spine by a neck bone, which controls its rotation.
- **Fingers and Toes**: These often require extra bones for fine-grained control over their animation.

Skinning the Mesh to the Skeleton

Once the skeleton is in place, the next step is to attach the mesh (the 3D model) to the bones. This process, known as **skinning**, involves assigning weights to the vertices of the mesh. Each vertex can be influenced by one or more bones, and the weights determine the extent to which each bone affects the vertex.

- **Weight Painting**: In 3D modeling software (such as Blender or Maya), skinning is often done using weight painting, where the artist paints weights onto the mesh, indicating how strongly each bone influences different parts of the mesh. For example, the vertices of a character's arm might be mostly influenced by the upper arm bone, with some influence from the shoulder and lower arm bones.
- **Bone Influence**: A vertex can be influenced by multiple bones, and the influence is defined by a set of weights (usually normalized between 0 and 1). These weights control how much each bone affects the vertex's position and deformation.

Defining Bone Hierarchy and Constraints

Once the bones are set up and the mesh is skinning, the bone hierarchy must be defined. This involves specifying the relationships between bones, such as parent-child relationships. For example, the elbow joint will be the child of the upper arm bone and the parent of the lower arm bone.

Additionally, constraints such as limits on rotation or movement might be applied to bones to prevent unnatural movements (e.g., preventing a bone from rotating beyond a certain angle).

Testing the Rig

After the rig is complete, it is important to test the rig by moving the bones and observing how the mesh deforms. Ideally, the mesh should move naturally and in accordance with the bone movements. If any areas of the mesh deform unnaturally (such as stretching or collapsing), the skinning weights and bone influences may need to be adjusted.

3. Animating a Rigged Model

Once a model is rigged, it can be animated using the skeleton. Animation is done by applying **keyframes** to the bones, similar to how keyframe animation works with other transformations. However, instead of animating positions, rotations, and scales directly, you are animating the rotation and movement of bones over time.

To animate a skeleton in OpenGL:

1. **Define the Keyframes**: For each bone, define keyframes for rotation and position at specific points in time.
2. **Interpolate Between Keyframes**: Use interpolation (such as **SLERP** for rotation) to smoothly transition between keyframes.
3. **Apply Bone Transformations**: For each frame, compute the transformation matrix for each bone based on the keyframe data and the interpolation factor. These matrices are then applied to the mesh, deforming it according to the bone movements.
4. **Rendering**: In the shader, pass the bone transformations to the vertex shader, which will apply the transformations to each vertex, based on its bone influences, to create the final animated mesh.

4. Implementing Skeletal Animation in OpenGL

To implement skeletal animation in OpenGL, you will need to:

- **Load the Skeleton and Mesh**: Import the skeleton and mesh into your OpenGL application, along with the bone weights and vertex influences.
- **Bone Transformation Matrices**: Calculate the transformation matrix for each bone using the current animation state (i.e., using keyframe data and interpolation).
- **Shader Communication**: Pass the transformation matrices for each bone to the vertex shader, where they will be used to calculate the final position of each vertex.
- **Skinning in the Shader**: In the vertex shader, perform the skinning by

multiplying the vertex position by the appropriate bone transformation matrices, weighted by the influence of the bones on the vertex.

Rigging and skeletal animation are powerful techniques for animating complex characters and objects. By using a hierarchical bone structure to control the deformation of a mesh, skeletal animation allows for highly efficient and realistic movements. Mastering rigging and skeletal animation in OpenGL opens the door to creating dynamic, lifelike characters and environments, bringing your 3D projects to life in a way that simple keyframe animation cannot achieve.

As you progress in your 3D graphics journey, understanding the underlying principles of skeletal animation will be critical for creating advanced animations, such as character actions, facial expressions, and even crowd simulations. By combining rigging, skinning, and animation techniques, you can create highly interactive and immersive 3D experiences that will captivate your audience.

Skinning and Blending Animations

After rigging a 3D model with a skeleton, the next crucial steps involve **skinning** the model to the bones and animating it. Skinning is the process of binding the 3D mesh (the model's surface) to the skeleton, so when the skeleton moves, the mesh deforms accordingly. Blending animations, on the other hand, allows for smooth transitions between different animation states, such as walking, running, or jumping, providing a more realistic and fluid animation experience. In this section, we will explore the techniques of skinning, blending animations, and how these processes are implemented in OpenGL.

1. Skinning: Binding the Mesh to the Skeleton

As mentioned earlier, **skinning** is the process of assigning the mesh to the skeleton's bones. When you move or rotate a bone in the skeleton, the vertices in the mesh (the 3D model) will be influenced accordingly, making it appear as if the mesh is moving naturally.

Vertex Weights

In smooth skinning, each vertex of the mesh is influenced by one or more bones. To determine how much influence each bone has on a given vertex, we use **vertex weights**. These weights define the degree to which a bone affects a vertex, with each weight ranging from 0 to 1. If a vertex is affected by multiple bones, the weights must add up to 1.0.

For example:

- A vertex near the shoulder might be primarily influenced by the upper arm bone, with a small amount of influence from the chest bone.
- A vertex near the elbow would be primarily influenced by the lower arm bone, with some influence from the upper arm.

The **skinning process** calculates how each vertex is transformed based on the influence of the bones.

Bone Transformation Matrices

Each bone in the skeleton has a transformation matrix that defines its position, rotation, and scale in 3D space. The vertex transformation is computed by multiplying the bone's transformation matrix by the skinning weights of each vertex.

The basic procedure for transforming a vertex is:

1. For each bone that influences the vertex, apply the bone's transformation matrix.
2. Multiply the bone's transformation matrix by the corresponding vertex weight.
3. Sum the transformed vertices for all bones that influence the vertex.
4. Update the position of the vertex based on the summed transformation.

This process ensures that vertices follow the bones' movements and rotations in a smooth, organic way.

Matrix Skinning:

In OpenGL, the transformation of each bone is represented as a 4x4 matrix. The process of updating the vertex position is carried out in the vertex shader by applying the bone transformations to each vertex.

For example, in GLSL (OpenGL Shading Language), skinning is typically done as follows:

```cpp
// Vertex Shader: Apply bone transformations to the vertex
position
#version 330 core

layout(location = 0) in vec3 position;    // Vertex position
layout(location = 1) in vec3 normal;      // Vertex normal
layout(location = 2) in ivec4 boneIDs;    // Bone indices
layout(location = 3) in vec4 weights;     // Bone weights

uniform mat4 bones[100]; // Array of bone transformation matrices

void main()
{
    mat4 finalTransformation = mat4(0.0);

    // Apply the bone transformations
    for (int i = 0; i < 4; ++i)
    {
        int boneID = boneIDs[i];
        float weight = weights[i];

        // Add weighted transformation to final transformation
        matrix
        finalTransformation += weight * bones[boneID];
    }
```

```
// Apply the final transformation to the vertex position
vec4 worldPosition = finalTransformation * vec4(position,
1.0);
gl_Position = projectionMatrix * viewMatrix * worldPosition;
}
```

This vertex shader uses bone indices (boneIDs) and weights (weights) to compute the final transformed position of each vertex by applying the bone transformations.

2. Blending Animations: Creating Smooth Transitions

Blending animations is the process of combining multiple animations in such a way that the transition between them appears smooth and seamless. For example, transitioning from a walking animation to a running animation, or blending a character's idle animation into a jumping animation. This technique is crucial for creating fluid, realistic motion, especially in interactive applications like games.

Animation Blending Overview

The idea behind animation blending is to mix the results of two or more animation states. These animation states are typically represented as **keyframe animations** (for example, a "walk" animation, a "run" animation, or a "jump" animation). Animation blending is often controlled by a **blend weight** parameter that determines the influence of each animation state on the final output.

For example:

- **Idle to Walk Blend**: The blend weight gradually transitions from 0 (only idle animation) to 1 (full walking animation).
- **Walk to Run Blend**: The character transitions from walking to running, with blend weights adjusting the influence of the two animations over time.

Linear Blending

The simplest form of animation blending is **linear interpolation** (lerp) between the keyframe poses of two animations. Linear blending involves interpolating between the keyframe data of two animations based on the current blend weight. The blend weight controls how much of each animation is shown at any given time.

For example, if you have two animations A and B (walking and running), and a blend weight t that goes from 0 to 1, you can blend between the two animations using linear interpolation:

$$\text{Final Pose} = (1 - t) \cdot A + t \cdot B$$

Where:

- A is the pose from animation A (e.g., walking).

- B is the pose from animation B (e.g., running).

- t is the blend factor, typically between 0 and 1.

When t = 0, the final pose will be entirely from animation A (walking). When t = 1, the final pose will be entirely from animation B (running). For values of t between 0 and 1, the final pose will be a blend of both animations.

Crossfading and Smooth Transitions

A more advanced technique in animation blending is **crossfading**, which creates smoother transitions between animations. Crossfading involves gradually fading out one animation while fading in another, as opposed to simply linearly blending between two keyframes. This results in a more natural transition, particularly when switching between drastically different animations.

Crossfading is particularly useful for transitions like:

- Transitioning from a standing animation to walking.
- Switching from a normal walk cycle to a sprint.
- Blending idle animations with environmental reactions (e.g., reacting to obstacles).

To implement crossfading, you typically need to calculate a set of intermediate frames between two keyframe sequences, effectively "mixing" the two animations together in a more fluid manner.

3. Managing Multiple Animations with Animation State Machines

When working with skeletal animation, particularly in complex 3D applications like games, managing multiple animation states (such as walking, running, jumping, crouching, etc.) becomes essential. To manage these animations effectively, developers often use **animation state machines** (ASM). An animation state machine tracks the current animation state of the character and handles smooth transitions between those states.

An **animation state machine** works by defining a set of states (e.g., walking, running, jumping) and transitions between them. Each state corresponds to a specific animation, and each transition defines when and how to switch between those animations (e.g., from walking to running when the player presses the sprint key).

The transition logic can involve factors like:

- **Input triggers**: Key presses or mouse events.
- **Time-based transitions**: Automatically changing states after a certain amount of time (e.g., after a jump animation ends).
- **Blend weights**: Determining how much influence each animation has over the final output.

4. Performance Considerations for Skeletal Animation

While skeletal animation is an efficient and powerful technique, it does come with performance overhead. Key performance considerations include:

- **Bone Count**: The more bones you have in a skeleton, the more calculations you need to perform. Complex characters (e.g., those with many limbs) will require more transformations per frame.
- **Mesh Complexity**: High-resolution meshes with many vertices will require more work to skin and animate.
- **Animation Blending**: Blending multiple animations can introduce computational overhead, particularly when blending many animations at once.

To optimize skeletal animation:

- Use **Level of Detail (LOD)** techniques for models (simplifying models at a distance).
- Optimize the number of bones in the skeleton (only use as many bones as necessary).
- Implement **instancing** techniques to animate large numbers of objects efficiently.

Skeletal animation, combined with effective skinning and animation blending techniques, is a powerful way to bring 3D models to life in OpenGL. By rigging a model with a skeleton and animating it using a combination of bone transformations and smooth interpolation, you can create realistic, flexible animations for characters and objects. With proper management of animations using state machines and blending, you can create dynamic, engaging 3D animations for interactive applications like games, simulations, and films.

Handling Multiple Animations and Transitions

Once you've set up skeletal animation with skinning, the next step is to handle **multiple animations** and create **smooth transitions** between them. Characters in games or simulations typically go through various states—walking, running, jumping, sitting, etc. Managing these different animation states and switching between them seamlessly is essential for creating realistic and fluid animation behavior.

In this section, we will explore how to handle multiple animations, manage their transitions, and blend them for smooth changes between different animation states.

1. Organizing and Managing Multiple Animations

In most real-time applications like video games or simulations, a character may need to switch between several different animations based on its actions or environment. These animations, such as "idle," "run," "jump," and "walk," are typically predefined as animation clips, each representing a series of poses or movements over time.

Each animation clip is essentially a set of keyframes, where each keyframe describes the state of each bone at a given point in time. These keyframes may represent positions, rotations, and scales of the bones. In skeletal animation, the keyframes are mapped to the bones in the skeleton, causing the 3D model to move in specific ways.

Animation States

To manage multiple animations, it's common to define **animation states**. Each state represents a particular animation, and the state machine can transition between these animations based on certain conditions (e.g., user input, game logic, or physics). For example:

- **Idle**: The character stands still or performs minor idle movements.
- **Walk**: The character is walking.
- **Run**: The character is running.
- **Jump**: The character is in the air.
- **Attack**: The character performs an attack animation.

These states can be organized in a **state machine**, where each state is an animation and can transition to other states based on triggers.

Managing Animations in OpenGL

To manage multiple animations in OpenGL, you'll typically need an **animation controller** that stores the current state and the corresponding animation. Here's how to structure it:

1. **Load Animation Clips**: Each animation is usually stored in a separate file, and each file contains keyframes for the bones of the skeleton.
2. **Assign Animations to States**: Each animation clip is assigned to a state (e.g., "idle," "walk," "jump").
3. **Transition Triggers**: Define conditions or events that trigger transitions between animations, such as the player pressing a key or reaching a certain point in the game world.
4. **Play Animation**: The controller keeps track of the current animation, updates the animation time, and passes the information to the GPU to render the correct keyframe.

For example, to implement an animation controller, you could have:

```cpp
struct Animation {
    std::vector<Keyframe> keyframes;  // Keyframes for the
    animation
    float duration;                    // Total duration of the
    animation
    float speed;                       // Speed factor for
    playback
};

class AnimationController {
public:
    Animation* currentAnimation;
    float timeElapsed;
```

```
void update(float deltaTime) {
    if (currentAnimation) {
        timeElapsed += deltaTime * currentAnimation->speed;
        if (timeElapsed > currentAnimation->duration) {
            timeElapsed = 0.0f;  // Loop animation or switch
        }
        // Update the skeleton based on the current
        animation and timeElapsed
    }
}

void setAnimation(Animation* animation) {
    currentAnimation = animation;
    timeElapsed = 0.0f;
}
};
```

In this simple setup:

- Animation contains the keyframes and playback properties.
- AnimationController keeps track of the current animation, the elapsed time, and manages the transition between different animation states.

2. Blending Animations for Smooth Transitions

Often, it's not enough to simply switch from one animation to another; instead, we want a **smooth transition** between different states, such as from running to walking, or from jumping to landing. **Animation blending** is the process of combining multiple animations over time, allowing for smoother transitions between them.

Linear Blending

Linear blending is the simplest form of animation blending. In linear blending, two animations are interpolated together based on a blending factor. This factor ranges from 0 to 1, where 0 represents the first animation fully, and 1 represents the second animation fully. Intermediate values smoothly mix the two animations.

For example, if you want to blend a **walk** animation with a **run** animation, you can use the blending factor to interpolate between the two animations:

- When the blending factor is 0, the walk animation is played.
- When the blending factor is 1, the run animation is played.
- Intermediate values (e.g., 0.5) blend the two animations.

The blending formula looks like this:

$$\text{Final Pose} = \text{Walk Pose} \times (1 - \text{blend factor}) + \text{Run Pose} \times \text{blend factor}$$

Crossfading

One of the most common and powerful techniques for blending animations is **crossfading**. Crossfading gradually blends between two animations over a set period of time. This technique can be used to smooth transitions between two animations by **fading out** one animation while simultaneously **fading in** another.

For example, when transitioning from a running animation to a walking animation, you may want to slow down the run animation gradually until it reaches the desired walking speed, rather than immediately jumping between two different animations.

In a crossfade, the blending factor is typically controlled by the time spent transitioning from one animation to the next. The amount of blending is determined by the **blend time**.

Here's a conceptual approach to implementing crossfade:

cpp

```
void AnimationController::crossfade(Animation* targetAnimation,
float blendTime) {
    if (currentAnimation != targetAnimation) {
        // Start the blending process
        blendProgress = 0.0f; // Start blending from the
        beginning
        targetAnimationTime = 0.0f;  // Reset the target
        animation's time
    }

    // Update the blending factor based on elapsed time
    blendProgress += deltaTime / blendTime;

    // Ensure blend progress stays within 0 and 1
    blendProgress = std::min(1.0f, blendProgress);

    // Blend the two animations based on blendProgress
    float factor = 1.0f - blendProgress;  // Blend from current
    to target
    // Interpolate between the two animations' poses based on
    factor
}
```

In this example:

- blendProgress tracks the blending state.
- The crossfade function allows smooth transitions from one animation to another by gradually blending over a set time (blendTime).
- You can adjust factor to mix animations based on the current time in the blend process.

Layered Blending

Sometimes, you might want to blend animations not just in a linear fashion, but on different parts of the character simultaneously. This is called **layered blending**, and it's useful when you want to animate one part of the body independently of others. For example, you might want to blend a walking animation for the legs with an idle animation for the arms.

In layered blending, each part of the character's body can have its own animation, and the body parts can be blended independently. The transformation matrices for each bone are computed separately for each layer, and then they are combined to produce the final pose.

Layered blending can be achieved by separating the character's skeleton into different layers (e.g., upper body, lower body, head) and blending the animations for each part individually.

3. Animation Transitions and Finite State Machines (FSMs)

Managing transitions between animations is often done using a **Finite State Machine (FSM)**, which is a system that tracks the current animation state and defines how to transition between different states based on specific conditions.

In the context of animation, a finite state machine might be responsible for managing transitions such as:

- **Idle to Walk**: When the player starts moving.
- **Walk to Run**: When the player accelerates.
- **Jump to Land**: When the player finishes a jump and lands on the ground.

The FSM is typically driven by inputs (e.g., user commands), triggers (e.g., reaching a certain point in time), or game events (e.g., collisions). By using an FSM, you can define specific rules for transitioning between animations while applying blending to ensure that transitions feel natural.

Handling multiple animations and blending transitions is a crucial part of creating fluid and believable animations in 3D graphics. By organizing animations into states, blending them smoothly, and using state machines to manage transitions, you can create characters that move in a natural and responsive way. Whether you're working on a video game, simulation, or interactive application, mastering animation blending and transitions will significantly enhance the realism and interactivity of your animations.

Physics-Based Animation Techniques: Rigid Body Dynamics and Beyond

While skeletal animation focuses on animating a character's bones and mesh, **physics-based animation** involves simulating the physical behaviors of objects and characters in a 3D environment. Instead of manually keyframing each movement, physics-based animation uses physical laws—such as gravity, friction, and mass—to determine how objects move, interact, and respond to forces. This creates animations that are more dynamic, realistic, and reactive to changes in the environment.

In this section, we will delve into the concept of **rigid body dynamics**, which is one of the most common and useful physics-based animation techniques, and explain how to incorporate it into a 3D graphics application using OpenGL. We will also touch on other physics-based animation techniques, including soft body dynamics, cloth simulation, and particle systems.

1. Rigid Body Dynamics: The Basics

Rigid body dynamics simulates the motion of solid, non-deformable objects. These objects are considered "rigid," meaning they don't bend, stretch, or compress under stress. Instead, they only rotate or translate (move in space) based on forces and torques applied to them. Common examples of rigid bodies in animations include cubes, spheres, vehicles, and other hard objects.

Rigid body simulation involves calculating the forces, velocities, and accelerations that affect an object's motion, taking into account its mass, inertia, and external forces such as gravity or collisions with other objects. This kind of animation is crucial for achieving realism in actions like falling, bouncing, sliding, or rotating objects.

Core Principles of Rigid Body Dynamics

The two key concepts in rigid body dynamics are:

- **Force and Torque**: A force is a vector that pushes or pulls an object in space, while torque is a rotational force that causes an object to spin around an axis.
- **Mass and Inertia**: Mass determines the resistance an object has to being moved, while inertia dictates how hard it is to change the object's state of motion (e.g., rotating an object depends on its moment of inertia).

To simulate rigid body dynamics, you need to calculate the position, velocity, and angular velocity of each object over time, applying forces and torques as needed. The position and rotation of each object can be updated using **Newton's Laws of Motion**.

Updating Object Position and Rotation

At each frame, you need to update the position and rotation of the object based on the forces and torques applied to it. This requires basic physics calculations, which can be done using numerical integration methods like **Euler's method** or **Verlet integration**.

Position update (translation):

$$\vec{p}(t + 1) = \vec{p}(t) + \vec{v}(t)\Delta t$$

where:

- $\vec{p}(t)$ is the position at time t,
- $\vec{v}(t)$ is the velocity at time t,
- Δt is the time step between frames.

Velocity update:

$$\vec{v}(t+1) = \vec{v}(t) + \frac{\vec{F}(t)}{m}\Delta t$$

where:

- $\vec{F}(t)$ is the force applied at time t,
- m is the mass of the object.

Rotation update:

$$\vec{\omega}(t+1) = \vec{\omega}(t) + \frac{\vec{\tau}(t)}{I}\Delta t$$

where:

- $\vec{\omega}(t)$ is the angular velocity at time t,
- $\vec{\tau}(t)$ is the torque applied at time t,
- I is the moment of inertia of the object.

Collision Detection and Response

For rigid body simulation, **collision detection** and **collision response** are essential to prevent objects from passing through one another and to simulate physical interactions.

- **Collision detection** involves checking if two objects in the scene intersect or are close enough to each other to cause a collision.
- **Collision response** is the process of calculating how objects react when they collide, typically involving applying forces to push them apart while considering properties like elasticity and friction.

There are various methods for detecting collisions, such as:

- **Bounding Box (AABB)**: A simple but fast method that checks if objects' axis-aligned bounding boxes intersect.
- **Bounding Sphere**: A method where objects are represented as spheres, making collision detection faster for spherical objects.
- **Triangle-Triangle or Mesh Collision**: For more complex objects, where detailed geometry is used to check for intersection between mesh surfaces.

Once a collision is detected, you must calculate the **collision response**, which determines how objects bounce or slide after a collision based on physical properties like **restitution** (elasticity) and **friction**.

2. Implementing Rigid Body Dynamics in OpenGL

While OpenGL is primarily used for rendering, you can integrate physics simulations like rigid body dynamics into your application by using a physics engine such as **Bullet Physics**, **PhysX**, or **Havok**. However, it's also possible to implement basic rigid body dynamics directly in your OpenGL-based engine.

Here's a basic example of how rigid body dynamics can be implemented:

1. **Initialize the Object's Properties**: Assign initial position, velocity, mass, and moment of inertia.
2. **Apply Forces**: Update forces like gravity, friction, or user-defined forces.
3. **Integrate the Physics**: Use Euler's method or Verlet integration to update the position and velocity over time.
4. **Detect and Handle Collisions**: Check for collisions with other objects and apply appropriate responses.

```cpp
cpp

struct RigidBody {
    glm::vec3 position;
    glm::vec3 velocity;
    glm::vec3 force;
    float mass;

    // Time step
    float deltaTime = 0.016f; // Assume 60 FPS

    void update() {
        // Apply forces (e.g., gravity)
        applyForces();

        // Update velocity and position
        velocity += force / mass * deltaTime;
        position += velocity * deltaTime;

        // Reset forces for the next frame
        force = glm::vec3(0.0f);
    }

    void applyForces() {
        // Example: Apply gravity
        force += glm::vec3(0.0f, -9.8f * mass, 0.0f);
    }
};
```

In this simplified example:

- The RigidBody structure represents an object with position, velocity, force, and mass.
- Forces (like gravity) are applied to the object each frame.
- The object's velocity and position are updated using basic physics equations, ensuring the object moves according to the forces applied.

3. Advanced Physics-Based Techniques

While rigid body dynamics is a powerful tool for simulating solid objects, there are several other advanced techniques for simulating different types of animations and interactions:

- **Soft Body Dynamics**: Unlike rigid bodies, soft bodies can deform and bend. Soft body dynamics simulate objects like cloth, rubber, or jelly, where the object's shape changes over time based on forces like stretching, compression, and shear. This is achieved using techniques like **finite element analysis (FEA)** or **mass-spring systems**.
- **Cloth Simulation**: Cloth simulation uses a grid of particles connected by springs (representing the fabric) to simulate the natural folding and stretching behavior of cloth. Algorithms like **Position Based Dynamics (PBD)** are commonly used to calculate cloth dynamics in real-time.
- **Particle Systems**: Particle systems simulate a large number of small particles that interact in simple ways, often used for effects like fire, smoke, rain, or explosions. Each particle behaves according to basic physics laws (e.g., gravity, velocity) but is typically not influenced by complex interactions with other particles or objects.
- **Fluid Simulation**: Simulating liquids and gases requires complex numerical methods, often involving computational fluid dynamics (CFD). Techniques like **smoothed particle hydrodynamics (SPH)** and **lattice Boltzmann methods** are used for real-time fluid simulation in interactive applications.

Physics-based animation techniques, such as rigid body dynamics, provide a powerful tool for animating objects that behave according to real-world laws. By incorporating forces, collisions, and realistic motion, physics-based animations bring a sense of dynamism and realism to 3D environments. While integrating such simulations into OpenGL might require combining physics engines and shaders, the results—realistic object interactions and animations—greatly enhance the user experience. For more complex scenarios, such as soft bodies, cloth, and fluids, additional simulation techniques will be required, but even basic rigid body dynamics will add significant realism to any 3D animation project.

Interactivity and User Input

In any interactive 3D application, especially games or simulations, **user input** is a critical aspect of the experience. How a program responds to keyboard presses, mouse movements, and gamepad actions determines the interactivity and user experience. Whether you're controlling a character, navigating a 3D scene, or manipulating objects, understanding how to handle user input is fundamental.

In this chapter, we will explore how to handle **keyboard**, **mouse**, and **gamepad** input in OpenGL, and how to integrate these inputs to create a responsive and engaging 3D environment. We'll look at the tools available for handling user input, how to process these inputs in a structured way, and provide a foundation for implementing interactive 3D scenes.

1. Introduction to User Input Handling

User input involves capturing actions performed by the user through physical devices like keyboards, mice, and gamepads, and translating these actions into commands that the program can process. For OpenGL applications, user input can be used to:

- **Control camera movement** (e.g., for exploring 3D environments),
- **Manipulate 3D objects** (e.g., rotating, scaling, or translating an object),
- **Trigger actions or animations** (e.g., character movements or effects).

Handling user input is essential for creating any interactive 3D experience, but it's not just about detecting key presses. It's also about **mapping** these inputs to meaningful actions within the application. For example, a user might move the mouse to rotate a camera or use a keyboard to move a character. To achieve this, it's important to understand how to capture, process, and respond to the various types of input.

2. Handling Keyboard Input in OpenGL

The **keyboard** is one of the most common input devices used to control interactive applications. In OpenGL, handling keyboard input involves detecting when keys are pressed or released and mapping those actions to specific in-game commands or camera controls.

Using GLFW for Keyboard Input

In OpenGL, the most commonly used library for window creation, input handling, and events is **GLFW**. GLFW provides built-in functionality to handle key events, such as key presses and releases.

Here is an example of how to capture keyboard input using GLFW:

```cpp
cpp

// GLFW window and key callback function setup
GLFWwindow* window = glfwCreateWindow(800, 600, "OpenGL Window",
NULL, NULL);

glfwSetKeyCallback(window, keyCallback);

// Key callback function to capture key events
void keyCallback(GLFWwindow* window, int key, int scancode, int
action, int mods)
{
    if (action == GLFW_PRESS) {
        if (key == GLFW_KEY_W) {
            // Move forward
        }
        if (key == GLFW_KEY_A) {
            // Move left
        }
```

```
    if (key == GLFW_KEY_S) {
        // Move backward
    }
    if (key == GLFW_KEY_D) {
        // Move right
    }
}
}
```

In this example, the keyCallback function is triggered whenever a key is pressed or released. The GLFW_KEY_W, GLFW_KEY_A, GLFW_KEY_S, and GLFW_KEY_D constants represent the W, A, S, and D keys on the keyboard, commonly used for character movement. You can map these key presses to camera or object movements in your 3D scene.

Modifying Input States

You can also track the state of keys, whether they are **held down** or just pressed once. GLFW provides the function glfwGetKey(window, key) that can be used to check whether a key is currently pressed:

cpp

```
if (glfwGetKey(window, GLFW_KEY_W) == GLFW_PRESS) {
    // Continuously move forward
}
```

This function checks whether a particular key is being pressed, allowing you to implement continuous movement or actions as long as the key is held down.

3. Handling Mouse Input in OpenGL

The **mouse** is another crucial input device for interacting with a 3D environment. It is often used for camera controls (e.g., rotating, zooming) or manipulating objects (e.g., dragging and dropping). Handling mouse events in OpenGL typically involves capturing mouse movement and

235

button presses.

Using GLFW for Mouse Input

GLFW provides mouse input handling capabilities, including mouse position, button presses, and scrolling events.

- **Mouse Position**: To get the mouse position, you can use glfwGetCursorPos(). This function retrieves the current cursor position relative to the window's coordinates.

cpp

```cpp
double xpos, ypos;
glfwGetCursorPos(window, &xpos, &ypos);
```

- **Mouse Button Press**: GLFW also handles mouse button events, which you can use to trigger interactions such as selecting or dragging objects.

cpp

```cpp
glfwSetMouseButtonCallback(window, mouseButtonCallback);

void mouseButtonCallback(GLFWwindow* window, int button, int
action, int mods)
{
    if (button == GLFW_MOUSE_BUTTON_LEFT && action ==
    GLFW_PRESS) {
        // Handle left-click event
    }
}
```

- **Mouse Movement for Camera Control**: To implement mouse-controlled camera movement (e.g., rotating the camera), you can capture the mouse position to detect movement over time.

Here's an example of how to use the mouse to control camera rotation:

```cpp
double lastX = 0, lastY = 0;
glfwGetCursorPos(window, &lastX, &lastY);

// In the update loop
double xpos, ypos;
glfwGetCursorPos(window, &xpos, &ypos);

// Calculate the change in mouse position
double deltaX = xpos - lastX;
double deltaY = ypos - lastY;

camera.rotate(deltaX * sensitivity, deltaY * sensitivity);
lastX = xpos;
lastY = ypos;
```

In this example, we track the change in the mouse position between frames to rotate the camera. The rotate() function would modify the camera's orientation based on the movement.

- **Mouse Scroll for Zoom**: To implement zooming, you can handle the scroll wheel input:

```cpp
glfwSetScrollCallback(window, scrollCallback);

void scrollCallback(GLFWwindow* window, double xoffset, double yoffset)
```

```
{
    camera.zoom(yoffset * zoomSpeed);
}
```

This allows you to zoom in and out by scrolling the mouse wheel.

4. Handling Gamepad Input

For more complex interactions, especially in games or simulations, **gamepad** input can provide an immersive experience. Gamepads typically have several buttons and analog sticks that are used for controlling movement, actions, or camera behavior.

Using GLFW for Gamepad Input

GLFW also supports gamepad input through the glfwGetGamepadState() function, which retrieves the current state of the gamepad.

cpp

```
GLFWgamepadstate state;
if (glfwGetGamepadState(GLFW_JOYSTICK_1, &state)) {
    if (state.buttons[GLFW_GAMEPAD_BUTTON_A] == GLFW_PRESS) {
        // Perform action for 'A' button press
    }
    float leftX = state.axes[GLFW_GAMEPAD_AXIS_LEFT_X];  // Left
    thumbstick X-axis
    float leftY = state.axes[GLFW_GAMEPAD_AXIS_LEFT_Y];  // Left
    thumbstick Y-axis
}
```

- **Buttons**: Each button on the gamepad is represented by an index in the state.buttons array. The values can be GLFW_PRESS or GLFW_RELEASE, depending on whether the button is pressed or released.
- **Analog Sticks**: Analog sticks are represented as axes, where values

range from -1.0 to 1.0. You can use this information to implement smooth movement or control.

```cpp
float leftX = state.axes[GLFW_GAMEPAD_AXIS_LEFT_X];
float leftY = state.axes[GLFW_GAMEPAD_AXIS_LEFT_Y];

camera.move(leftX, leftY); // Move camera based on analog stick
input
```

5. Combining Inputs for Complex Interactions

To create a truly interactive experience, you'll often need to combine input from multiple devices. For example, you might use the keyboard for basic movement controls, the mouse for camera rotation, and the gamepad for precise aiming or character actions.

A typical strategy for handling complex inputs is to prioritize different input devices based on the context. For example:

- When a gamepad is connected, prioritize gamepad input for movement.
- If the user is using the keyboard, fall back to keyboard-based movement.
- If the user is using the mouse, enable camera controls and object manipulation.

This dynamic approach ensures a seamless user experience.

6. Handling Input in a Game Loop

In OpenGL, input handling typically occurs inside the main game loop, where you continuously poll for input events and respond accordingly. Here is a simplified structure for handling input within the game loop:

cpp

```cpp
while (!glfwWindowShouldClose(window)) {
    // Poll for input events (keyboard, mouse, gamepad)
    glfwPollEvents();

    // Update game state based on input
    processKeyboardInput(window);
    processMouseInput(window);
    processGamepadInput(window);

    // Render scene
    renderScene();

    // Swap buffers
    glfwSwapBuffers(window);
}
```

In this loop:

- glfwPollEvents() processes all input events (key presses, mouse movements, gamepad actions).
- Input-processing functions (processKeyboardInput(), processMouseInput(), processGamepadInput()) map the user input to actions or commands within the game.
- The game continues to render and update the scene based on the user's actions.

The **mouse** plays an important role in interactivity, particularly when navigating a 3D environment or manipulating objects. In OpenGL, mouse input can be used for various purposes, such as camera control (e.g., rotating the camera with the mouse), picking objects (e.g., selecting objects in a 3D scene), or triggering actions like shooting or drawing.

Using GLFW for Mouse Input

Just like keyboard input, **GLFW** provides a convenient interface for handling mouse events. GLFW can capture mouse button presses, mouse movements, and scroll wheel events.

Here's an example of handling mouse movement and button clicks:

cpp

```cpp
// GLFW window and mouse callback function setup
glfwSetCursorPosCallback(window, mouseCallback);
glfwSetMouseButtonCallback(window, mouseButtonCallback);

// Mouse callback function for mouse movement
void mouseCallback(GLFWwindow* window, double xpos, double ypos)
{
    // Process mouse movement
    float deltaX = xpos - lastX;
    float deltaY = ypos - lastY;
    lastX = xpos;
    lastY = ypos;

    // Use deltaX and deltaY to rotate the camera or objects
    camera.ProcessMouseMovement(deltaX, deltaY);
}

// Mouse button callback function to capture mouse button clicks
void mouseButtonCallback(GLFWwindow* window, int button, int
action, int mods)
{
    if (action == GLFW_PRESS) {
        if (button == GLFW_MOUSE_BUTTON_LEFT) {
            // Left mouse button clicked
            // Trigger object selection or action
        }
        if (button == GLFW_MOUSE_BUTTON_RIGHT) {
            // Right mouse button clicked
            // Trigger context menu or other action
        }
    }
}
```

In this example:

- The **mouseCallback** function captures the mouse's position relative to the window. This is commonly used to implement **camera look** functionality, where moving the mouse changes the camera's orientation.

- The **mouseButtonCallback** function captures mouse button clicks, such as left-click and right-click events. This can be used for object selection or triggering specific interactions within your application.

Mouse Movement for Camera Control

A common use case for mouse movement in 3D applications is controlling the camera. For example, moving the mouse horizontally can rotate the camera left or right, while moving the mouse vertically can tilt it up or down. This is a basic form of **first-person** or **free-look** camera control.

Here's how you might use the mouse movement to rotate the camera:

cpp

```
// Process mouse movement to control camera orientation
float lastX = 400, lastY = 300;  // Initial mouse position
(center of the window)
float sensitivity = 0.05f;

void mouseCallback(GLFWwindow* window, double xpos, double ypos)
{
    // Calculate change in mouse position
    float deltaX = xpos - lastX;
    float deltaY = lastY - ypos;  // Invert Y-axis for intuitive
    control
    lastX = xpos;
    lastY = ypos;

    // Apply sensitivity factor
    deltaX *= sensitivity;
    deltaY *= sensitivity;

    // Rotate the camera based on mouse movement
```

```
    camera.ProcessMouseMovement(deltaX, deltaY);
}
```

In this example:

- The deltaX and deltaY values represent how much the mouse has moved from the previous frame.
- The camera.ProcessMouseMovement() function adjusts the camera's orientation based on the mouse's movement.
- The sensitivity factor scales the mouse movement to control the speed of rotation.

This technique is frequently used in games or simulations to allow players to look around the scene by simply moving the mouse.

Mouse Wheel for Zooming

The **mouse wheel** is often used for zooming in or out, especially in 3D applications. In OpenGL, you can use the scroll wheel to adjust the camera's field of view or zoom level.

Here's an example of handling mouse wheel input to zoom the camera in and out:

cpp

```
// GLFW window and scroll callback function setup
glfwSetScrollCallback(window, scrollCallback);

// Scroll callback function to handle zooming
void scrollCallback(GLFWwindow* window, double xOffset, double yOffset)
{
    // Zoom the camera by adjusting the field of view (FOV)
    camera.ProcessMouseScroll(yOffset);
}
```

In this example:

- The scrollCallback function detects the mouse scroll event and adjusts the camera's **field of view** (FOV) based on the vertical scroll offset (yOffset).
- This results in a zoom-in or zoom-out effect when the user scrolls the mouse wheel.

Handling Gamepad Input in OpenGL

While mouse and keyboard inputs are commonly used in many applications, **gamepads** are often preferred in gaming or simulations where players need precise control. Gamepad input allows for **analog** control (e.g., using joysticks to move a character or camera) and **button presses** (e.g., for jumping, shooting, or other actions).

Using GLFW for Gamepad Input

GLFW provides support for gamepad input, allowing you to capture button presses and joystick movements. You can use glfwGetGamepadSta te() to retrieve the current state of the gamepad, including button states and joystick positions.

Here's an example of handling gamepad input:

```cpp
GLFWgamepadstate state;
if (glfwGetGamepadState(GLFW_JOYSTICK_1, &state)) {
    if (state.buttons[GLFW_GAMEPAD_BUTTON_A] == GLFW_PRESS) {
        // Jump action
    }

    // Use left joystick to move character
    float moveX = state.axes[GLFW_GAMEPAD_AXIS_LEFT_X];
    float moveY = state.axes[GLFW_GAMEPAD_AXIS_LEFT_Y];

    // Process movement based on joystick input
```

```cpp
    character.Move(moveX, moveY);
}
```

In this example:

- The glfwGetGamepadState() function retrieves the current state of the gamepad.
- The state.buttons array contains the status of each gamepad button (e.g., GLFW_GAMEPAD_BUTTON_A for the "A" button).
- The state.axes array contains the positions of each joystick axis (e.g., GLFW_GAMEPAD_AXIS_LEFT_X for the horizontal axis of the left joystick).

You can map the gamepad's input to various actions within your application, such as character movement or triggering specific events (e.g., jumping, attacking).

Analog Joystick Control

One of the benefits of using a gamepad is the **analog input** from the joysticks. The joysticks provide continuous input values (ranging from -1.0 to 1.0), which can be used for smooth control of movement, rotation, or other actions. For example, the left joystick might control character movement along the X and Y axes, while the right joystick could control the camera's rotation.

cpp

```cpp
// Get the left joystick input for moving the character
float moveX = state.axes[GLFW_GAMEPAD_AXIS_LEFT_X];  // 
Horizontal movement
float moveY = state.axes[GLFW_GAMEPAD_AXIS_LEFT_Y];  // Vertical
movement

// Apply movement based on joystick input
```

245

```cpp
character.Move(moveX, moveY);
```

In this code, the moveX and moveY values represent the horizontal and vertical positions of the left joystick. These values can be mapped to move a character or camera smoothly through the scene.

Implementing Multiple Input Devices Simultaneously

In many applications, it's common to handle multiple input devices simultaneously. For instance, a user might use the mouse to look around the scene, the keyboard to move, and the gamepad to control an in-game character or vehicle.

To implement this, you would need to integrate inputs from all devices into a unified control system, ensuring that the user experience remains seamless. For example, a **user input manager** could be used to monitor and process input from all devices at once, allowing the game or application to respond accordingly.

Here's a simplified approach to handling multiple devices:

cpp

```cpp
void processInput(GLFWwindow* window, GamepadState&
gamepadState) {
    // Handle keyboard input
    if (glfwGetKey(window, GLFW_KEY_W) == GLFW_PRESS) {
        camera.MoveForward();
    }
    if (glfwGetKey(window, GLFW_KEY_S) == GLFW_PRESS) {
        camera.MoveBackward();
    }

    // Handle mouse input
    if (glfwGetMouseButton(window, GLFW_MOUSE_BUTTON_LEFT) ==
GLFW_PRESS) {
        // Perform mouse click action
    }
```

```
    // Handle gamepad input
    if (gamepadState.isButtonPressed(GLFW_GAMEPAD_BUTTON_A)) {
        // Trigger gamepad action
    }
}
```

This processInput() function handles input from multiple devices (keyboard, mouse, and gamepad) in a unified way, ensuring the application responds to all inputs in a consistent and intuitive manner.

Handling user input is a fundamental part of creating interactive 3D applications. By understanding how to handle keyboard, mouse, and gamepad input, you can create dynamic and responsive experiences that allow users to fully engage with your program. OpenGL, when combined with libraries like **GLFW**, offers powerful tools for capturing and processing input, making it easier than ever to integrate interactivity into your 3D environments.

Implementing Interactive 3D Environments

Creating an interactive 3D environment involves integrating various user input methods (keyboard, mouse, gamepad) to manipulate objects, control cameras, and trigger actions within a 3D world. The goal is to build a dynamic experience where the user feels in control of the environment, objects, and characters. This process includes handling object interactions, navigating the 3D space, and responding to various events that the user triggers.

In this section, we will focus on how to use input devices to manipulate objects, control the camera, and implement interactive features like object selection and navigation, which are essential for making your OpenGL application engaging and dynamic.

1. Interactive Camera Control

One of the most fundamental interactive elements in a 3D environment is the **camera**. A well-designed camera system allows users to navigate

247

the scene and observe the world from different perspectives. Typically, 3D applications use either a **first-person camera** (where the camera is controlled by the user's view, similar to looking through a character's eyes) or a **third-person camera** (where the camera follows an object or character in the scene).

First-Person Camera

A **first-person camera** allows the user to look around the environment as if they were the character. The camera's orientation is controlled by mouse movement (for looking around), and movement is typically done through keyboard input (e.g., WASD keys for walking).

Here's an example of how you can create a basic first-person camera system using **GLFW** and OpenGL:

```cpp
cpp

class Camera {
public:
    glm::vec3 position;
    glm::vec3 front;
    glm::vec3 up;
    glm::vec3 right;
    float yaw, pitch;
    float speed, sensitivity;

    Camera(glm::vec3 startPosition)
        : position(startPosition), front(glm::vec3(0.0f, 0.0f,
        -1.0f)),
          up(glm::vec3(0.0f, 1.0f, 0.0f)), yaw(-90.0f),
          pitch(0.0f),
          speed(2.5f), sensitivity(0.1f) {}

    void ProcessKeyboardInput(GLFWwindow* window, float
    deltaTime) {
        float velocity = speed * deltaTime;

        if (glfwGetKey(window, GLFW_KEY_W) == GLFW_PRESS)
```

```
            position += front * velocity;
        if (glfwGetKey(window, GLFW_KEY_S) == GLFW_PRESS)
            position -= front * velocity;
        if (glfwGetKey(window, GLFW_KEY_A) == GLFW_PRESS)
            position -= right * velocity;
        if (glfwGetKey(window, GLFW_KEY_D) == GLFW_PRESS)
            position += right * velocity;
    }

    void ProcessMouseMovement(float xOffset, float yOffset) {
        xOffset *= sensitivity;
        yOffset *= sensitivity;

        yaw += xOffset;
        pitch -= yOffset;

        if (pitch > 89.0f) pitch = 89.0f;
        if (pitch < -89.0f) pitch = -89.0f;

        updateCameraVectors();
    }

private:
    void updateCameraVectors() {
        glm::vec3 newFront;
        newFront.x = cos(glm::radians(yaw)) *
        cos(glm::radians(pitch));
        newFront.y = sin(glm::radians(pitch));
        newFront.z = sin(glm::radians(yaw)) *
        cos(glm::radians(pitch));
        front = glm::normalize(newFront);

        right = glm::normalize(glm::cross(front, up));
    }
};
```

In this example:

- The Camera class holds the camera's position, orientation, and movement speed.

- **ProcessKeyboardInput()** handles the user's keyboard input (WASD) to move the camera.
- **ProcessMouseMovement()** adjusts the camera's orientation based on mouse movement, allowing the user to look around the environment.
- The **updateCameraVectors()** function updates the direction vectors (front, right, and up) based on the yaw and pitch angles.

You would need to call these functions within your main loop to update the camera's position and orientation based on user input:

```cpp
// In the main loop
float deltaTime = glfwGetTime() - lastFrame;
lastFrame = glfwGetTime();

camera.ProcessKeyboardInput(window, deltaTime);
camera.ProcessMouseMovement(xOffset, yOffset);  // Capture mouse
movement

// Update the camera projection
view = glm::lookAt(camera.position, camera.position +
camera.front, camera.up);
```

The glm::lookAt function is used to generate a **view matrix** that transforms the world into camera space, allowing the camera to follow the user's movements.

Third-Person Camera

A **third-person camera** follows an object or character from behind, allowing the user to move and rotate the camera around that object. It is common in games like platformers or action games, where you control a character and view them from a fixed angle.

```cpp
cpp

class ThirdPersonCamera {
public:
    glm::vec3 position;
    glm::vec3 target;
    float distance;  // Camera distance from target
    float angleX, angleY;

    ThirdPersonCamera(glm::vec3 initialPosition, glm::vec3
    targetPosition)
        : position(initialPosition), target(targetPosition),
        distance(5.0f), angleX(0.0f), angleY(0.0f) {}

    void updateCameraPosition(GLFWwindow* window) {
        // Allow the user to adjust camera distance and angles
        if (glfwGetKey(window, GLFW_KEY_UP) == GLFW_PRESS) {
            angleY += 1.0f;
        }
        if (glfwGetKey(window, GLFW_KEY_DOWN) == GLFW_PRESS) {
            angleY -= 1.0f;
        }

        // Adjust the position based on angles and distance
        position.x = target.x + distance *
        cos(glm::radians(angleX)) * sin(glm::radians(angleY));
        position.y = target.y + distance *
        sin(glm::radians(angleY));
        position.z = target.z + distance *
        cos(glm::radians(angleX)) * cos(glm::radians(angleY));
    }

    glm::mat4 getViewMatrix() {
        return glm::lookAt(position, target, glm::vec3(0.0f,
        1.0f, 0.0f));
    }
};
```

In this example:

- The camera's position is updated based on the distance and angles relative to a target object (e.g., a character).
- **updateCameraPosition()** adjusts the camera's position based on keypresses that control the camera's angle and distance.
- **getViewMatrix()** generates the view matrix to render the scene from the camera's point of view.

2. Object Interaction and Manipulation

Once the camera system is in place, you may want to allow the user to interact with the environment. This includes **selecting**, **moving**, and **rotating** objects. In OpenGL, this typically involves ray casting or picking techniques that detect which objects are under the mouse cursor or screen coordinates.

Object Picking (Ray Casting)

Ray casting involves shooting an invisible ray from the camera (based on the mouse position) into the scene and determining which object the ray intersects. This is essential for selecting or interacting with 3D objects.

cpp

```cpp
// Assuming camera and mouse position are available
glm::vec3 rayOrigin = camera.position;
glm::vec3 rayDirection = glm::normalize(mousePosition -
camera.position);

// Perform intersection tests with scene objects
for (auto& object : sceneObjects) {
    if (rayIntersectsObject(rayOrigin, rayDirection, object)) {
        // Object picked, perform action
    }
}
```

In this example:

- rayOrigin is the camera's position, and rayDirection is the direction in which the camera is pointing, based on the mouse's screen position.

- **rayIntersectsObject()** checks if the ray intersects any object in the scene, triggering interaction if an intersection occurs.

3. UI Interactions and Event Handling

In addition to camera control and object manipulation, OpenGL applications often require handling UI elements like buttons, sliders, or menus. These UI elements can be manipulated using mouse input and keyboard commands. Integrating **GUI libraries** such as **ImGui** or **GLFW**'s native input system allows you to easily implement menus and control interfaces.

Implementing interactive 3D environments in OpenGL requires integrating various input systems (keyboard, mouse, gamepad) to create a dynamic, engaging user experience. By understanding how to process and respond to user input—whether it's controlling a camera, manipulating objects, or interacting with the UI—you can create fully interactive, real-time 3D applications. Whether you're building a game, a simulation, or any other 3D environment, mastering these techniques is essential for creating an intuitive and enjoyable experience.

Creating an Interactive 3D Scene Viewer

An **interactive 3D scene viewer** is a foundational element for many 3D applications, such as CAD software, architectural visualizations, and games. This system allows users to navigate and interact with a 3D environment, manipulating the view or objects within it in real time. The ability to seamlessly rotate, zoom, and pan through a scene provides a dynamic and immersive experience for users.

To build an interactive 3D scene viewer in OpenGL, you need to integrate several key components:

- **Camera Control**: To navigate the scene.
- **User Input Handling**: For mouse, keyboard, and possibly gamepad

inputs.

- **Object Interaction**: Such as rotating, scaling, or translating objects in the scene.
- **Rendering and Display**: Efficiently drawing the scene, updating it as the user interacts, and applying transformations.

In this section, we'll explore how to implement a basic interactive 3D scene viewer that includes the ability to control the camera, manipulate objects, and display a scene. We'll focus on setting up the environment, handling user inputs, and drawing objects dynamically.

1. Setting Up the Scene: Creating a Basic 3D Scene

Before allowing the user to interact with the 3D scene, it's important to set up a basic environment. This involves creating the initial objects in the scene, such as simple geometric shapes (e.g., cubes, spheres) and a background or terrain.

Creating the Objects

Start by defining simple geometric shapes (e.g., cubes, spheres, pyramids) to populate the scene. These shapes will be the "actors" in the 3D world. You can create the models for these objects using vertex buffers and shaders, or load more complex models using external libraries like **Assimp** (which allows you to load 3D models in formats like OBJ, FBX, etc.).

For example, to create a simple cube:

cpp

```
// Define vertices for a cube
float vertices[] = {
    -0.5f, -0.5f, -0.5f,  // Bottom-left-front
     0.5f, -0.5f, -0.5f,  // Bottom-right-front
     0.5f,  0.5f, -0.5f,  // Top-right-front
    -0.5f,  0.5f, -0.5f,  // Top-left-front
    -0.5f, -0.5f,  0.5f,  // Bottom-left-back
```

```
    0.5f, -0.5f,  0.5f,    // Bottom-right-back
    0.5f,  0.5f,  0.5f,    // Top-right-back
   -0.5f,  0.5f,  0.5f     // Top-left-back
};

// Define the indices to create faces from the vertices
unsigned int indices[] = {
    0, 1, 2, 2, 3, 0, // Front face
    4, 5, 6, 6, 7, 4, // Back face
    0, 1, 5, 5, 4, 0, // Bottom face
    2, 3, 7, 7, 6, 2, // Top face
    0, 3, 7, 7, 4, 0, // Left face
    1, 2, 6, 6, 5, 1  // Right face
};
```

Here, the cube is made up of 8 vertices and 12 triangles (since each face is a quadrilateral made from 2 triangles), which are indexed into the **indices array**. You can create a Vertex Array Object (VAO) and Vertex Buffer Object (VBO) to store and render these shapes in OpenGL.

cpp

```cpp
GLuint VBO, VAO, EBO;
glGenVertexArrays(1, &VAO);
glGenBuffers(1, &VBO);
glGenBuffers(1, &EBO);

glBindVertexArray(VAO);

// Bind the VBO and EBO
glBindBuffer(GL_ARRAY_BUFFER, VBO);
glBufferData(GL_ARRAY_BUFFER, sizeof(vertices), vertices,
GL_STATIC_DRAW);
glBindBuffer(GL_ELEMENT_ARRAY_BUFFER, EBO);
glBufferData(GL_ELEMENT_ARRAY_BUFFER, sizeof(indices), indices,
GL_STATIC_DRAW);

// Define the vertex position attribute
```

255

```cpp
glVertexAttribPointer(0, 3, GL_FLOAT, GL_FALSE, 3 *
sizeof(float), (void*)0);
glEnableVertexAttribArray(0);

glBindBuffer(GL_ARRAY_BUFFER, 0);
glBindVertexArray(0);
```

In this example:

- A **VBO** is used to store the vertex data for the cube.
- An **EBO** (Element Buffer Object) is used to store the index data for rendering.
- The **VAO** binds the VBO and EBO together, ensuring that they are used correctly during rendering.

Rendering the Scene

Once the objects are created, you can render the scene using OpenGL shaders. A basic rendering loop can look like this:

cpp

```cpp
while (!glfwWindowShouldClose(window)) {
    // Clear the screen
    glClear(GL_COLOR_BUFFER_BIT | GL_DEPTH_BUFFER_BIT);

    // Use the shader program
    shader.use();

    // Set up transformations (rotation, scaling, translation)
    glm::mat4 model = glm::mat4(1.0f);
    model = glm::translate(model, glm::vec3(0.0f, 0.0f, -5.0f));
    // Move the object
    model = glm::rotate(model, glm::radians(20.0f),
    glm::vec3(1.0f, 0.0f, 0.0f)); // Rotate the object

    // Pass the model matrix to the shader
    unsigned int modelLoc = glGetUniformLocation(shader.ID,
```

```
    "model");
    glUniformMatrix4fv(modelLoc, 1, GL_FALSE,
    glm::value_ptr(model));

    // Draw the object (cube)
    glBindVertexArray(VAO);
    glDrawElements(GL_TRIANGLES, 36, GL_UNSIGNED_INT, 0);
    glBindVertexArray(0);

    // Swap buffers and poll events
    glfwSwapBuffers(window);
    glfwPollEvents();
}
```

This loop continuously clears the screen, updates object transformations, and draws the scene. The object can be moved, rotated, and scaled by manipulating the **model matrix**.

2. Handling User Interactions

Once the scene is set up and rendering correctly, the next step is to allow users to interact with the environment. Interactivity often involves **camera controls** and **object manipulation** through user input. This section discusses integrating camera movement and object interaction into the viewer.

Camera Movement

For navigating the scene, the camera must respond to keyboard and mouse input. As discussed in the previous section, using **WASD keys** for movement and **mouse movement** for looking around is a common approach. You can modify the ProcessKeyboardInput and ProcessMouse-Movement functions to move the camera smoothly through the scene.

For example, pressing the **W key** will move the camera forward, while **A** and **D** will strafe left and right, respectively.

Object Interaction

Another aspect of interactivity is **object manipulation**. This could involve dragging objects around the scene, rotating them, or scaling them. For instance, if the user clicks on an object with the mouse, they could drag it across the screen. Implementing this functionality requires detecting when the mouse clicks on an object and applying transformations based on mouse movement.

You can achieve this through **raycasting**, which is a technique for shooting a "ray" from the camera's viewpoint to check for intersections with objects in the scene. When a user clicks on an object, you cast a ray from the mouse position to find which object the ray intersects. Then, you can apply transformations like translation or rotation based on the user's drag movements.

Example: Object Selection Using Raycasting

cpp

```
// Cast a ray from the camera based on the mouse position
glm::vec3 rayOrigin = camera.position;
glm::vec3 rayDirection = camera.front;  // Direction of the ray
(camera's front vector)

// Perform ray-object intersection tests here...
```

Raycasting will allow you to detect which objects are under the mouse cursor, and from there, you can implement dragging or other object manipulation features.

3. Enhancing Interactivity: UI and Feedback

Adding **visual feedback** can significantly improve the user experience. For instance, providing on-screen indicators when objects are selected, or showing the camera's position in the world, can help users understand their current context within the scene.

Additionally, incorporating **UI elements** (such as buttons, sliders, and menus) allows users to perform actions like toggling lighting, changing object textures, or adjusting camera settings.

Libraries like **ImGui** are commonly used for creating interactive graphical user interfaces in OpenGL applications. You can integrate such libraries to provide users with intuitive controls for managing the 3D scene.

Responding to User Interactions (Clicks, Drags, and Gestures)

In an interactive 3D environment, responding to user actions such as **clicks**, **drags**, and **gestures** is essential for creating a dynamic and immersive experience. These interactions allow users to select, move, or manipulate objects in the 3D world, as well as control the camera or trigger specific events. In this section, we will focus on handling mouse events (clicks and drags) and gestures in OpenGL to implement user interactions.

1. Mouse Clicks and Object Selection

Mouse clicks are commonly used for **object selection** in 3D environments. This allows the user to click on an object to select it, move it, or interact with it in other ways (e.g., dragging, rotating, or applying transformations). In OpenGL, handling mouse clicks involves capturing the mouse's position in the window and determining which 3D object the user clicked on.

To handle object selection, you must convert the 2D screen coordinates of the mouse into 3D world coordinates. This process is called **picking**. Picking can be performed using **ray casting**, which involves casting a ray from the camera through the mouse position and checking for intersections with objects in the 3D scene.

Here's a simple overview of how to implement object picking using ray casting:

1. **Capture the Mouse Position**: Get the mouse's 2D screen coordinates (using GLFW or another input library).
2. **Convert 2D to 3D**: Using the camera's projection and view matrices, convert the mouse position into a ray in 3D space.
3. **Test for Intersections**: For each object in the scene, check if the ray intersects the object's geometry.

259

4. **Select Object**: If an intersection is detected, select the object and trigger any relevant actions (e.g., highlight the object, initiate object movement, etc.).

```cpp
// Function to convert screen coordinates to world coordinates
(ray casting)
glm::vec3 screenToWorldRay(double xpos, double ypos, const
glm::mat4& projection, const glm::mat4& view)
{
    // Convert screen coordinates to normalized device
    coordinates (-1 to 1)
    float x = (2.0f * xpos) / windowWidth - 1.0f;
    float y = 1.0f - (2.0f * ypos) / windowHeight;

    // Create the ray from the camera's perspective
    glm::vec4 rayClipSpace(x, y, -1.0f, 1.0f);
    glm::mat4 invViewProjection = glm::inverse(projection *
    view);
    glm::vec4 rayWorldSpace = invViewProjection * rayClipSpace;
    rayWorldSpace /= rayWorldSpace.w;  // Normalize the ray

    // Return the ray direction in world space
    return glm::vec3(rayWorldSpace);
}
```

In this example:

- The screenToWorldRay() function converts the 2D screen coordinates of the mouse position (xpos, ypos) into a ray in 3D world space.
- The ray can then be used to check if it intersects with any 3D objects in the scene.

Once you have the ray, you can perform intersection tests with the 3D objects in your scene using algorithms like **AABB (Axis-Aligned**

Bounding Box) intersection or Ray-Triangle Intersection.

2. Dragging Objects with Mouse

Another common interaction is **dragging**. Dragging typically involves selecting an object and then clicking and holding the mouse button to move the object around in the 3D scene. Once the object is selected, the user can drag it by moving the mouse, and the object will follow the mouse's movement.

To implement dragging, you must track the mouse's position while the user holds down the mouse button and update the object's position accordingly.

Here's an approach for implementing basic object dragging:

1. **Select an Object**: Use the ray-casting technique described earlier to detect when an object is clicked.
2. **Track Mouse Movement**: Once the object is selected, track the mouse's movements to update the object's position in 3D space.
3. **Update Object Position**: The object's position is updated based on the change in mouse position.

Here's a simplified implementation of the drag functionality:

```cpp
bool isDragging = false;
glm::vec3 lastMousePosition;

void mouseButtonCallback(GLFWwindow* window, int button, int action, int mods)
{
    if (button == GLFW_MOUSE_BUTTON_LEFT) {
        if (action == GLFW_PRESS) {
            // Start dragging
            isDragging = true;
            // Get the initial mouse position in world space
```

261

```
            lastMousePosition = screenToWorldRay(lastX, lastY,
            projectionMatrix, viewMatrix);
        }
        else if (action == GLFW_RELEASE) {
            // Stop dragging
            isDragging = false;
        }
    }
}

void mouseCallback(GLFWwindow* window, double xpos, double ypos)
{
    if (isDragging) {
        // Calculate the change in mouse position
        glm::vec3 newMousePosition = screenToWorldRay(xpos,
        ypos, projectionMatrix, viewMatrix);
        glm::vec3 dragOffset = newMousePosition -
        lastMousePosition;

        // Update the object's position based on the mouse
        movement
        draggedObject->position += dragOffset;

        // Update the last mouse position
        lastMousePosition = newMousePosition;
    }
}
```

In this example:

- When the left mouse button is pressed, the drag operation starts, and the current mouse position is recorded.
- When the mouse moves while dragging, the object's position is updated by calculating the change in the mouse's 3D position.
- When the mouse button is released, the drag operation ends.

3. Implementing Gestures for Touch Devices

If your application is intended to run on touch-enabled devices (e.g., tablets, smartphones, or touchscreens), you may want to implement **gestures** such as pinch-to-zoom, swipe, or rotation. These gestures are common in mobile games, interactive media, and other touch-based 3D applications.

For gestures, handling **multi-touch input** is necessary. While OpenGL does not have built-in support for touch inputs, libraries like **GLFW** or **SDL** can handle touch events, or you can use platform-specific APIs for mobile devices to detect multi-touch input.

For example, you could implement **pinch-to-zoom** by detecting the distance between two touch points and adjusting the camera's zoom level accordingly.

Here's a basic example of pinch-to-zoom:

1. **Track Two Finger Positions**: Capture the positions of two touch points.
2. **Calculate Distance Between Points**: Calculate the distance between the two touch points.
3. **Zoom In or Out**: Adjust the camera's field of view (FOV) based on the distance between the touch points.

cpp

```
float lastDistance = 0.0f;

void handleTouchInput(glm::vec2 touch1, glm::vec2 touch2)
{
    // Calculate the distance between the two touch points
    float currentDistance = glm::length(touch1 - touch2);

    // If the distance has changed, adjust the zoom level
    if (lastDistance != 0.0f) {
        float zoomFactor = currentDistance - lastDistance;
        camera.Zoom += zoomFactor * sensitivity;
        if (camera.Zoom < 1.0f) camera.Zoom = 1.0f;
```

```
        if (camera.Zoom > 45.0f) camera.Zoom = 45.0f;
    }

    // Update the last distance for the next frame
    lastDistance = currentDistance;
}
```

In this example:

- touch1 and touch2 represent the two touch points on the screen.
- The distance between the touch points is calculated and used to adjust the camera's **zoom level**.
- The zoom level is constrained between 1.0 and 45.0 degrees for practical use.

Implementing responsive user interactions in OpenGL is vital for creating immersive and engaging 3D applications. By effectively handling mouse clicks, drags, and touch gestures, you can allow users to manipulate objects, navigate the 3D environment, and trigger meaningful actions within the scene. Integrating these interactive elements helps build a dynamic user experience, whether you're creating a game, simulation, or any other interactive 3D application.

Optimizing OpenGL Applications

1. Minimizing Draw Calls and Reducing GPU Workload

When developing an OpenGL-based application, performance is often a critical concern, particularly for real-time 3D graphics such as video games or interactive simulations. One of the most effective ways to optimize OpenGL applications is to **minimize draw calls** and reduce the workload on the GPU. **Draw calls** represent the number of times the CPU requests the GPU to render something to the screen. Each draw call involves considerable overhead, and excessive draw calls can lead to significant performance bottlenecks, especially on mobile devices or lower-end hardware.

In this section, we will explore strategies for minimizing draw calls, which will help optimize the rendering pipeline and improve performance, and also discuss ways to reduce the GPU workload to make rendering more efficient.

2. Understanding Draw Calls in OpenGL

A **draw call** is an instruction issued from the CPU to the GPU to render a set of primitives (such as triangles or lines) to the frame buffer. Each draw call typically involves:

- Setting up the appropriate vertex buffers (VBOs), index buffers (IBOs), and shaders.
- Sending commands to the GPU to process the geometry and shaders.
- Updating the framebuffer or texture with the final output.

While OpenGL can render multiple objects at once using a single draw call (e.g., by using instancing), every new draw call adds additional overhead to the CPU. The CPU must switch between different pipeline states (e.g., shaders, textures, or buffer bindings), and this state-switching is costly. Therefore, reducing the number of draw calls in an OpenGL application can significantly improve performance.

Factors Contributing to Draw Call Overhead:

- **State changes**: Every time you change a shader, texture, or buffer, the GPU must reconfigure itself, leading to additional overhead.
- **CPU-GPU communication**: Each draw call requires a communication cycle between the CPU and GPU. More draw calls result in more frequent synchronization between the two.
- **Geometry complexity**: Larger, more complex objects require more computational resources for rendering. Optimizing these objects can reduce the need for multiple draw calls.

3. Strategies to Minimize Draw Calls

Reducing the number of draw calls in OpenGL applications often requires **batching** techniques, where multiple objects or parts of a scene are grouped together to be rendered in a single draw call. Here are several strategies to minimize draw calls effectively:

1. Use of Instancing

Instancing is one of the most effective techniques for reducing draw calls. It allows you to render multiple copies of the same object using a single draw call by providing an array of transformation matrices or other per-instance data to the GPU. This is especially useful when rendering large numbers of identical objects, such as trees, enemies, or buildings, where each object shares the same mesh and texture.

In OpenGL, instancing can be achieved using the glDrawArraysInstanced() or glDrawElementsInstanced() functions. Here's a simple example of using instancing:

cpp

```cpp
// Set up a buffer to store instance transformation data (e.g.,
positions, rotations)
GLuint instanceVBO;
glGenBuffers(1, &instanceVBO);
glBindBuffer(GL_ARRAY_BUFFER, instanceVBO);
glBufferData(GL_ARRAY_BUFFER, sizeof(glm::mat4) * numInstances,
&instanceData[0], GL_STATIC_DRAW);

// Specify the transformation matrix for each instance in the
vertex shader
glVertexAttribPointer(1, 4, GL_FLOAT, GL_FALSE,
sizeof(glm::mat4), (void*)0);
glEnableVertexAttribArray(1);
glVertexAttribPointer(2, 4, GL_FLOAT, GL_FALSE,
sizeof(glm::mat4), (void*)(sizeof(glm::vec4)));
glEnableVertexAttribArray(2);
glVertexAttribPointer(3, 4, GL_FLOAT, GL_FALSE,
sizeof(glm::mat4), (void*)(2 * sizeof(glm::vec4)));
glEnableVertexAttribArray(3);
glVertexAttribPointer(4, 4, GL_FLOAT, GL_FALSE,
sizeof(glm::mat4), (void*)(3 * sizeof(glm::vec4)));
glEnableVertexAttribArray(4);

// Draw all instances with a single call
glDrawElementsInstanced(GL_TRIANGLES, numIndices,
GL_UNSIGNED_INT, 0, numInstances);
```

In this example:

- The transformation data for each instance (position, rotation, scale) is stored in an instance buffer.
- The glDrawElementsInstanced() function is called to render all instances in a single draw call.

Using instancing drastically reduces the number of draw calls when rendering large numbers of identical objects.

267

2. Use of Texture Atlases

A **texture atlas** is a single large texture that contains multiple smaller textures used by different objects in your scene. By combining several textures into a single texture, you can reduce the need to switch between multiple textures during rendering. This reduces the number of texture bindings and, therefore, the number of draw calls.

For example, instead of using different texture files for each object, you can map several objects' textures onto different regions of a single texture atlas and use that texture across multiple objects.

Here's how you might implement a texture atlas:

- **Pack** multiple textures (e.g., diffuse maps for different objects) into one large texture image.
- **Adjust UV coordinates** for each object so they correctly reference the region of the atlas that corresponds to their texture.

Using texture atlases is particularly beneficial in games and applications with many small assets that share similar textures.

3. Combine Meshes and Objects

If objects in your scene share the same material or texture, **combining meshes** into one larger mesh can drastically reduce the number of draw calls. This technique works best when objects are part of the same static scene and do not need to be rendered separately.

You can use this approach when dealing with static objects or when rendering large batches of objects that share the same material, such as furniture in a room, multiple trees in a forest, or props in a game environment.

To combine meshes:

Merge the geometry of all objects into a single vertex buffer.

If the objects have different positions or rotations, apply these transformations in the vertex shader or combine them into one transformation matrix.

4. Batch Drawing by Material

In OpenGL, state changes (such as switching between shaders, textures, and buffers) can be costly. A good optimization technique is to **batch objects** that share the same material (e.g., texture and shader) together and render them in a single draw call.

For example:

- Group objects that use the same shader program and texture into one batch.
- Sort objects by material type before rendering, so the shader and texture bindings are minimized.

You can use a **material sorting technique** to first sort all the objects by their materials and then draw them together.

4. Reducing GPU Workload

Reducing GPU workload goes hand-in-hand with minimizing draw calls. Even if you manage to reduce the number of draw calls, the workload on the GPU can still be significant if the geometry is complex or if there are unnecessary calculations happening in the shaders. Here are some methods to reduce GPU workload:

1. Level of Detail (LOD)

The **Level of Detail (LOD)** technique is used to decrease the number of polygons that need to be rendered for objects that are far from the camera. For example, instead of rendering a high-polygon model of a building at a distance, you can render a lower-polygon version of the same model, significantly reducing the GPU's workload.

LOD can be implemented by using multiple versions of a model with different levels of detail, and then switching between these versions based on the distance from the camera.

2. Use of Culling Techniques

Culling is the process of **not rendering objects** that are outside the camera's view frustum or hidden behind other objects. There are two common types of culling:

- **Frustum culling**: Objects outside the camera's view are not rendered.
- **Backface culling**: For objects that are made up of triangles, faces that are not visible to the camera (i.e., back faces) are not rendered.

In OpenGL, backface culling can be easily enabled with the following command:

```cpp
glEnable(GL_CULL_FACE);
glCullFace(GL_BACK);
```

Frustum culling is more complex and typically requires checking if an object's bounding box is within the camera's frustum. These techniques ensure that the GPU isn't wasting time rendering unnecessary objects.

3. Efficient Shaders

A well-optimized shader is key to reducing the workload on the GPU. Avoid unnecessary computations and keep shaders simple and efficient. For instance, calculations that can be precomputed on the CPU should not be done in the shader, and any complex math that can be simplified should be optimized.

Optimizing OpenGL applications involves more than just reducing draw calls; it requires carefully managing GPU resources and minimizing computational overhead at every stage of the rendering pipeline. By using techniques like **instancing**, **texture atlases**, and **mesh batching**, as well as applying strategies for reducing GPU workload through **LOD**, **culling**, and **efficient shaders**, you can significantly improve the performance of your OpenGL applications.

A well-optimized application will not only run faster but will also scale better across a variety of hardware, from high-end gaming PCs to mobile devices, ensuring a smooth and responsive user experience.

Efficient Memory Management: Vertex Buffers, Textures, and Framebuffers

Efficient memory management is a critical aspect of optimizing any OpenGL application. Managing how you store and access data—such as vertex data, textures, and framebuffers—can significantly impact performance, especially in complex 3D applications. By carefully handling memory allocation, data transfer, and resource management, you can reduce CPU-GPU communication overhead, minimize memory usage, and improve overall performance.

In this section, we'll explore strategies for efficient memory management in OpenGL, focusing on **vertex buffers**, **textures**, and **framebuffers**. We'll discuss best practices for allocating, using, and cleaning up these resources to ensure your application runs smoothly and efficiently.

1. Vertex Buffers: Efficient Storage and Access

Vertex buffers store the geometry data of 3D models, such as positions, normals, textures, and colors. These buffers are used by the GPU to render objects in the scene. Efficiently managing vertex buffers is essential for minimizing draw calls and ensuring smooth performance.

Vertex Buffer Objects (VBOs)

In OpenGL, **Vertex Buffer Objects (VBOs)** are used to store vertex data on the GPU, rather than on the CPU. This allows the GPU to access the data directly, reducing the need for repeated data transfers from the CPU to the GPU during rendering.

To ensure efficient memory usage with VBOs:

Create and Use Static VBOs: If your geometry doesn't change (static geometry), you can create static VBOs and store them in GPU memory permanently. Use GL_STATIC_DRAW when creating the buffer to hint to OpenGL that the buffer will not change frequently.

cpp

```cpp
GLuint VBO;
glGenBuffers(1, &VBO);
glBindBuffer(GL_ARRAY_BUFFER, VBO);
glBufferData(GL_ARRAY_BUFFER, sizeof(vertices), vertices,
GL_STATIC_DRAW);
```

Use Dynamic VBOs for Changing Data: For dynamic objects that change frequently (e.g., animated characters, particles), you should use GL_DYNAMIC_DRAW. This allows OpenGL to optimize for updates to the buffer.

cpp

```cpp
glBufferData(GL_ARRAY_BUFFER, sizeof(newVertices), newVertices,
GL_DYNAMIC_DRAW);
```

Use Multiple Buffers: For efficient memory management, use multiple buffers when dealing with complex geometry. For instance, use separate buffers for positions, normals, and texture coordinates to reduce redundancy.

Buffer Subdata for Updates: If only a portion of your buffer changes, use glBufferSubData() instead of re-uploading the entire buffer. This minimizes data transfer and speeds up rendering.

cpp

```cpp
glBufferSubData(GL_ARRAY_BUFFER, offset, size, data);
```

Binding and Unbinding Buffers: OpenGL uses **VAOs** (Vertex Array Objects) to manage multiple vertex buffers efficiently. A VAO stores the state of all the vertex attribute bindings for a specific object, so you don't need to re-bind the buffers each time you render.

```cpp
GLuint VAO;
glGenVertexArrays(1, &VAO);
glBindVertexArray(VAO);
glBindBuffer(GL_ARRAY_BUFFER, VBO);
// Enable and configure vertex attributes
glBindVertexArray(0); // Unbind VAO when done
```

By using VAOs and VBOs efficiently, you can ensure that the GPU directly accesses the vertex data without needing to re-upload it every frame.

2. Textures: Optimizing Memory Usage and Access

Textures are used to map image data (like diffuse maps, normal maps, etc.) to 3D objects in the scene. Texture memory management is vital because large textures can quickly consume significant amounts of GPU memory, leading to performance degradation.

Texture Types and Memory Usage

OpenGL supports several types of textures, each optimized for specific purposes:

- **2D Textures**: Standard textures applied to objects, such as diffuse maps.
- **Cubemaps**: Used for environment mapping and skyboxes. A cubemap consists of six 2D textures arranged as a cube.
- **Array Textures**: These are used for storing multiple layers of 2D textures in a single texture object, useful for handling large batches of similar textures (e.g., for sprites or terrain tiles).
- **Mipmap Textures**: Mipmaps are lower-resolution versions of a texture that OpenGL can use based on the distance of the object from the camera, improving performance when objects are far away.

Texture Optimization Tips

Use Mipmaps for Textures: Mipmaps improve performance by providing lower-resolution versions of textures when objects are distant from the camera. This reduces memory bandwidth usage and avoids texture aliasing.

```cpp
glGenerateMipmap(GL_TEXTURE_2D);
```

Texture Compression: Compressing textures helps save memory and reduce GPU load. OpenGL supports compressed texture formats, such as **S3TC** (DXT), **ETC**, and **PVRTC**, which provide high-quality textures with smaller file sizes. You can load compressed textures using libraries like **stb_image** or **Assimp**.

Use Texture Atlases: Instead of using multiple separate textures for different objects or materials, combine several textures into a single large texture (a texture atlas). This reduces texture bindings and minimizes state changes during rendering, leading to fewer draw calls and better performance.

Texture Streaming: For large textures, especially in open-world games, **texture streaming** involves loading textures into memory only when needed. Textures for distant objects can be loaded asynchronously while the user is exploring the environment.

Use the Right Texture Format: Choose the appropriate texture format based on the target platform and performance needs. For instance, using 8-bit textures instead of 32-bit textures can save memory when high color depth is not required.

Reduce the Number of Textures: Use as few textures as necessary. Merging textures into a single atlas or reusing existing textures for multiple objects can help reduce the number of textures loaded into memory.

3. Framebuffers: Optimizing Offscreen Rendering

Framebuffers in OpenGL allow rendering to offscreen targets (such as textures) instead of the default framebuffer (the screen). This is essential for techniques like shadow mapping, post-processing effects, and reflections. Efficient management of framebuffers is crucial for reducing GPU workload and optimizing rendering performance.

Framebuffer Objects (FBOs)

A **Framebuffer Object (FBO)** is a container for multiple rendering attachments, such as color buffers, depth buffers, and stencil buffers. FBOs are used to render to textures or offscreen buffers for post-processing or multi-pass effects.

Here's how to set up a basic FBO with color and depth attachments:

cpp

```
GLuint framebuffer, textureColorbuffer, renderbuffer;
glGenFramebuffers(1, &framebuffer);
glBindFramebuffer(GL_FRAMEBUFFER, framebuffer);

// Create a color texture attachment
glGenTextures(1, &textureColorbuffer);
glBindTexture(GL_TEXTURE_2D, textureColorbuffer);
glTexImage2D(GL_TEXTURE_2D, 0, GL_RGB, width, height, 0, GL_RGB,
GL_UNSIGNED_BYTE, NULL);
glGenerateMipmap(GL_TEXTURE_2D);
glFramebufferTexture2D(GL_FRAMEBUFFER, GL_COLOR_ATTACHMENT0,
GL_TEXTURE_2D, textureColorbuffer, 0);

// Create a renderbuffer for depth attachment
glGenRenderbuffers(1, &renderbuffer);
glBindRenderbuffer(GL_RENDERBUFFER, renderbuffer);
glRenderbufferStorage(GL_RENDERBUFFER, GL_DEPTH24_STENCIL8,
width, height);
glFramebufferRenderbuffer(GL_FRAMEBUFFER,
GL_DEPTH_STENCIL_ATTACHMENT, GL_RENDERBUFFER, renderbuffer);

// Check if framebuffer is complete
if (glCheckFramebufferStatus(GL_FRAMEBUFFER) !=
```

```
GL_FRAMEBUFFER_COMPLETE) {
    std::cout << "ERROR::FRAMEBUFFER:: Framebuffer is not
    complete!" << std::endl;
}
glBindFramebuffer(GL_FRAMEBUFFER, 0);
```

Optimizing FBO Usage

1. **Use Multiple Render Targets (MRT)**: When rendering to multiple textures (e.g., for post-processing effects), you can use MRT to write to several textures in a single pass, reducing the number of draw calls. In OpenGL, MRT is supported by binding multiple textures to different color attachments.

2. **Minimize FBO Switching**: FBO switching introduces overhead because each framebuffer may have different attachments (textures or renderbuffers). Try to minimize the number of times you switch between different framebuffers in a single frame.

3. **Reusing Framebuffers**: If possible, reuse framebuffers for multiple passes or effects. For example, you can render shadows, then use the same FBO for reflections, without needing to allocate separate framebuffers for each effect.

4. **Texture Size Optimization**: Avoid rendering large textures when smaller ones are sufficient. For example, use lower-resolution textures for intermediate effects or shadows to reduce memory and GPU workload.

5. **Clear Buffers Only When Needed**: Clearing buffers (color, depth, or stencil) in every frame is computationally expensive. If possible, avoid unnecessary clears or clear only parts of the buffer that need resetting.

4. Memory Cleanup and Resource Management

Proper memory management is not just about allocation but also about ensuring resources are cleaned up when they are no longer needed. Leaking resources (e.g., textures, buffers, shaders) can quickly degrade performance and cause crashes.

1. Clean Up Resources

Make sure to delete any OpenGL resources when they are no longer in use:

cpp

```cpp
glDeleteBuffers(1, &VBO);
glDeleteVertexArrays(1, &VAO);
glDeleteTextures(1, &texture);
glDeleteFramebuffers(1, &framebuffer);
```

2. Use Efficient Resource Management Systems

For more complex applications, consider using a resource manager that tracks the lifecycle of resources like textures, buffers, and shaders. This way, resources are only loaded once, reused where appropriate, and automatically cleaned up when no longer needed.

Efficient memory management is crucial to optimizing OpenGL applications. By understanding how to manage vertex buffers, textures, and framebuffers effectively, you can reduce GPU workload, minimize memory usage, and significantly improve rendering performance. Implementing techniques such as **vertex buffer optimizations**, **texture atlases**, **framebuffer reuse**, and **efficient resource cleanup** will ensure that your OpenGL application performs optimally, even on resource-constrained devices or complex scenes. Proper memory management, combined with other optimization techniques like minimizing draw calls, is key to achieving smooth and responsive real-time graphics.

Using Framebuffers for Post-Processing Effects

Post-processing effects are an essential part of modern computer graphics, adding visual effects like bloom, motion blur, depth of field, and color correction to enhance the user experience. OpenGL allows you to perform these effects efficiently using **framebuffers** to render to offscreen targets. By rendering the scene to an offscreen framebuffer first and then applying effects in a post-processing pass, you can achieve a wide range of high-quality visual enhancements.

In this section, we will explore how to use **framebuffers** for post-processing effects, including the setup of **offscreen rendering**, and how to apply common post-processing techniques using the **framebuffer** in OpenGL.

1. What is Post-Processing?

Post-processing refers to the application of visual effects after the scene has been rendered. These effects modify the final image in various ways, often to create stylized looks or add realism to the scene. Post-processing effects are usually applied as a second rendering pass, where the result of the initial scene rendering (the "framebuffer") is read and processed by a shader.

Some common post-processing effects include:
- **Bloom**: A glowing effect for bright areas of the scene.
- **Motion Blur**: Simulates the blur caused by fast-moving objects or camera movements.
- **Depth of Field**: Simulates the blur of objects out of the camera's focus range.
- **Color Correction**: Adjusting the colors of the scene, such as brightness, contrast, and saturation.

These effects are typically applied after the main scene is rendered to the screen. To achieve this, the scene is first rendered to an offscreen framebuffer, then the texture from this framebuffer is passed to a post-processing shader where various effects are applied.

2. Setting Up a Framebuffer for Post-Processing

To implement post-processing in OpenGL, you first need to render the scene to a texture rather than directly to the screen. This is done using an **offscreen framebuffer**, where the result of rendering the scene is stored in a texture, and then this texture is used as input for post-processing shaders.

Creating a Framebuffer Object (FBO)

A **Framebuffer Object (FBO)** allows OpenGL to render to offscreen targets such as textures or renderbuffers. The basic steps to create an FBO for post-processing are:

1. **Create a texture** that will store the rendered image.
2. **Create a framebuffer** and attach the texture to it.
3. **Bind the framebuffer** before rendering the scene.
4. **Render to the texture** as if it were the screen.
5. **Use the texture for post-processing** in the next render pass.

Here's how to set up a basic framebuffer for post-processing:

cpp

```
// 1. Create the framebuffer
GLuint framebuffer;
glGenFramebuffers(1, &framebuffer);
glBindFramebuffer(GL_FRAMEBUFFER, framebuffer);

// 2. Create a texture to store the scene
GLuint texture;
glGenTextures(1, &texture);
glBindTexture(GL_TEXTURE_2D, texture);
glTexImage2D(GL_TEXTURE_2D, 0, GL_RGBA, width, height, 0,
GL_RGBA, GL_UNSIGNED_BYTE, nullptr);
glTexParameteri(GL_TEXTURE_2D, GL_TEXTURE_MIN_FILTER, GL_LINEAR);
glTexParameteri(GL_TEXTURE_2D, GL_TEXTURE_MAG_FILTER, GL_LINEAR);

// 3. Attach the texture to the framebuffer
glFramebufferTexture2D(GL_FRAMEBUFFER, GL_COLOR_ATTACHMENT0,
```

```
GL_TEXTURE_2D, texture, 0);

// 4. Create a renderbuffer for depth and stencil buffers
(optional, but improves rendering quality)
GLuint rbo;
glGenRenderbuffers(1, &rbo);
glBindRenderbuffer(GL_RENDERBUFFER, rbo);
glRenderbufferStorage(GL_RENDERBUFFER, GL_DEPTH24_STENCIL8,
width, height);
glFramebufferRenderbuffer(GL_FRAMEBUFFER,
GL_DEPTH_STENCIL_ATTACHMENT, GL_RENDERBUFFER, rbo);

// 5. Check if the framebuffer is complete
if (glCheckFramebufferStatus(GL_FRAMEBUFFER) !=
GL_FRAMEBUFFER_COMPLETE)
    std::cerr << "ERROR: Framebuffer not complete!" << std::endl;

glBindFramebuffer(GL_FRAMEBUFFER, 0);  // Unbind the framebuffer
after setup
```

This framebuffer stores the scene's rendered output in a texture. This texture can later be used in post-processing shaders.

3. Rendering to the Framebuffer

After setting up the framebuffer, you need to render the scene to it. To do so, bind the framebuffer, perform the usual rendering steps (e.g., rendering your scene with your shaders and objects), and then unbind the framebuffer once the scene has been rendered.

```cpp
// Bind the framebuffer for rendering
glBindFramebuffer(GL_FRAMEBUFFER, framebuffer);
glClear(GL_COLOR_BUFFER_BIT | GL_DEPTH_BUFFER_BIT);  // Clear
the framebuffer
```

```cpp
// Render your scene (objects, models, etc.)
renderScene();  // Your rendering logic

// Unbind the framebuffer to return to the default framebuffer
glBindFramebuffer(GL_FRAMEBUFFER, 0);
```

At this point, the scene has been rendered to the texture attached to the framebuffer. You can now use this texture in subsequent post-processing passes.

4. Applying Post-Processing Effects

Once you have rendered the scene to a texture using the framebuffer, you can apply various post-processing effects using fragment shaders. These shaders read the texture from the framebuffer and apply modifications such as bloom, motion blur, or color grading.

The basic idea is to pass the texture you created in the previous step to a post-processing shader and perform operations on it.

Here is an example of how to apply a simple post-processing effect (e.g., converting the scene to grayscale) in OpenGL:

Post-Processing Shader (Grayscale Example)

cpp

```
// Simple fragment shader for grayscale effect
#version 330 core
out vec4 FragColor;

in vec2 TexCoords;

uniform sampler2D screenTexture;  // The texture from the
framebuffer

void main()
{
    // Get the color of the fragment from the texture
```

```
    vec3 color = texture(screenTexture, TexCoords).rgb;

    // Apply grayscale effect
    float gray = dot(color, vec3(0.299, 0.587, 0.114));   //
    Luminosity method
    FragColor = vec4(vec3(gray), 1.0);   // Output the grayscale
    color
}
```

In this shader:

- The screenTexture is the texture from the framebuffer that contains the rendered scene.
- The TexCoords are the texture coordinates passed from the vertex shader.
- The color is converted to grayscale by calculating the weighted average of the RGB channels.

Applying the Post-Processing Shader

Now, to apply this post-processing shader, you can render a full-screen quad (a rectangle that covers the entire screen) with the texture attached to it:

cpp

```
// Set up a full-screen quad (just a simple rectangle)
float vertices[] = {
    // Positions         // Texture coordinates
    -1.0f, -1.0f,  0.0f,  0.0f, 0.0f,
     1.0f, -1.0f,  0.0f,  1.0f, 0.0f,
     1.0f,  1.0f,  0.0f,  1.0f, 1.0f,

    -1.0f, -1.0f,  0.0f,  0.0f, 0.0f,
     1.0f,  1.0f,  0.0f,  1.0f, 1.0f,
    -1.0f,  1.0f,  0.0f,  0.0f, 1.0f
};
```

```
// Set up the VAO and VBO for the full-screen quad
GLuint quadVAO, quadVBO;
glGenVertexArrays(1, &quadVAO);
glGenBuffers(1, &quadVBO);
glBindVertexArray(quadVAO);
glBindBuffer(GL_ARRAY_BUFFER, quadVBO);
glBufferData(GL_ARRAY_BUFFER, sizeof(vertices), vertices,
GL_STATIC_DRAW);
glVertexAttribPointer(0, 3, GL_FLOAT, GL_FALSE, 5 *
sizeof(float), (void*)0);
glEnableVertexAttribArray(0);
glVertexAttribPointer(1, 2, GL_FLOAT, GL_FALSE, 5 *
sizeof(float), (void*)(3 * sizeof(float)));
glEnableVertexAttribArray(1);

// Now render the quad with the post-processing shader
glUseProgram(postProcessingShader);
glBindTexture(GL_TEXTURE_2D, texture);  // Bind the framebuffer
texture
glBindVertexArray(quadVAO);
glDrawArrays(GL_TRIANGLES, 0, 6);  // Render the full-screen quad
```

This renders the texture created by the framebuffer as a full-screen quad, applying the post-processing shader to modify its appearance. In this case, it converts the scene to grayscale.

5. Common Post-Processing Effects

Now that you understand the basic process of applying a post-processing effect, let's explore a few common post-processing effects you can implement:

Bloom

Bloom simulates the glowing of bright parts of a scene, making light sources appear as if they emit a glow. This is typically done by extracting the bright parts of the scene and applying a Gaussian blur.

cpp

```cpp
// Extract bright fragments
vec3 brightColor = (color > vec3(1.0)) ? color : vec3(0.0);

// Apply Gaussian blur to bright fragments in a subsequent pass
```

Motion Blur

Motion blur simulates the blur caused by fast-moving objects. It can be applied by accumulating the previous frames' pixel data and averaging it with the current frame.

cpp

```cpp
// In the shader, blend the current pixel with the previous one
FragColor = mix(texture(screenTexture, TexCoords),
previousFrameTexture, blurAmount);
```

Depth of Field

Depth of field simulates the focus effect seen in real-world cameras, where objects at a certain distance from the camera are blurred. This effect can be achieved by sampling from the depth buffer and applying a blur based on the depth.

cpp

```cpp
// Sample depth buffer and apply blur based on depth
float depth = texture(depthTexture, TexCoords).r;
vec3 blurredColor = applyBlur(color, depth);
```

Using **framebuffers** for post-processing effects is a powerful technique that enables a wide range of visual enhancements in OpenGL applications. By rendering the scene to an offscreen framebuffer and applying shaders to manipulate the texture, you can create realistic effects like bloom, motion blur, depth of field, and color correction. Optimizing post-processing by using techniques like framebuffer reuse, efficient shader operations, and reducing redundant calculations ensures that these effects run smoothly on a wide range of hardware, contributing to a visually stunning and immersive experience.

Profiling and Debugging OpenGL Applications

Profiling and debugging are crucial aspects of optimizing and ensuring the correctness of OpenGL applications. With complex graphics rendering pipelines and potentially large amounts of data being processed, identifying performance bottlenecks or errors can be challenging. However, by utilizing the right tools and techniques, you can improve both the **performance** and **stability** of your OpenGL applications.

In this section, we'll explore various methods for profiling and debugging OpenGL applications, from understanding performance metrics to using debugging tools and techniques to identify errors and inefficiencies.

1. Profiling OpenGL Applications

Profiling is the process of measuring the performance of an application to identify bottlenecks and inefficiencies. In the context of OpenGL, profiling helps you understand how efficiently the GPU is processing the rendered scene and how to optimize the application to make it run smoother, especially in real-time applications like games.

Performance Counters

OpenGL exposes **performance counters** that allow you to track the GPU's behavior and measure various performance metrics, such as the number of vertices processed, the number of fragment shader invocations, and memory usage. These metrics can help identify where the GPU is spending its time, allowing you to optimize specific stages of the rendering pipeline.

You can use **OpenGL queries** to measure the time taken by specific operations. For example, you can measure the time taken by rendering calls or shader executions. Here's how you can use an OpenGL query to measure GPU time:

```cpp
GLuint queryID;
glGenQueries(1, &queryID);

// Begin query to measure GPU time for a specific operation
glBeginQuery(GL_TIME_ELAPSED, queryID);

// Perform OpenGL rendering here
// For example, a draw call
glDrawArrays(GL_TRIANGLES, 0, 3);

// End query
glEndQuery(GL_TIME_ELAPSED);

// Retrieve the results
GLuint64 elapsedTime;
glGetQueryObjectui64v(queryID, GL_QUERY_RESULT, &elapsedTime);
std::cout << "Time elapsed: " << elapsedTime << " nanoseconds"
<< std::endl;
```

In this example:

- The glBeginQuery() function starts tracking the time elapsed during a specific OpenGL call (in this case, a glDrawArrays() call).
- glEndQuery() stops the query, and glGetQueryObjectui64v() retrieves the elapsed time.

By performing such queries at different stages of your rendering pipeline, you can identify where the bottlenecks are occurring.

GPU Profiling Tools

Several third-party tools are available to profile OpenGL applications and give you deep insights into GPU performance. Some popular tools include:

1. **NVIDIA Nsight**: A powerful tool for debugging and profiling applications using NVIDIA GPUs. It provides detailed information on GPU usage, memory utilization, and API calls, helping you optimize performance.
2. **AMD Radeon GPU Profiler**: AMD's tool for GPU profiling offers insights into GPU usage, draw call counts, and more. It helps developers identify performance bottlenecks on AMD hardware.
3. **RenderDoc**: A graphics debugger that captures OpenGL frame data and allows you to inspect and debug the rendering process step by step. It is highly useful for identifying issues with shaders, textures, or geometry.
4. **gDEBugger**: Another OpenGL debugger that provides GPU performance metrics, API call tracking, and the ability to inspect the OpenGL call stack.

Using these tools, you can get real-time insights into performance metrics and visualize your rendering pipeline, making it easier to detect issues.

2. Debugging OpenGL Applications

Debugging OpenGL applications can be a challenging task, especially when working with low-level API calls and complex shaders. Below are some common debugging techniques and tools to help you identify and resolve issues in your OpenGL applications.

OpenGL Debug Output

OpenGL provides a debug output feature that can help you identify issues in your application. The debug output provides detailed error messages, warnings, and performance-related messages directly from the OpenGL implementation. It can be invaluable for detecting problems during development.

To enable debug output in OpenGL, you need to create a context that supports debugging, and then set up a callback to capture OpenGL errors:

```cpp

// Set the OpenGL context to debug mode
glEnable(GL_DEBUG_OUTPUT);
glEnable(GL_DEBUG_OUTPUT_SYNCHRONOUS);

// Define a callback function to handle debug messages
glDebugMessageCallback(MessageCallback, nullptr);

// The callback function that will be called for OpenGL messages
void GLAPIENTRY MessageCallback(GLenum source, GLenum type,
GLuint id, GLenum severity,
                                GLsizei length, const GLchar*
                                message, const void* userParam)
{
    std::cout << "OpenGL Debug Message: " << message <<
    std::endl;
}
```

This callback will receive detailed OpenGL error messages and warnings related to your application. It helps to identify common issues like invalid state, wrong bindings, and shader compilation errors.

Shader Debugging

Shaders are often the source of errors in OpenGL applications, as they can fail to compile or run incorrectly. To debug shaders, OpenGL provides functions for checking the compilation and linking status of shaders.

Here's how to check for shader compilation errors:

```cpp

GLuint shader = glCreateShader(GL_VERTEX_SHADER);
glShaderSource(shader, 1, &shaderSource, nullptr);
glCompileShader(shader);
```

```cpp
// Check for shader compilation errors
GLint success;
glGetShaderiv(shader, GL_COMPILE_STATUS, &success);
if (!success)
{
    GLint logLength;
    glGetShaderiv(shader, GL_INFO_LOG_LENGTH, &logLength);
    char* log = new char[logLength];
    glGetShaderInfoLog(shader, logLength, nullptr, log);
    std::cout << "Shader Compilation Failed: " << log <<
    std::endl;
    delete[] log;
}
```

This will print any compilation errors related to the shader code, making it easier to debug issues like invalid syntax or unsupported features.

Similarly, you should check the program linking status to ensure that shaders are linked correctly:

cpp

```cpp
GLuint shaderProgram = glCreateProgram();
glAttachShader(shaderProgram, vertexShader);
glAttachShader(shaderProgram, fragmentShader);
glLinkProgram(shaderProgram);

// Check for linking errors
glGetProgramiv(shaderProgram, GL_LINK_STATUS, &success);
if (!success)
{
    GLint logLength;
    glGetProgramiv(shaderProgram, GL_INFO_LOG_LENGTH,
    &logLength);
    char* log = new char[logLength];
    glGetProgramInfoLog(shaderProgram, logLength, nullptr, log);
    std::cout << "Shader Program Linking Failed: " << log <<
    std::endl;
    delete[] log;
```

```
}
```

This approach ensures that your shaders are compiled and linked correctly, which is crucial for debugging graphical issues in your scene.

3. Common Debugging Tips and Techniques

Here are some general OpenGL debugging tips to help you resolve common issues:

1. Simplify the Scene

If you encounter graphical errors, try simplifying the scene to isolate the issue. For example, render just one object (e.g., a cube or a simple triangle) to see if the problem persists. This will help narrow down the potential causes, whether it's geometry, textures, shaders, or transformations.

2. Enable Wireframe Mode

In some cases, visualizing the geometry in **wireframe mode** can help identify issues with the mesh, such as inverted normals, missing faces, or incorrect transformations. You can enable wireframe mode in OpenGL like this:

cpp

```cpp
glPolygonMode(GL_FRONT_AND_BACK, GL_LINE);  // Switch to
wireframe mode
```

3. Check for State Issues

OpenGL is a **state machine**, and small state changes can have large effects on rendering. Ensure that the correct **state** is set for each rendering pass (e.g., correct blending mode, depth test, or culling mode). Use OpenGL debug output or tools like **gDEBugger** to track state changes and identify where issues arise.

4. Use OpenGL Debugging Tools

As mentioned earlier, tools like **RenderDoc, gDEBugger**, and **Nsight** can capture frame data and allow you to step through the rendering process.

These tools help inspect buffer contents, shader variables, and rendering calls at each stage of the pipeline.

Profiling and debugging are essential steps in ensuring that your OpenGL application runs efficiently and correctly. By using performance counters, GPU profiling tools, OpenGL debug output, and shader debugging techniques, you can identify and resolve performance bottlenecks and rendering issues. Proper memory management, minimizing draw calls, and optimizing the use of framebuffers will also improve overall performance, making your OpenGL applications smoother and more responsive.

Advanced Rendering Techniques for Performance

Instancing and Dynamic Meshes

When developing graphics applications with OpenGL, ensuring that your rendering pipeline is both efficient and scalable is crucial. As the complexity of the scene increases — whether through additional objects, more intricate animations, or dynamic environments — performance can quickly degrade. Two key techniques that can drastically improve the efficiency of your rendering pipeline are **instancing** and **dynamic meshes**. These methods allow you to render large numbers of objects or complex scenes while keeping GPU workloads manageable and reducing CPU-GPU communication overhead.

In this section, we'll explore **instancing** and **dynamic meshes** in detail, discussing their advantages, implementation, and how to use them effectively to enhance rendering performance in OpenGL applications.

1. Instancing: Efficiently Rendering Multiple Identical Objects

Instancing is a technique used to render multiple copies of the same object or mesh in a scene with minimal overhead. Instead of sending the vertex data for each object individually, instancing allows you to send the vertex data once and use it to render many instances of the object at different locations, scales, or orientations within the scene. This technique is highly beneficial when you need to render a large number of identical objects, such as trees, rocks, or characters.

Instancing works by sending a **single draw call** to the GPU, where the only variation between instances is typically data like position, scale, rotation, and sometimes color or other attributes. The GPU can handle these instances in parallel, which can significantly reduce the cost of multiple draw calls.

How Instancing Works in OpenGL

In OpenGL, instancing is achieved using the glDrawArraysInstanced() or glDrawElementsInstanced() functions. These functions allow you to render multiple instances of an object with a single call to the GPU. The key advantage is that the geometry of the object is uploaded only once, and OpenGL takes care of rendering multiple copies of that object.

Here's a basic implementation of instancing in OpenGL:

Define Vertex Data for the Object

First, you create the vertex data for the object that you want to instance. This is typically done with a Vertex Buffer Object (VBO) and Vertex Array Object (VAO), just like in regular rendering.

cpp

```
GLuint VAO, VBO;
glGenVertexArrays(1, &VAO);
glBindVertexArray(VAO);
glGenBuffers(1, &VBO);
glBindBuffer(GL_ARRAY_BUFFER, VBO);
glBufferData(GL_ARRAY_BUFFER, sizeof(vertices), vertices,
GL_STATIC_DRAW);
```

Create a Buffer for Instance Data

Next, you create a separate VBO to store the instance-specific data, such as positions, rotations, and scales. This buffer will contain an array of data for each instance.

cpp

```cpp
GLuint instanceVBO;
glGenBuffers(1, &instanceVBO);
glBindBuffer(GL_ARRAY_BUFFER, instanceVBO);
glBufferData(GL_ARRAY_BUFFER, sizeof(glm::mat4) * instanceCount,
nullptr, GL_DYNAMIC_DRAW);
```

Configure Instance Attribute Pointers

After creating the instance buffer, you must tell OpenGL how to access the data for each instance. In this case, you will access a glm::mat4 (4x4 matrix) for each instance, which stores the position, rotation, and scale of each object. These matrices are passed as attributes to the vertex shader.

cpp

```cpp
glEnableVertexAttribArray(3);  // Enable the instance position
attribute
glVertexAttribPointer(3, 4, GL_FLOAT, GL_FALSE,
sizeof(glm::mat4), (void*)0);
glEnableVertexAttribArray(4);  // Enable the instance rotation
attribute
glVertexAttribPointer(4, 4, GL_FLOAT, GL_FALSE,
sizeof(glm::mat4), (void*)(sizeof(GLfloat) * 4));
glEnableVertexAttribArray(5);  // Enable the instance scale
attribute
glVertexAttribPointer(5, 4, GL_FLOAT, GL_FALSE,
sizeof(glm::mat4), (void*)(sizeof(GLfloat) * 8));
```

Render Instances with a Single Draw Call

Once the buffers are set up, you can render all instances using glDrawArr aysInstanced() or glDrawElementsInstanced() with a single call to the GPU. OpenGL will handle drawing each instance in parallel, using the transformation data (position, rotation, scale) from the instance buffer.

```cpp
glBindVertexArray(VAO);
glBindBuffer(GL_ARRAY_BUFFER, instanceVBO);
glDrawArraysInstanced(GL_TRIANGLES, 0, vertexCount,
instanceCount);
```

This approach allows you to render thousands of identical objects with a single GPU call, vastly improving performance compared to making individual draw calls for each object.

2. Dynamic Meshes: Optimizing Mesh Updates and Animation

While instancing is great for rendering large numbers of identical objects, **dynamic meshes** are used when objects in the scene are frequently updated, such as animated meshes or objects with changing vertices (e.g., deforming characters, particle systems, destructible objects, or terrain deformation).

A **dynamic mesh** refers to a mesh that is modified during runtime, often in real-time. Instead of keeping static data in memory, dynamic meshes allow for efficient updating and rendering of changing geometry. This is particularly useful in cases where objects are animated or constantly changing shape.

Dynamic Vertex Buffers for Mesh Updates

To render dynamic meshes efficiently, you need to manage vertex buffers that can be updated frequently. OpenGL provides two primary ways to handle dynamic meshes:

Buffer Subdata

The glBufferSubData() function allows you to update only a portion of an existing buffer without reallocating memory. If only a small portion of a mesh changes (e.g., a small section of a character's animation), you can use this function to efficiently modify the data on the GPU.

295

cpp

```
glBindBuffer(GL_ARRAY_BUFFER, dynamicVBO);
glBufferSubData(GL_ARRAY_BUFFER, offset, size, newData);
```

By updating only the modified portion of the buffer, you reduce the overhead of re-uploading the entire mesh and ensure that the system remains efficient.

Persistent Mapping

Another method for managing dynamic meshes is **persistent mapping**, which allows you to directly map the GPU buffer to the CPU's memory space. This method reduces the need to copy data back and forth, enabling faster mesh updates.

cpp

```
glBindBuffer(GL_ARRAY_BUFFER, dynamicVBO);
void* ptr = glMapBufferRange(GL_ARRAY_BUFFER, 0, size,
GL_MAP_WRITE_BIT | GL_MAP_INVALIDATE_BUFFER_BIT);
// Update the mesh data in-place
memcpy(ptr, newData, size);
glUnmapBuffer(GL_ARRAY_BUFFER);
```

Persistent mapping is particularly useful for frequently updated data, such as dynamic animations or simulations.

3. Combining Instancing and Dynamic Meshes

In some advanced rendering scenarios, you may need to combine **instancing** and **dynamic meshes** to achieve optimal performance. For example, you may want to render multiple copies of a dynamic object (such as a character that's animating) in different locations within the scene.

In this case, you would:

1. Use **instancing** to handle rendering multiple identical objects with minimal overhead.
2. Use **dynamic meshes** to update the geometry of each instance, such as modifying the vertex data for animated characters.

This combination allows for efficient rendering of multiple animated objects with minimal CPU-GPU communication, while still enabling complex dynamic content like character animation or terrain deformation.

4. Benefits of Instancing and Dynamic Meshes

Both instancing and dynamic meshes offer several performance benefits:

- **Reduced Draw Calls**: Instancing significantly reduces the number of draw calls, which is one of the biggest performance bottlenecks in real-time graphics.
- **Efficient Memory Usage**: Instancing allows for memory-efficient rendering of large numbers of objects, as only one copy of the geometry is stored on the GPU.
- **Optimized Updates**: Dynamic meshes allow for efficient updates of frequently changing data, reducing the need for re-uploading the entire mesh.
- **Parallelism**: Instancing allows the GPU to process instances in parallel, which increases throughput and reduces latency.

By combining these two techniques, you can achieve high-performance rendering even in large, dynamic scenes.

Instancing and **dynamic meshes** are powerful techniques for optimizing rendering performance in OpenGL. Instancing is particularly effective for rendering large numbers of identical objects, while dynamic meshes enable efficient updates to frequently changing geometry. By implementing these techniques thoughtfully and understanding how to manage GPU memory and data transfers, you can create highly performant and scalable graphics applications capable of rendering complex 3D scenes in real time.

Level of Detail (LOD) for Distant Objects

Level of Detail (LOD) is a technique used to optimize the rendering performance of objects that are distant from the camera. As objects move further away from the camera in a 3D scene, the level of detail required to render them diminishes. By reducing the complexity of distant objects, LOD helps reduce the computational load, improve rendering performance, and maintain a smooth frame rate, especially in large-scale scenes such as open-world games or simulations.

What is LOD?

The concept behind LOD is simple: as an object moves farther from the camera, it appears smaller on screen, and therefore, the level of detail required to represent it can be decreased without sacrificing visual quality. LOD techniques vary in how the level of detail is reduced, but the general idea is to use **simpler** models for objects that are farther away and **more detailed** models for objects closer to the camera.

In OpenGL, LOD can be implemented using different methods such as **mesh simplification** (reduced polygon count), **texture resolution reduction**, or even **different geometric representations** for distant objects.

How LOD Works in OpenGL

In a typical LOD implementation, multiple versions of the same object are created with varying levels of detail. These versions of the object, known as **LOD models**, are pre-generated or dynamically simplified during runtime. When rendering a scene, the appropriate LOD version is selected based on the **distance to the camera**.

Here's a step-by-step breakdown of how to implement LOD:

Create Multiple LOD Models

For each object in your scene, create multiple versions with varying levels of detail. This could range from a high-poly model (for close distances) to a low-poly model (for distant objects). The simplest version could be a basic shape (e.g., a cube or sphere) to represent the object when it's far away.

Example of three LOD models for a tree:

- **LOD 0**: High-detail model with many branches and leaves (used when the tree is close).
- **LOD 1**: Medium-detail model with fewer branches (used when the tree is at an intermediate distance).
- **LOD 2**: Low-detail model with a simple trunk and few branches (used when the tree is very far).

Calculate the Distance to the Camera

In your rendering loop, you calculate the distance from the camera to each object. This distance is used to determine which LOD model to render. The farther the object, the lower the LOD.

Here's how you can compute the distance between an object and the camera:

cpp

```
glm::vec3 cameraPosition = camera.GetPosition();
glm::vec3 objectPosition = glm::vec3(objectModelMatrix[3]); //
Assuming position is stored in the model matrix

float distance = glm::length(cameraPosition - objectPosition);
```

Determine Which LOD to Use

Based on the calculated distance, select the appropriate LOD model for each object. This selection can be done using simple conditional checks or more advanced algorithms that consider screen space size, object importance, or other factors.

299

cpp

```cpp
if (distance < 50.0f) {
    // Use high-detail LOD model
    glBindVertexArray(LOD0_VAO);
} else if (distance < 200.0f) {
    // Use medium-detail LOD model
    glBindVertexArray(LOD1_VAO);
} else {
    // Use low-detail LOD model
    glBindVertexArray(LOD2_VAO);
}
```

Render the Object with the Selected LOD

Once the appropriate LOD model is selected, you can render it just like any other object. The performance benefits arise from the fact that the GPU processes a simpler model for distant objects, reducing the number of vertices and fragments that need to be processed.

cpp

```cpp
glDrawElements(GL_TRIANGLES, LOD_Vertices_Count,
GL_UNSIGNED_INT, 0);
```

Dynamic LOD Adjustment

In many cases, you don't want to manually create all the different LOD models. You can implement **dynamic LOD generation** algorithms, where the level of detail is adjusted in real-time based on distance. For example, this might involve dynamically simplifying geometry (reducing polygon count) or even reducing the resolution of textures as objects move farther from the camera.

Dynamic LOD can be achieved through algorithms like:

- **Mesh Decimation**: Reducing the number of vertices and polygons in an object based on distance.

- **Texture Mipmapping**: Using lower-resolution textures for objects at greater distances. OpenGL's **mipmapping** automatically generates lower-resolution versions of a texture, and the appropriate level is selected based on the distance to the camera.

Example of Using Mipmaps for Texture LOD

Mipmaps are a series of precomputed texture levels at different resolutions, which OpenGL can use for efficient rendering. When an object is far from the camera, OpenGL can select a lower-resolution texture to avoid wasting GPU resources on high-resolution textures that won't be noticeable at that distance.

Here's how you can generate mipmaps for a texture in OpenGL:

```cpp
GLuint texture;
glGenTextures(1, &texture);
glBindTexture(GL_TEXTURE_2D, texture);
glTexImage2D(GL_TEXTURE_2D, 0, GL_RGB, width, height, 0, GL_RGB,
GL_UNSIGNED_BYTE, data);

// Generate mipmaps
glGenerateMipmap(GL_TEXTURE_2D);
```

This automatically generates multiple levels of detail for the texture and ensures that the appropriate level is used during rendering, depending on the distance to the camera.

3. Benefits of LOD

1. **Improved Performance**: By rendering fewer polygons and textures for distant objects, LOD reduces the GPU workload, improving frame rates.
2. **Memory Efficiency**: LOD helps reduce memory usage by storing only the necessary level of detail for each object. You can store

multiple versions of an object (or texture) at different resolutions and select them based on the camera's distance.

3. **Visual Consistency**: LOD helps maintain a visually consistent performance even in large scenes, ensuring that distant objects don't unnecessarily consume GPU resources, but still appear as detailed as needed when close to the camera.

4. **Scalability**: LOD can be particularly beneficial for large-scale applications, such as open-world games or simulations, where the number of objects in the scene can vary greatly.

4. LOD Challenges

While LOD is a powerful optimization technique, there are a few challenges you need to keep in mind:

1. **Pop-in Artifacts**: As objects transition between different LOD levels, you may notice a "pop-in" effect, where an object suddenly becomes more or less detailed. This can be minimized by using **cross-fading** techniques or **continuous LOD transitions**, where objects gradually shift to a different LOD level instead of switching abruptly.

2. **Memory Management**: Storing multiple LOD models can increase memory usage, especially if you have a large number of objects in the scene. Efficient memory management and streaming techniques are essential to ensure that the memory footprint stays manageable.

3. **Complexity in Handling Animations**: If an object is animated, it may be difficult to maintain smooth transitions between LOD models, especially if animations are tied to the mesh topology. In these cases, **skeletal animation** combined with LOD can provide a more consistent result, though it requires careful management.

Level of Detail (LOD) is a critical technique for rendering efficiency, especially in large, complex scenes. By dynamically adjusting the level of detail based on the camera's distance, you can significantly reduce rendering time, improving overall performance. Whether you use simple geometric simplification or more complex techniques like dynamic mesh decimation and mipmapping, LOD ensures that your OpenGL applications can scale well while maintaining visual fidelity.

By combining LOD with other performance-enhancing techniques, such as **instancing** and **dynamic meshes,** you can create optimized, visually stunning applications that run smoothly even in resource-intensive 3D environments.

Efficient Texture Mapping: Mipmap Generation and Texture Compression

Efficient **texture mapping** is a key component in optimizing the rendering performance of 3D scenes, especially in real-time applications like games or simulations. As textures are applied to 3D objects, the process of fetching and applying these textures can be a performance bottleneck, particularly when dealing with high-resolution textures. To address this, techniques like **mipmap generation** and **texture compression** are essential to improving both visual quality and rendering performance.

In this section, we will explore **mipmaps** and **texture compression,** two powerful techniques that help optimize texture mapping in OpenGL.

1. Mipmap Generation: Optimizing Texture Fetching

Mipmaps are precomputed sets of textures at multiple levels of detail (LOD), which are designed to improve performance and reduce visual artifacts when textures are mapped onto objects. The key benefit of mipmaps is that they allow the GPU to select the most appropriate texture size based on the distance of the object from the camera. This process reduces the number of texture fetches and allows for more efficient

303

memory usage.

What is Mipmap?

A **mipmap** is a collection of textures in various sizes, typically starting from the original texture and progressively halving the resolution with each level. For example, if the original texture is 1024x1024 pixels, the mipmap levels would include textures of sizes like 512x512, 256x256, 128x128, and so on.

When rendering a scene, the GPU selects the appropriate mipmap level based on the screen-space size of the textured object. Objects that are farther away from the camera use smaller mipmaps, while closer objects use higher-resolution textures. This results in faster rendering and better visual quality, as it prevents the aliasing effects that can occur when a high-resolution texture is applied to a small object.

How Mipmaps Work in OpenGL

OpenGL provides an easy way to generate and manage mipmaps. When you load a texture into OpenGL, you can automatically generate mipmaps using the glGenerateMipmap() function. Here's how to generate mipmaps for a texture:

Load the Texture

Load the texture data (e.g., from an image file) into a texture object using glTexImage2D().

```cpp
GLuint texture;
glGenTextures(1, &texture);
glBindTexture(GL_TEXTURE_2D, texture);
glTexImage2D(GL_TEXTURE_2D, 0, GL_RGBA, width, height, 0,
GL_RGBA, GL_UNSIGNED_BYTE, data);
```

Generate Mipmaps

After loading the texture, you can generate mipmaps using glGener-

304

ateMipmap(). OpenGL automatically computes the mipmap levels and stores them in GPU memory.

```cpp
glGenerateMipmap(GL_TEXTURE_2D);
```

Set Texture Filtering

When using mipmaps, it's important to specify the appropriate texture filtering methods. For most situations, **mipmap filtering** is used, which combines **minification** and **magnification** filters for different levels of detail.

```cpp
glTexParameteri(GL_TEXTURE_2D, GL_TEXTURE_MIN_FILTER,
GL_LINEAR_MIPMAP_LINEAR); // For minification
glTexParameteri(GL_TEXTURE_2D, GL_TEXTURE_MAG_FILTER,
GL_LINEAR); // For magnification
```

- GL_LINEAR_MIPMAP_LINEAR is the most common filter for smooth transitions between mipmap levels.
- GL_LINEAR is used for magnification, and it ensures that the texture is filtered for pixels that need to be enlarged.

Benefits of Mipmaps

- **Improved performance**: By reducing the size of textures when objects are far away from the camera, mipmaps reduce the amount of texture data that needs to be processed, improving rendering performance.
- **Reduced aliasing**: Mipmaps help to minimize aliasing artifacts (such as shimmering) when objects are viewed from a distance.

305

• **Efficient memory usage**: By storing multiple levels of texture detail, mipmaps make better use of the available GPU memory.

Choosing the Right Mipmap Level

OpenGL automatically selects the appropriate mipmap level based on the size of the object on screen. However, you can also implement your own logic for selecting mipmap levels manually if needed. For example, you can adjust the mipmap level based on factors like object importance, camera distance, or frame rate.

```cpp
// Calculate the level of detail (LOD)
float lod = log2f(distance / objectSize);

// Use the calculated LOD for mipmap selection
glTexParameteri(GL_TEXTURE_2D, GL_TEXTURE_LOD_BIAS, lod);
```

2. Texture Compression: Reducing Texture Memory Usage

Texture compression is another critical technique for optimizing the use of textures in OpenGL applications. High-resolution textures can consume a significant amount of memory, which can slow down rendering performance, especially on lower-end devices or GPUs with limited memory. **Texture compression** reduces the memory footprint of textures without sacrificing too much visual quality.

There are several texture compression formats available in OpenGL, each suited for different use cases. The most commonly used formats include **S3TC (DXT)**, **ETC**, and **ASTC**.

What is Texture Compression?

Texture compression algorithms reduce the size of texture data by encoding it in a way that uses fewer bits per texel (texture element). These algorithms compress the data so that less memory is required to store the texture, reducing both GPU memory usage and bandwidth.

Some common texture compression formats include:

- **S3TC (DXT1/DXT5)**: Widely used in older graphics hardware (DirectX 9 and OpenGL 4.x). It offers a good balance between compression and quality but is somewhat outdated.
- **ETC (ETC1/ETC2)**: A format supported by most mobile devices (Android). ETC2, the newer version, supports alpha transparency.
- **ASTC (Adaptive Scalable Texture Compression)**: A newer compression format that provides better quality and flexibility, supporting a range of bit rates and is supported on modern hardware (including consoles and mobile).

How Texture Compression Works in OpenGL

In OpenGL, you can compress textures either when loading them or during the creation of the texture object. The process typically involves using compressed texture formats when loading the texture into OpenGL. Here's an example of how to load a compressed texture:

Load the Compressed Texture

When you load a compressed texture, OpenGL expects the texture data to be in a compressed format. If you have a texture file in a compressed format (e.g., .dds with DXT compression), you can load it as follows:

```cpp
GLuint texture;
glGenTextures(1, &texture);
glBindTexture(GL_TEXTURE_2D, texture);

// Assuming 'data' is a pointer to the compressed texture data
glCompressedTexImage2D(GL_TEXTURE_2D, 0,
GL_COMPRESSED_RGBA_S3TC_DXT1_EXT, width, height, 0, dataSize,
data);
```

Set Texture Parameters

You can still set the usual texture parameters like filtering and wrapping.

However, with compressed textures, you may need to adjust filtering methods based on the compression format.

cpp

```
glTexParameteri(GL_TEXTURE_2D, GL_TEXTURE_MIN_FILTER, GL_LINEAR);
glTexParameteri(GL_TEXTURE_2D, GL_TEXTURE_MAG_FILTER, GL_LINEAR);
```

Benefits of Texture Compression

- **Reduced memory usage**: Compressed textures use less memory, which is particularly important for devices with limited GPU memory.
- **Faster texture loading**: Compressed textures are smaller in size, which can speed up the process of loading textures into GPU memory.
- **Reduced bandwidth**: Compressed textures require less bandwidth when being transferred between CPU and GPU, improving overall rendering performance.

Texture Compression Considerations

While texture compression reduces memory usage and increases performance, there is a trade-off in terms of quality. The amount of detail preserved depends on the compression algorithm and the quality settings you choose. **Higher compression** typically results in lower quality, so it's important to find a balance that suits your application's needs.

In general, it's a good practice to use **higher-quality compression formats** (like ASTC) for close-up objects and **lower-quality formats** (like DXT1) for distant objects, where the loss in quality is less noticeable.

Both **mipmap generation** and **texture compression** are powerful techniques that help optimize the rendering performance and memory usage in OpenGL applications. Mipmaps improve performance by reducing texture fetches for distant objects, while texture compression reduces the memory footprint of textures without sacrificing too much visual quality. By leveraging these techniques effectively, you can ensure that your 3D scenes are rendered efficiently, even with a large number of textures and complex scenes.

Multi-threading and Asynchronous Rendering

In modern graphics applications, performance is a critical concern, particularly as the complexity of 3D scenes and rendering pipelines increases. One of the most effective strategies for improving performance, especially for CPU-bound tasks, is **multi-threading**. By utilizing multiple CPU cores for tasks such as scene processing, physics simulation, or even managing OpenGL rendering commands, you can achieve a significant boost in efficiency and responsiveness. When combined with **asynchronous rendering** techniques, multi-threading allows for more efficient use of the GPU and a smoother overall experience for users.

In this section, we'll dive into **multi-threading** and **asynchronous rendering** in OpenGL, and explain how these techniques can be leveraged to significantly improve the performance of your applications.

1. Multi-threading in Graphics Applications

Multi-threading refers to the ability to execute multiple parts of a program simultaneously across multiple CPU cores. This is particularly important in modern applications, as many CPUs have multiple cores, and multi-threading allows you to take full advantage of these resources. For graphics applications, multi-threading can be used to parallelize tasks like loading assets, processing data, managing resources, and even preparing OpenGL commands.

Multi-threading Benefits in OpenGL

1. **Parallel Data Processing:** Multi-threading allows you to prepare assets, load textures, process meshes, and handle physics simulations in parallel with the rendering process. This reduces the overall time spent waiting for these tasks to complete, especially when large datasets or complex computations are involved.

2. **Improved Frame Rate:** By distributing the load across multiple threads, the main rendering thread remains free to issue drawing commands to the GPU, which can help maintain a smooth frame rate. For example, loading textures or calculating physics in parallel can prevent bottlenecks that would otherwise cause frame drops.

3. **Better CPU Utilization:** By making use of multiple CPU cores, multi-threading ensures that the system's resources are fully utilized. In OpenGL, this can help reduce the time spent preparing rendering commands and make the graphics pipeline more efficient.

How to Implement Multi-threading in OpenGL

While OpenGL itself is not inherently multi-threaded, it does allow for multi-threaded resource management and command preparation. This can be achieved by using a **multi-threaded context**, where different threads handle separate tasks but still communicate with the OpenGL context as needed.

Creating and Managing OpenGL Contexts: OpenGL contexts are the primary mechanism for interacting with the GPU. In a multi-threaded application, each thread that needs to interact with OpenGL will have its own context. One thread is responsible for issuing OpenGL commands, while other threads handle tasks like loading resources or preparing data.

OpenGL allows **shared contexts**, where resources like textures and buffers are shared between multiple contexts. This can be useful for tasks like asynchronously loading textures while the main thread handles rendering.

Example:

cpp

```
// Create a new OpenGL context in a new thread
GLFWwindow* window = glfwCreateWindow(800, 600, "OpenGL
Multi-threading", nullptr, nullptr);
glfwMakeContextCurrent(window);  // Make the new context current
```

Loading Assets in Parallel: A common use case for multi-threading in OpenGL is loading assets (like textures or meshes) in parallel with rendering. For example, while the main thread renders the scene, another thread can load new textures or prepare mesh data. Once the assets are loaded, they can be transferred to the GPU for rendering.

Example of parallel texture loading:

cpp

```
std::thread textureThread([&]() {
    // Load textures in parallel
    loadTexture("texture.png");
});

textureThread.detach(); // Detach the thread so it runs
independently
```

Synchronizing Threads: When using multiple threads, it's important to manage synchronization to avoid race conditions or inconsistencies in rendering. OpenGL provides synchronization mechanisms like **fences** or **semaphores**, which can be used to ensure that commands are executed in the correct order.

Example of synchronization using OpenGL:

cpp

```
GLuint fence = glFenceSync(GL_SYNC_GPU_COMMANDS_COMPLETE, 0);
glWaitSync(fence, 0, GL_TIMEOUT_IGNORED);  // Wait until GPU
commands are completed
glDeleteSync(fence);
```

2. Asynchronous Rendering

Asynchronous rendering is the practice of performing rendering tasks in the background, independent of the main thread. This allows you to prepare and submit rendering commands to the GPU while the CPU continues executing other tasks. Asynchronous rendering significantly

311

improves the overall frame rate and responsiveness of the application, especially when rendering large scenes with complex assets.

In OpenGL, several techniques can be used to implement asynchronous rendering, including **double buffering**, **triple buffering**, and **GPU-based compute shaders**.

Benefits of Asynchronous Rendering

Reduced CPU-GPU Wait Time: Asynchronous rendering can reduce the idle time between CPU and GPU. By preparing rendering commands in parallel with rendering the previous frame, the CPU does not have to wait for the GPU to finish before starting the next frame.

Improved Frame Rate: By decoupling the CPU and GPU tasks, asynchronous rendering allows both to work concurrently, leading to higher frame rates and a smoother experience. This is particularly useful when dealing with heavy scenes or objects that require significant computational resources.

Efficient Use of GPU Resources: Asynchronous rendering helps maximize the GPU's potential by ensuring that it is always working on a task. Instead of waiting for the CPU to finish preparing the next batch of commands, the GPU can begin processing commands that were prepared earlier.

How to Implement Asynchronous Rendering in OpenGL

Double and Triple Buffering: Double and triple buffering are common techniques for improving the efficiency of rendering pipelines by reducing **screen tearing** and optimizing GPU utilization. In double buffering, one frame is being drawn to the back buffer while the previous frame is being displayed on the screen. Triple buffering adds an additional buffer, allowing for even smoother transitions between frames.

Example of setting up double buffering in OpenGL:

cpp

```cpp
glfwWindowHint(GLFW_DOUBLEBUFFER, GL_TRUE);
```

Using OpenGL Framebuffer Objects (FBOs): Framebuffers in OpenGL allow you to render to off-screen targets, such as textures or other framebuffers. You can render scenes asynchronously by offloading the rendering to an FBO, which can then be displayed or further processed in subsequent frames.

Example of using a framebuffer for off-screen rendering:

cpp

```cpp
GLuint framebuffer;
glGenFramebuffers(1, &framebuffer);
glBindFramebuffer(GL_FRAMEBUFFER, framebuffer);

GLuint texture;
glGenTextures(1, &texture);
glBindTexture(GL_TEXTURE_2D, texture);
glTexImage2D(GL_TEXTURE_2D, 0, GL_RGBA, width, height, 0,
GL_RGBA, GL_UNSIGNED_BYTE, nullptr);
glFramebufferTexture2D(GL_FRAMEBUFFER, GL_COLOR_ATTACHMENT0,
GL_TEXTURE_2D, texture, 0);

// Perform rendering to the framebuffer asynchronously
```

GPU Compute Shaders: GPU-based compute shaders allow you to perform general-purpose computations on the GPU, freeing up the CPU for other tasks. Compute shaders can be used to handle tasks like physics simulations, particle systems, or any computation that can benefit from parallel processing.

Example of using a compute shader for asynchronous computations:

cpp

```
GLuint computeShader = glCreateShader(GL_COMPUTE_SHADER);
glShaderSource(computeShader, 1, &computeShaderSource, nullptr);
glCompileShader(computeShader);

GLuint program = glCreateProgram();
glAttachShader(program, computeShader);
glLinkProgram(program);
glUseProgram(program);

// Dispatch compute shader work in parallel
glDispatchCompute(1024, 1, 1); // Execute 1024 parallel threads
```

3. Combining Multi-threading and Asynchronous Rendering

To achieve optimal performance, many modern applications combine **multi-threading** and **asynchronous rendering**. For instance, you can use multiple threads to load resources in the background while simultaneously rendering the scene using techniques like double or triple buffering. Additionally, asynchronous rendering can be used to prepare and submit rendering commands while the CPU is free to perform other tasks, such as updating object positions, physics calculations, or handling user input.

By combining both techniques, you can maximize the use of both your CPU and GPU, resulting in a smoother, more responsive rendering experience.

In summary, **multi-threading** and **asynchronous rendering** are critical techniques for optimizing OpenGL applications. By leveraging multi-threading, you can offload computational tasks to other CPU cores, while asynchronous rendering ensures that the GPU is always active and ready to process the next frame. Together, these techniques allow you to create more efficient, performant applications that can handle complex scenes and real-time rendering tasks with minimal latency and improved frame rates.

Building a 3D Game Engine with OpenGL

The Architecture of a Basic 3D Game Engine

Building a **3D game engine** from scratch can seem like a daunting task, but with OpenGL as your rendering backend, it becomes a highly rewarding project that can provide a deep understanding of how modern 3D graphics systems operate. A game engine serves as the backbone of most 3D games, providing essential features like rendering, physics, user input, scene management, and more. The goal of a basic 3D game engine is to provide a platform that allows game developers to efficiently create, modify, and render complex 3D environments in real-time.

In this chapter, we'll explore the key components and architectural structure of a basic 3D game engine. We'll discuss the foundational layers of the engine, focusing on core concepts such as rendering, physics, scene management, and asset loading. Along the way, we'll outline how to integrate these components into a cohesive system that can render 3D objects, handle user input, and perform fundamental game logic.

1. Core Components of a 3D Game Engine

A typical 3D game engine comprises several interconnected components that together handle the complexity of creating a 3D experience. At a high level, the core components of a game engine can be broken down into the following modules:

- **Rendering Engine (Graphics Pipeline)**: Responsible for drawing 3D objects, handling shaders, textures, lighting, and more.
- **Physics Engine**: Manages interactions between objects, including collision detection, rigid body dynamics, and other physical simulations.
- **Input Management**: Captures user input from devices like the keyboard, mouse, or gamepad.
- **Scene Management**: Handles the creation and management of objects, cameras, lights, and other elements in a 3D world.
- **Audio System**: Responsible for handling sound effects, music, and other audio elements.
- **Asset Management**: Loads and manages game assets like textures, models, and sounds.
- **Game Logic/Controller**: Manages the flow of the game, including the logic that governs the progression and behavior of the game world.

Together, these components form the architecture of a game engine, with each module focusing on a specific aspect of the game's functionality.

2. Rendering Engine (Graphics Pipeline)

At the heart of every game engine is the **rendering engine**, which uses OpenGL to render the 3D world. The rendering engine is responsible for translating the game world's data (such as models, textures, lighting, and shaders) into images that are displayed on the screen.

In a 3D game engine, the rendering system can be divided into multiple stages, including:

- **Scene Graph**: A hierarchical structure that organizes the 3D objects in the game world. It helps in efficiently managing and rendering objects based on their spatial relationships (i.e., parent-child relationships in the scene).
- **Camera and Projection**: The camera is responsible for viewing the scene from a particular perspective. The game engine must handle camera transformations, projection matrices, and viewport settings.

OpenGL uses the **model-view** and **projection** matrices to transform 3D coordinates into 2D screen coordinates.

- **Shaders and Materials**: The rendering engine uses vertex and fragment shaders to manipulate vertex data and calculate the final pixel color. Materials, which consist of properties like diffuse color, specularity, and texture maps, are applied to objects during the rendering process.

- **Lighting**: The lighting module simulates different light sources (point lights, directional lights, and spotlights) and how they interact with surfaces in the scene. Lighting calculations are often done in shaders to achieve realistic results, including normal mapping, shadow mapping, and advanced lighting effects.

Example Code for Basic Rendering Engine Structure

cpp

```cpp
// Initializing OpenGL and creating shaders
GLuint shaderProgram = createShaderProgram("vertex_shader.glsl",
"fragment_shader.glsl");

// Set up camera, lighting, and scene data
Camera camera;
Lighting lighting;

// Set up the scene graph to manage 3D objects
SceneGraph sceneGraph;

// Game loop
while (!glfwWindowShouldClose(window)) {
    // Process input
    handleInput();

    // Update scene (transformations, physics)
    sceneGraph.update(deltaTime);
```

```
// Render the scene
glClear(GL_COLOR_BUFFER_BIT | GL_DEPTH_BUFFER_BIT);

// Set up camera and view matrix
camera.updateViewMatrix();
glUniformMatrix4fv(viewMatrixLocation, 1, GL_FALSE,
glm::value_ptr(camera.getViewMatrix()));

// Render objects
sceneGraph.render(shaderProgram);

// Swap buffers
glfwSwapBuffers(window);
glfwPollEvents();
}
```

3. Physics Engine

The **physics engine** is another vital component of any game engine. It simulates real-world physical interactions such as object movement, gravity, collision detection, and response.

In a basic game engine, the physics engine typically handles:

- **Rigid Body Physics**: The basic simulation of objects as solid, non-deformable bodies. This includes handling forces like gravity, velocity, and applying transformations (movement, rotation).
- **Collision Detection**: The physics engine determines when objects intersect or collide. It uses algorithms like **AABB (Axis-Aligned Bounding Box)**, **OBB (Oriented Bounding Box)**, and **sphere-based collisions** to detect these intersections.
- **Collision Response**: Once a collision is detected, the physics engine determines how to react to the interaction (e.g., applying a force to objects, bouncing, sliding, or stopping).

While implementing a full-featured physics engine can be quite complex, basic collision detection and response can be achieved through a combination of bounding volume checks and simple physics calculations.

319

Example of a Basic Physics Engine Setup

cpp

```cpp
class PhysicsObject {
public:
    glm::vec3 position;
    glm::vec3 velocity;
    float mass;

    void update(float deltaTime) {
        // Apply basic physics calculations (e.g., gravity,
        movement)
        velocity += glm::vec3(0.0f, -9.81f, 0.0f) * deltaTime;
        // Gravity
        position += velocity * deltaTime; // Update position
    }

    bool checkCollision(PhysicsObject& other) {
        // Basic AABB collision detection
        return glm::length(position - other.position) <
        collisionThreshold;
    }
};
```

4. Input Management

A game engine must handle user input efficiently to allow interaction with the game world. This includes capturing input from the **keyboard, mouse**, and **gamepad**. Input management usually involves a system that listens for events and translates them into actions that affect the game world.

- **Keyboard Input**: Captures key presses for controlling game characters, triggering actions, or navigating menus.
- **Mouse Input**: Captures mouse movement for camera control, object interaction, or selection.
- **Gamepad Input**: Often used in console games, gamepads provide a

more tactile method of interacting with the game world.

In OpenGL, input events are typically handled by libraries like **GLFW**, **SDL**, or **GLUT**. These libraries provide convenient methods for polling input events and querying the state of input devices.

5. Asset Management

Efficient **asset management** is crucial for loading and storing game assets such as textures, 3D models, sound files, and shaders. A game engine must be able to load assets from disk into memory, organize them in a way that makes them easy to access during runtime, and ensure they are optimized for performance.

Some key tasks involved in asset management include:

- **Loading assets** from files (e.g., .obj for 3D models, .png or .jpg for textures).
- **Caching assets** in memory to avoid reloading them unnecessarily.
- **Handling resource dependencies**, ensuring that assets are loaded in the correct order and that textures and models are correctly linked.

6. Game Logic and Scene Management

The **game logic** dictates the flow of the game, defining how entities interact with one another, how the game world evolves, and how the player progresses. Scene management, on the other hand, is responsible for organizing and handling objects within the game world.

A basic game engine uses a **scene graph**, a tree-like data structure that represents the hierarchy of all game objects and their transformations. This is crucial for efficiently rendering and updating game objects.

```cpp
cpp

class SceneGraph {
public:
```

```cpp
    void addObject(GameObject* object) {
        objects.push_back(object);
    }

    void update(float deltaTime) {
        for (auto& object : objects) {
            object->update(deltaTime);
        }
    }

    void render(GLuint shaderProgram) {
        for (auto& object : objects) {
            object->render(shaderProgram);
        }
    }

private:
    std::vector<GameObject*> objects;
};
```

In this chapter, we've outlined the fundamental architecture of a basic 3D game engine using OpenGL. We explored key components such as the rendering engine, physics engine, input management, asset handling, and game logic. By structuring a game engine in this modular fashion, developers can create powerful and flexible systems that can be easily expanded to incorporate more advanced features as needed. Building a game engine from the ground up is an excellent way to understand the inner workings of both 3D graphics and game development, and it provides a solid foundation for creating complex interactive experiences.

Integrating Physics Engines (like Bullet or PhysX)

An essential feature of any 3D game engine is its ability to simulate realistic physics. Physics engines are responsible for simulating the movement and interaction of objects in the 3D world, including collisions, gravity, friction, and forces. Without physics, a game world can feel unrealistic and disconnected from the player's actions.

Physics engines, such as **Bullet** and **NVIDIA PhysX**, are commonly used in 3D game engines to handle these calculations in real time. These engines provide highly optimized, efficient algorithms for simulating rigid body dynamics, soft body physics, and collision detection. In this section, we'll explore how to integrate a physics engine into your 3D game engine and provide an overview of the core concepts involved.

1. What is a Physics Engine?

A **physics engine** is a software framework designed to simulate the physical behaviors of objects in a game environment. The most basic functions of a physics engine include:

- **Rigid Body Dynamics**: Simulating solid, unchanging objects that can move, rotate, and collide with other objects.
- **Collision Detection**: Determining when and where objects in the game world collide.
- **Forces**: Handling forces such as gravity, friction, drag, and user-applied forces like explosions or impacts.
- **Joints and Constraints**: Managing complex interactions between objects, such as attaching two objects together with a hinge joint, or restricting their movements in some way.

For a 3D game engine, integrating a physics engine requires a combination of scene management (for tracking objects and their positions), rendering (for drawing objects based on their physics transformations), and input handling (for interacting with physics objects).

2. Bullet Physics Engine

The **Bullet** physics engine is an open-source, high-performance physics library used in many 3D games and simulations. It supports rigid body dynamics, soft body dynamics, and collision detection.

Basic Steps to Integrating Bullet Physics into Your Engine:

Setting Up Bullet Physics: To use Bullet, you'll need to include its header files and link to the Bullet libraries. Bullet provides a set of classes for managing rigid bodies, collision shapes, and world simulations.

cpp

```
#include <btBulletDynamicsCommon.h>

btDefaultCollisionConfiguration* collisionConfiguration;
btCollisionDispatcher* dispatcher;
btDbvtBroadphase* overlappingPairCache;
btSequentialImpulseConstraintSolver* solver;
btDiscreteDynamicsWorld* dynamicsWorld;
```

Creating a Bullet Physics World: The Bullet physics world is where all objects are simulated. To create the physics world, you need to initialize the necessary components, such as the collision configuration, the broadphase algorithm (for detecting potential collisions), the solver (for solving physical constraints), and the dispatcher (for dispatching collision detection).

cpp

```
collisionConfiguration = new btDefaultCollisionConfiguration();
dispatcher = new btCollisionDispatcher(collisionConfiguration);
overlappingPairCache = new btDbvtBroadphase();
solver = new btSequentialImpulseConstraintSolver();
dynamicsWorld = new btDiscreteDynamicsWorld(dispatcher,
overlappingPairCache, solver, collisionConfiguration);
dynamicsWorld->setGravity(btVector3(0, -9.8, 0)); // Set gravity
to simulate Earth's gravity
```

Adding Rigid Bodies: To simulate objects in your world, you need to create **rigid bodies**. A rigid body represents an object with mass, position, and velocity. You also need to specify its shape and whether it's static or dynamic.

```cpp
btCollisionShape* groundShape = new
btStaticPlaneShape(btVector3(0, 1, 0), 1); // A static ground
plane
btDefaultMotionState* groundMotionState = new
btDefaultMotionState(btTransform(btQuaternion(0, 0, 0, 1),
btVector3(0, -1, 0)));
btRigidBody::btRigidBodyConstructionInfo groundRigidBodyCI(0,
groundMotionState, groundShape);
btRigidBody* groundRigidBody = new
btRigidBody(groundRigidBodyCI);
dynamicsWorld->addRigidBody(groundRigidBody);

// Add a dynamic rigid body (e.g., a falling box)
btCollisionShape* boxShape = new btBoxShape(btVector3(1, 1, 1));
btDefaultMotionState* boxMotionState = new
btDefaultMotionState(btTransform(btQuaternion(0, 0, 0, 1),
btVector3(0, 50, 0)));
btScalar mass = 1.0f;
btVector3 fallInertia(0, 0, 0);
boxShape->calculateLocalInertia(mass, fallInertia);
btRigidBody::btRigidBodyConstructionInfo boxRigidBodyCI(mass,
boxMotionState, boxShape, fallInertia);
btRigidBody* fallingBox = new btRigidBody(boxRigidBodyCI);
dynamicsWorld->addRigidBody(fallingBox);
```

Simulating the World: The Bullet physics world is updated every frame. This is where the actual physics calculations occur, including collision detection and the movement of rigid bodies based on forces applied (e.g., gravity).

```cpp
dynamicsWorld->stepSimulation(1.f / 60.f, 10); // Step the
simulation
```

Retrieving Physics Data: Once the simulation is updated, you can retrieve the updated positions and orientations of objects to pass them to the

325

rendering system.

```cpp
btTransform trans;
fallingBox->getMotionState()->getWorldTransform(trans);
btScalar* pos = trans.getOrigin().getX();
```

3. NVIDIA PhysX

Another popular physics engine is **NVIDIA PhysX**, which is widely used in the gaming industry for its performance and ease of integration. PhysX is available both for CPU and GPU-based calculations, and it supports a range of physics simulations, including rigid body dynamics, cloth simulation, and particle systems.

Basic Setup for PhysX:

Initialize the PhysX SDK: PhysX requires setting up a few core components, including the **Physics SDK**, **Scene**, and **Material**. Here's how to initialize the engine:

```cpp
#include <PxPhysicsAPI.h>

using namespace physx;

PxDefaultAllocator gAllocator;
PxDefaultErrorCallback gErrorCallback;
PxFoundation* gFoundation =
PxCreateFoundation(PX_PHYSICS_VERSION, gAllocator,
gErrorCallback);
PxPhysics* gPhysics = PxCreatePhysics(PX_PHYSICS_VERSION,
*gFoundation, PxTolerancesScale());
```

Creating a Scene and Materials: After initializing PhysX, you can create a **Scene** where all your physics objects will reside. You can also define the **material** properties for objects, such as friction and restitution.

```cpp
PxSceneDesc sceneDesc(gPhysics->getTolerancesScale());
PxDefaultCpuDispatcher* dispatcher =
PxDefaultCpuDispatcherCreate(4); // 4 threads
sceneDesc.cpuDispatcher = dispatcher;
sceneDesc.filterShader = PxDefaultSimulationFilterShader;
PxScene* gScene = gPhysics->createScene(sceneDesc);

PxMaterial* material = gPhysics->createMaterial(0.5f, 0.5f,
0.6f); // Define material properties (friction, restitution)
```

Creating Rigid Bodies and Adding Forces: You can now create objects (rigid bodies) and add them to the scene. PhysX handles the simulation, and you can apply forces or let objects interact with each other according to the physics rules.

```cpp
PxRigidDynamic* dynamicActor =
gPhysics->createRigidDynamic(PxTransform(PxVec3(0, 50, 0)));
PxShape* shape =
PxRigidActorExt::createExclusiveShape(*dynamicActor,
*boxGeometry, *material);
gScene->addActor(*dynamicActor);
```

Simulating and Updating the Scene: As with Bullet, the PhysX simulation must be updated each frame. After the simulation is complete, the game engine can retrieve updated positions and apply them to the rendered objects.

```cpp
gScene->simulate(1.0f / 60.0f); // Step the simulation
gScene->fetchResults(true); // Fetch the results (i.e., updated
physics state)
```

327

4. Benefits of Using a Physics Engine

- **Realistic Interactions**: Physics engines like Bullet and PhysX provide highly realistic interactions between objects, making the game world feel more immersive and interactive.
- **Performance Optimization**: Physics engines are highly optimized for real-time simulation, enabling the simulation of large numbers of objects without significant performance drops.
- **Ease of Use**: Both Bullet and PhysX offer comprehensive APIs for handling common physics tasks like collision detection, rigid body dynamics, and constraint systems, saving you from writing complex physics code from scratch.

By integrating a physics engine like **Bullet** or **PhysX** into your 3D game engine, you can simulate realistic object behaviors, collisions, and forces, adding a layer of depth and interactivity that enhances the player's experience.

cpp

```cpp
btRigidBody* groundRigidBody = new
btRigidBody(groundRigidBodyCI);
dynamicsWorld->addRigidBody(groundRigidBody);

// Creating a dynamic object (e.g., a falling box)
btCollisionShape* boxShape = new btBoxShape(btVector3(1, 1,
1)); // A box with dimensions 2x2x2
btDefaultMotionState* boxMotionState = new
btDefaultMotionState(btTransform(btQuaternion(0, 0, 0, 1),
btVector3(0, 10, 0))); // Start at (0,10,0)
btScalar mass = 1.0f; // Mass of the box
btVector3 inertia(0, 0, 0); // No inertia initially
boxShape->calculateLocalInertia(mass, inertia); // Calculate
inertia based on mass
```

```cpp
btRigidBody::btRigidBodyConstructionInfo boxRigidBodyCI(mass,
boxMotionState, boxShape, inertia);
btRigidBody* boxRigidBody = new btRigidBody(boxRigidBodyCI);

dynamicsWorld->addRigidBody(boxRigidBody);
```

Simulating the Physics World: Once the objects are added to the physics world, you need to update the world on each frame to simulate their behavior. Bullet provides a simple interface for stepping through the physics simulation and updating the positions of objects based on their physics properties.

cpp

```cpp
dynamicsWorld->stepSimulation(1.f / 60.f, 10); // Simulate the
physics for 1/60th of a second
```

Handling Collisions and Responses: Bullet handles collision detection automatically. When a collision occurs between objects, Bullet calculates the collision response based on the mass, velocity, and other physical properties of the objects. You can further customize the collision response by implementing custom callbacks.

cpp

```cpp
// Get the collision object of the box
btTransform trans;
boxRigidBody->getMotionState()->getWorldTransform(trans);

// Access position
btVector3 boxPos = trans.getOrigin();
std::cout << "Box Position: " << boxPos.getX() << ", " <<
boxPos.getY() << ", " << boxPos.getZ() << std::endl;
```

Building a Simple 3D Game Prototype

329

Now that we've covered the essential aspects of integrating a physics engine (like Bullet or PhysX) into your 3D game engine, let's take a step back and see how we can build a simple prototype of a 3D game using OpenGL and the physics systems we've just set up.

Creating a **3D game prototype** involves combining your rendering system, physics engine, input handling, and scene management into a coherent gameplay experience. While a full-fledged game engine includes many advanced features (like AI, advanced physics, complex shaders, and multiplayer support), a simple prototype serves as a foundation from which you can iterate and expand.

In this section, we'll walk through the steps of building a very basic 3D game prototype, focusing on these core features:

- **A 3D world with interactive objects**
- **Physics-based interactions**
- **User input for controlling the player**
- **Simple game mechanics and gameplay**

By the end of this section, you'll have the groundwork for a basic 3D physics-based game, and from here, you can further build upon the prototype with additional features.

1. Setting Up the Scene and Objects

To begin with, you'll want to define the objects that will populate your game world. For a simple prototype, let's start with a few objects that the player can interact with—such as a cube (which the player can control) and a ground plane. We'll also create a few physics-based objects, such as falling boxes, to simulate interactions.

Setting Up the Scene:

- **Player-controlled object (cube)**
- **Ground (static plane)**
- **Falling boxes (dynamic objects)**

cpp

```
// Create a ground object (static plane)
btCollisionShape* groundShape = new
btStaticPlaneShape(btVector3(0, 1, 0), 0); // Horizontal plane
btDefaultMotionState* groundMotionState = new
btDefaultMotionState(btTransform(btQuaternion(0, 0, 0, 1),
btVector3(0, -10, 0)));
btRigidBody::btRigidBodyConstructionInfo groundRigidBodyCI(0,
groundMotionState, groundShape);
btRigidBody* groundRigidBody = new
btRigidBody(groundRigidBodyCI);
dynamicsWorld->addRigidBody(groundRigidBody);

// Create the player cube (dynamic object)
btCollisionShape* cubeShape = new btBoxShape(btVector3(1, 1,
1)); // A 2x2x2 cube
btDefaultMotionState* cubeMotionState = new
btDefaultMotionState(btTransform(btQuaternion(0, 0, 0, 1),
btVector3(0, 5, 0))); // Start above the ground
btScalar cubeMass = 1.0f;
btVector3 cubeInertia(0, 0, 0);
cubeShape->calculateLocalInertia(cubeMass, cubeInertia);
btRigidBody::btRigidBodyConstructionInfo
cubeRigidBodyCI(cubeMass, cubeMotionState, cubeShape,
cubeInertia);
btRigidBody* cubeRigidBody = new btRigidBody(cubeRigidBodyCI);
dynamicsWorld->addRigidBody(cubeRigidBody);
```

2. Handling Player Input

To make the prototype interactive, we need to allow the player to control the cube object using input devices such as the keyboard or mouse. We'll start by implementing basic movement controls (forward, backward, left, right, and jump) for the player-controlled cube.

Basic Input Controls:

We'll use **keyboard input** to control the movement of the cube. For example:

- **W, A, S, D** for forward, left, back, and right movement.
- **Space** for jumping.

To achieve this, you'll need to capture keyboard input and then apply forces or transformations to the cube based on the player's actions.

```cpp
// Check for player input (using a simple example for keyboard
control)
if (keyIsPressed(KEY_W)) {
    cubeRigidBody->applyCentralForce(btVector3(0, 0, -10));  //
    Move forward
}
if (keyIsPressed(KEY_S)) {
    cubeRigidBody->applyCentralForce(btVector3(0, 0, 10));   //
    Move backward
}
if (keyIsPressed(KEY_A)) {
    cubeRigidBody->applyCentralForce(btVector3(-10, 0, 0));  //
    Move left
}
if (keyIsPressed(KEY_D)) {
    cubeRigidBody->applyCentralForce(btVector3(10, 0, 0));   //
    Move right
}
if (keyIsPressed(KEY_SPACE)) {
    cubeRigidBody->applyCentralImpulse(btVector3(0, 10, 0));  //
    Jump (apply upward force)
}
```

Here, applyCentralForce() adds a force to the center of mass of the cube to make it move, and applyCentralImpulse() applies a sudden force to simulate a jump.

3. Game Logic and Mechanics

In this prototype, the game logic is minimal—there's a simple objective for the player to interact with the environment. For example, we can make it so that if the player cube collides with any falling boxes, the box will be destroyed (simulated by removing it from the physics world).

Basic Game Logic Example:

cpp

```
// Detect collisions and perform actions based on collision
for (int i = 0; i < dynamicsWorld->getNumCollisionObjects();
++i) {
    btCollisionObject* obj =
    dynamicsWorld->getCollisionObjectArray()[i];

    // Check if the cube has collided with any falling box
    if (obj != cubeRigidBody) { // Skip the player cube itself
        btRigidBody* otherRigidBody = btRigidBody::upcast(obj);
        if (otherRigidBody) {
            btVector3 otherPosition = otherRigidBody-
>getWorldTransform().getOrigin();

            // Check if the cube is near the falling box and
            destroy it
            if (otherPosition.distance(cubeRigidBody-
>getWorldTransform().getOrigin()) < 5.0) {
                dynamicsWorld->removeRigidBody(otherRigidBody);
                delete otherRigidBody;
            }
        }
    }
}
```

4. Rendering the Scene

Now that we have a physics-based environment and player input handling in place, we can focus on rendering the game objects—specifically, the cube and the falling boxes. OpenGL will handle the rendering process, and we'll need to set up the camera, lighting, and shaders for a basic visual display.

Setting up the Camera:

For this prototype, a basic third-person camera that follows the player cube might be a good start. Here's how you can set up the camera to follow the player:

cpp

```
// Camera follows the cube
btTransform cubeTransform;
cubeRigidBody->getMotionState()->getWorldTransform(cubeTransform);
btVector3 playerPosition = cubeTransform.getOrigin();

// Camera position set slightly behind and above the player cube
btVector3 cameraPosition = playerPosition + btVector3(0, 5, 10);
camera.lookAt(playerPosition);  // Point the camera at the
player cube
```

This simple camera setup makes the camera follow the cube and keeps the cube in the center of the screen while adjusting its position to be slightly behind and above the player.

5. Putting It All Together:

Finally, integrate the components (physics, input, scene setup, and rendering) to create a fully interactive 3D game prototype. The main loop would involve updating the physics simulation, handling input, updating the game world, and rendering the scene.

cpp

```
while (!windowShouldClose()) {
    // Step 1: Handle user input
    handleInput();

    // Step 2: Update the physics simulation
    dynamicsWorld->stepSimulation(1.f / 60.f, 10);

    // Step 3: Update game logic (e.g., collision detection)
    updateGameLogic();
```

```
    // Step 4: Render the scene
    renderScene();
}
```

Building a simple 3D game prototype is an exciting step toward understanding the mechanics of game development. By integrating the rendering pipeline, physics engine, input management, and game logic, you've created a solid foundation for building more complex game mechanics, adding animations, and implementing other advanced features.

This prototype can be extended further with additional gameplay features, such as more interactive objects, advanced AI, enhanced graphics effects, and even multiplayer support. Once the prototype is functioning smoothly, you can begin to refine and expand upon it, gradually adding complexity and optimizing performance.

Optimizing Game Performance with OpenGL

When developing a 3D game, performance is crucial. Even with an excellent physics engine and solid gameplay mechanics, a poorly optimized game can lead to low frame rates, stuttering, and an overall poor user experience. In this section, we'll explore various strategies to optimize performance in OpenGL, covering both rendering and physics aspects, and how to strike the right balance between quality and performance for your game prototype.

The primary areas where optimization can significantly improve performance are:

- **Reducing the number of draw calls**
- **Efficient texture management**
- **Level of Detail (LOD) techniques**
- **Optimizing shaders**

- **Leveraging GPU acceleration for physics**

Let's dive into these areas.

1. Reducing the Number of Draw Calls

One of the most significant performance bottlenecks in OpenGL is the **number of draw calls**. Every time you make a draw call, the GPU has to switch contexts, set up shaders, and draw the geometry. Too many draw calls can lead to **CPU-GPU synchronization issues** and an overall drop in performance, especially on less powerful hardware.

Batching and Instancing:

One way to optimize draw calls is by **batching** multiple objects into a single draw call or using **instancing** for repeated objects (such as trees, enemies, or other static geometry).

Instancing allows you to render multiple copies of the same object using a single draw call. This is incredibly useful for objects that share the same geometry and material but differ in transformation (position, rotation, scale).

cpp

```cpp
GLuint instanceVBO; // Vertex buffer object for instances
GLuint instanceVAO; // Vertex array object for instances
std::vector<glm::mat4> modelMatrices; // Matrices for
transformations

// Initialize instance buffers
glGenBuffers(1, &instanceVBO);
glBindBuffer(GL_ARRAY_BUFFER, instanceVBO);
glBufferData(GL_ARRAY_BUFFER, modelMatrices.size() *
sizeof(glm::mat4), &modelMatrices[0], GL_STATIC_DRAW);

// For instancing, set the transformation matrix attribute for
each instance
glVertexAttribPointer(1, 4, GL_FLOAT, GL_FALSE,
```

```
sizeof(glm::mat4), (void*)0);
glEnableVertexAttribArray(1);
glVertexAttribPointer(2, 4, GL_FLOAT, GL_FALSE,
sizeof(glm::mat4), (void*)(sizeof(glm::vec4)));
glEnableVertexAttribArray(2);
// Repeat for other components of the matrix if necessary

// Draw all instances in one call
glDrawArraysInstanced(GL_TRIANGLES, 0, numVertices,
modelMatrices.size());
```

With **instancing**, instead of calling glDrawElements or glDrawArrays for each object in the scene, you call it once for multiple objects with different transformations. This reduces the number of draw calls, thus improving performance.

2. Efficient Texture Management

Textures are another area where you can achieve considerable performance improvements. OpenGL allows you to load and manage textures, but inefficient use of textures can lead to memory bloat, increased loading times, and lower performance.

Texture Atlases:

One effective strategy for reducing the number of texture bindings is to use **texture atlases**. A texture atlas is a large texture that contains multiple smaller textures (e.g., textures for various game objects). Instead of binding different textures for each object, you can bind a single texture atlas and use **texture coordinates** to reference specific areas of the atlas.

cpp

```
// Instead of binding each texture individually, bind the
texture atlas once
glBindTexture(GL_TEXTURE_2D, textureAtlas);
```

```
// Set the texture coordinates to point to different parts of
the atlas for each object
```

Mipmapping:

Mipmaps are precomputed versions of a texture at different levels of detail. When rendering distant objects, OpenGL can select lower-resolution mipmaps to avoid using unnecessary high-detail textures, which saves both memory and rendering time.

You can enable mipmapping for your textures as follows:

cpp

```
glGenerateMipmap(GL_TEXTURE_2D); // Automatically generates
mipmaps for the texture
```

Texture Compression:

Another important optimization is **texture compression**. Modern GPUs support various compressed texture formats (like **DXT**, **ASTC**, **ETC2**), which reduce the amount of texture data that needs to be loaded into memory. Compressed textures can drastically improve memory usage and loading times.

To implement compressed textures:

cpp

```
// Load compressed texture (e.g., DXT1) directly
glTexImage2D(GL_TEXTURE_2D, 0, GL_COMPRESSED_RGB_S3TC_DXT1_EXT,
width, height, 0, GL_RGB, GL_UNSIGNED_BYTE, data);
```

3. Level of Detail (LOD) for Distant Objects

Level of Detail (LOD) is a technique used to reduce the complexity of rendering objects that are far away from the camera. Instead of rendering highly detailed models for distant objects, you can use simpler models (with fewer polygons), saving both memory and processing power.

LOD Strategy:

1. **Multiple Mesh Versions**: Create different versions of the same model, with varying levels of detail (LOD0, LOD1, LOD2, etc.). For example, LOD0 could be the highest resolution model, LOD1 a medium-res version, and LOD2 a low-res version.

2. **Distance-based Selection**: Based on the distance between the camera and the object, choose which LOD model to render. This selection can happen dynamically based on the camera's position.

```cpp
// Based on distance, choose the appropriate LOD level for an
object
float distanceToCamera = glm::length(cameraPosition -
objectPosition);
if (distanceToCamera < LOD0_threshold) {
    renderLOD0();
} else if (distanceToCamera < LOD1_threshold) {
    renderLOD1();
} else {
    renderLOD2();
}
```

By implementing LOD, you can ensure that the system isn't wasting resources on rendering distant objects with a high level of detail, improving both **GPU performance** and **frame rate**.

4. Optimizing Shaders

Shaders are another area where performance gains can be achieved. Complex shaders with multiple operations and high precision can cause significant overhead on the GPU. Optimizing shaders ensures that your game runs smoothly across various hardware.

Shader Optimization Techniques:

- **Use simpler shaders for less important objects**: For background objects, UI elements, and non-interactive elements, use simpler shaders that don't need as much computation.

- **Avoid unnecessary texture fetches**: Texture fetches can be costly. Only fetch textures when absolutely necessary and ensure you're not repeatedly fetching the same texture in a single frame.
- **Use lower precision**: In some cases, you can use lower precision types (e.g., mediump instead of highp for floating-point numbers) to reduce computation time, especially for mobile devices.
- **Combine multiple shaders into one**: Instead of using separate shaders for different materials, combine them into one program that can handle multiple materials with a single pass.

Example of switching to lower precision:

```cpp
precision mediump float; // For mobile devices, instead of highp
```

5. Leveraging GPU Acceleration for Physics

In addition to optimizing rendering, you can also leverage GPU acceleration for **physics computations**. Physics engines like **NVIDIA PhysX** can take advantage of **CUDA** (NVIDIA's GPU computing framework) to offload the physics computations onto the GPU. This can significantly reduce the CPU load, allowing it to focus on other tasks like AI or input handling.

Integrating **GPU-accelerated physics** into your game can lead to dramatic performance improvements, especially when dealing with large numbers of dynamic objects or complex simulations.

Optimizing your OpenGL-based game involves a combination of strategies across multiple areas—rendering, physics, texture management, and GPU usage. By reducing draw calls, efficiently managing textures, implementing

LOD, optimizing shaders, and leveraging GPU acceleration for physics, you can ensure that your game runs smoothly on a wide variety of hardware.

These optimizations not only improve performance but also create a more responsive and enjoyable experience for players. As you develop your 3D game prototype, always keep an eye on the performance implications of each decision you make, and continue testing and iterating to find the best balance between visual fidelity and frame rate.

Real-Time Visualizations and Simulations

Using OpenGL for Scientific Visualizations and Simulations

OpenGL is a powerful tool that can be used for a wide variety of applications beyond gaming, including **scientific visualizations** and **simulations**. Whether you are working with data from complex simulations, visualizing large datasets, or performing real-time simulations in physics, chemistry, or biology, OpenGL provides the necessary tools to render dynamic, real-time visualizations with high performance and flexibility.

In this chapter, we will discuss how to use OpenGL to create effective and efficient **scientific visualizations** and **real-time simulations**. We'll cover several key concepts, including rendering techniques, data handling, shaders, and optimization strategies. By the end of this chapter, you will have a comprehensive understanding of how OpenGL can be utilized to create interactive, real-time visualizations for scientific and engineering purposes.

1. Introduction to Scientific Visualizations

Scientific visualization involves the graphical representation of data to help scientists, engineers, and analysts understand complex datasets or phenomena. These visualizations play a critical role in many fields, including physics, chemistry, biology, and engineering, by transforming raw data into understandable, interactive visuals.

In scientific visualization, the goal is to represent multidimensional, often time-varying, data in ways that are meaningful and insightful. Typical examples of scientific visualizations include:

- **3D models** of molecules or anatomical structures in biology
- **Geospatial visualizations** such as terrain or ocean modeling
- **Weather simulations** and fluid dynamics
- **Physics simulations** like particle systems, molecular dynamics, and simulations of electromagnetic fields

OpenGL can help render these visualizations by efficiently processing large datasets and visualizing the data in real-time with interactive feedback.

2. Key Requirements for Scientific Visualization with OpenGL

When creating scientific visualizations with OpenGL, there are several key requirements:

1. **Real-Time Rendering**: Scientific simulations often involve large datasets that change over time (e.g., time-dependent fluid simulations or molecular dynamics). OpenGL allows us to render these datasets in real time and update the visualizations dynamically.
2. **3D Rendering**: Most scientific data is inherently three-dimensional, such as fluid dynamics or volume rendering. OpenGL excels at handling 3D data and rendering it in interactive environments.
3. **Large Datasets**: Scientific data can be massive, often requiring efficient memory usage and optimized rendering techniques to handle millions of points or complex geometries.
4. **Interactivity**: Many scientific applications require the ability to interact with the visualization, whether it's zooming in on a dataset, rotating a 3D model, or adjusting simulation parameters. OpenGL provides a great platform for these real-time interactions.

3. Rendering Techniques for Scientific Visualizations

OpenGL provides a wide array of rendering techniques that are useful for scientific visualizations. Below are some commonly used techniques:

Volume Rendering

Volume rendering is used to visualize volumetric data, such as MRI scans, fluid dynamics, and meteorological data. Unlike traditional surface rendering, volume rendering allows you to display data points within a volume rather than just the surfaces of objects.

Steps for Volume Rendering:

1. **Data Preparation**: You need to store the volumetric data in a 3D texture or voxel grid. Each voxel represents a data point in the volume, and the values can be anything from density to temperature.
2. **Ray Casting or Slicing**: The most common technique for rendering volumetric data is **ray casting**. Rays are cast through the volume from the camera's perspective, and the accumulated data along the ray path is used to determine the color and opacity of each pixel.
3. **Shaders**: Use fragment shaders to compute color and opacity based on voxel values along the ray. You can also implement techniques like **transfer functions**, where different voxel values are mapped to different colors and opacities.

```cpp
// Simple volume rendering using ray-casting
#version 330 core

in vec3 fragCoord; // Fragment coordinates in world space
uniform sampler3D volumeTexture; // 3D texture for volume data
uniform float opacityThreshold;

out vec4 FragColor;

void main() {
    vec3 rayOrigin = fragCoord;
    vec3 rayDirection = normalize(cameraPos - rayOrigin);
```

```
    float totalOpacity = 0.0;
    vec4 color = vec4(0.0);

    // Raycasting loop through the volume texture
    for (float t = 0.0; t < 1.0; t += 0.01) {
        vec3 samplePos = rayOrigin + t * rayDirection;
        vec4 sampleColor = texture(volumeTexture, samplePos);

        // Accumulate color and opacity
        color += (1.0 - totalOpacity) * sampleColor *
        sampleColor.a;
        totalOpacity += sampleColor.a;

        if (totalOpacity >= opacityThreshold) break;
    }

    FragColor = color;
}
```

Surface and Mesh Rendering

Another essential rendering technique is displaying **surfaces** or **meshes** derived from scientific data. For example, in physics simulations or molecular modeling, you might want to render the surface of a 3D model, such as the surface of a particle or molecule.

To render surfaces, you can use **triangular meshes** or **point clouds** to represent objects. OpenGL's efficiency in handling large meshes makes it ideal for these tasks.

1. **Surface Meshes**: Represent surfaces using vertices, and apply shaders for lighting, color, and texture.
2. **Point Clouds**: When visualizing large datasets (e.g., 3D scanning, particle systems), a point cloud visualization might be more suitable. OpenGL can efficiently render millions of points using **instancing** techniques.

cpp

```
// Rendering a mesh of scientific data points
glEnableVertexAttribArray(0);  // Vertex positions
glBindBuffer(GL_ARRAY_BUFFER, pointCloudVBO);
glVertexAttribPointer(0, 3, GL_FLOAT, GL_FALSE, 0, (void*)0);

glPointSize(5.0f); // Set point size
glDrawArrays(GL_POINTS, 0, numPoints);  // Draw points
```

Wireframe and Contour Rendering

Wireframe rendering is useful for visualizing the structure of a simulation or geometry. For example, when displaying a mesh or molecular structure, you might want to see just the edges without filling the faces. This technique is widely used in **finite element analysis** and **structural simulations**.

To render in wireframe, you can use OpenGL's **polygon mode**:

cpp

```
glPolygonMode(GL_FRONT_AND_BACK, GL_LINE);  // Render in
wireframe mode
glDrawArrays(GL_TRIANGLES, 0, numVertices); // Draw the mesh
```

You can also use **contour rendering** for visualizing scalar fields (e.g., temperature, pressure) by drawing lines or surfaces at specific scalar values.

4. Handling Large Datasets

When visualizing large scientific datasets, the amount of data to be rendered can easily exceed the available memory. OpenGL provides several methods to handle this efficiently:

Level of Detail (LOD) for Large Datasets

For large models or simulations, use **Level of Detail (LOD)** techniques to reduce the complexity of distant or less significant parts of the model. This involves using lower-resolution meshes or simplified models for objects that are far away from the camera or less important.

```cpp
// Select lower-resolution LOD for distant objects
if (distance > LOD_threshold) {
    renderLOD_low();  // Use simplified model for distant objects
} else {
    renderLOD_high();  // Use detailed model for close objects
}
```

Streaming Data

For datasets that are too large to fit into memory, you can use **streaming** to load and unload data dynamically based on what is needed. For example, if you are rendering a massive terrain, you can load portions of the terrain into memory only when they are within the camera's view.

Efficient Buffering with Vertex Buffer Objects (VBOs)

To render large datasets efficiently, you can use **Vertex Buffer Objects (VBOs)** to store vertex data directly in the GPU's memory. This avoids the need for sending data to the GPU every frame, thus improving performance.

```cpp
GLuint VBO, VAO;
glGenBuffers(1, &VBO);
glBindBuffer(GL_ARRAY_BUFFER, VBO);
glBufferData(GL_ARRAY_BUFFER, sizeof(vertices), vertices,
GL_STATIC_DRAW);
```

5. Real-Time Simulations

OpenGL is not only used for rendering static scenes but is also an excellent tool for **real-time simulations**. These simulations might involve physical models (e.g., fluid dynamics, molecular modeling) or mathematical models (e.g., weather prediction, atmospheric modeling).

Simulating Fluid Dynamics

Fluid simulations require handling complex physical interactions. While OpenGL is used for rendering, the simulation itself can run in parallel on the CPU or GPU (using CUDA or OpenCL for heavy calculations). For real-time interaction, visualizing fluid with shaders can give insight into behavior.

A basic simulation might use **particle systems** to represent fluid elements and **force fields** to simulate fluid motion. Shaders can then render these particles based on their physical properties, such as velocity and color (representing temperature, for example).

```cpp
cpp

// Shader for rendering particles in a fluid simulation
#version 330 core
in vec3 particlePos;
in vec3 particleColor;
out vec4 FragColor;

void main() {
    FragColor = vec4(particleColor, 1.0);
}
```

Rendering Dynamic Simulations

For simulations like **molecular dynamics** or **atomic collision** simulations, OpenGL's real-time rendering abilities are crucial for visualizing the interactions of thousands or even millions of particles in a single scene.

6. Optimizing Performance for Simulations

When dealing with large datasets or complex simulations, performance can quickly become a bottleneck. Here are some techniques for optimizing OpenGL-based scientific visualizations:

- **Instancing**: Use instancing to draw multiple particles or objects with the same geometry, reducing draw calls.

- **Level of Detail (LOD)**: Use LOD techniques to reduce the complexity of objects as they move farther from the camera.
- **Data Streaming**: Stream data into the GPU in chunks to avoid memory overload.
- **Parallel Computing**: Offload heavy simulation calculations to the GPU or use multi-threading to parallelize computations.

OpenGL provides a powerful platform for creating **real-time visualizations** and **simulations** across a wide range of scientific fields. Whether you are visualizing complex molecular structures, simulating fluid dynamics, or rendering massive terrain datasets, OpenGL's flexibility and performance make it an ideal choice for high-quality scientific visualization.

By combining OpenGL's rendering capabilities with optimized data management and efficient simulation techniques, you can create compelling, interactive visualizations that bring scientific data to life, providing insights that would otherwise be difficult to achieve. The integration of real-time rendering with scientific computations allows for the creation of dynamic, interactive environments that are both informative and visually appealing.

Building a Simulation Engine for Fluid Dynamics or Particle Systems

Real-time simulations, such as **fluid dynamics** or **particle systems**, are crucial in many scientific applications, from engineering to environmental science, and even graphics. OpenGL, with its powerful rendering pipeline, is ideal for visualizing such complex simulations. However, building a simulation engine involves not just rendering but also accurately modeling the physical systems and efficiently handling large numbers of dynamic entities in real time.

In this section, we'll discuss how to build a **fluid dynamics simulation engine** and a **particle system engine** using OpenGL. Both simulations are commonly used in scientific visualization and require a good understanding of physics, as well as effective data structures and algorithms.

1. Fluid Dynamics Simulation

Fluid dynamics simulations are a critical component in many scientific fields, from simulating the behavior of water in oceans to modeling airflows in wind tunnels. To simulate fluid dynamics in real-time, we need to solve a set of equations (such as the **Navier-Stokes equations**) that describe the motion of fluid substances.

However, solving the equations directly in real-time is computationally expensive. Instead, we often use simplified methods such as **smoothed-particle hydrodynamics (SPH)** or **lattice Boltzmann methods (LBM)**. These methods break the fluid into particles or grid cells and simulate their movement based on local interactions.

Smoothed-Particle Hydrodynamics (SPH)

In SPH, the fluid is represented by particles that interact with each other. Each particle has mass, position, velocity, and other attributes such as pressure and temperature. SPH simulates the physical behavior of the fluid by calculating the forces between neighboring particles.

Steps to implement SPH in OpenGL:

Define Particles: Each particle is represented by a structure that contains its position, velocity, mass, and density.

```cpp
struct Particle {
    glm::vec3 position;
    glm::vec3 velocity;
    float mass;
    float density;
    float pressure;
};
```

Calculate Forces: You need to calculate forces between particles. These forces can include pressure forces, viscosity forces, and external forces (e.g., gravity).

cpp

```cpp
glm::vec3 computePressureForce(const Particle& p1, const
Particle& p2) {
    // Compute force based on pressure difference between p1 and
    p2
    glm::vec3 direction = p2.position - p1.position;
    float distance = glm::length(direction);
    // Use a simple spring-like force model for the pressure
    force
    float forceMagnitude = (p1.pressure + p2.pressure) *
    distance;
    return glm::normalize(direction) * forceMagnitude;
}
```

Update Particle Positions: Once the forces are calculated, update the position and velocity of each particle.

cpp

```cpp
void updateParticlePositions(Particle& p, float dt) {
    // Use simple Euler integration for position update
    p.position += p.velocity * dt;
}
```

Visualization: Once the particle positions are updated, use OpenGL to render the particles. You can represent them as points or small spheres in 3D space.

cpp

```cpp
glBegin(GL_POINTS);
for (const Particle& p : particles) {
    glVertex3fv(glm::value_ptr(p.position));
}
glEnd();
```

Rendering with Shaders: To visualize fluid flow more effectively, you can use shaders to color the particles based on their velocity or pressure. For instance, you can use **velocity-based coloring** to highlight regions of high or low flow.

```cpp
cpp

#version 330 core
in vec3 velocity; // Particle velocity as input
out vec4 FragColor;

void main() {
    float speed = length(velocity);
    FragColor = vec4(speed, 0.0, 1.0 - speed, 1.0); // Color
    based on speed
}
```

2. Particle Systems

A **particle system** is a simulation technique used to simulate and render a large number of small, independent particles. These particles can represent phenomena like smoke, fire, water droplets, dust, and more. In scientific simulations, particle systems are often used to model things like the motion of atoms, diffusion processes, or the distribution of particles in a medium.

Building a Basic Particle System

A basic particle system includes the following components:

- **Particles**: Individual elements that move according to physical rules (e.g., velocity, acceleration, gravity).
- **Emitters**: The source that generates new particles (often in a burst or stream).
- **Forces**: Forces like gravity, wind, or drag that affect the particles.

Steps for creating a particle system:

Define the Particle Structure: Similar to fluid dynamics, each particle has properties such as position, velocity, color, size, and lifespan.

```cpp
struct Particle {
    glm::vec3 position;
    glm::vec3 velocity;
    glm::vec3 acceleration;
    float life;
    glm::vec4 color;
};
```

Emit Particles: The emitter generates new particles at regular intervals. Each new particle is initialized with random properties (e.g., position, velocity, and color).

```cpp
void emitParticles(std::vector<Particle>& particles, glm::vec3
emitterPosition) {
    Particle newParticle;
    newParticle.position = emitterPosition;
    newParticle.velocity = glm::vec3(rand() % 10, rand() % 10,
    rand() % 10);
    newParticle.acceleration = glm::vec3(0, -9.8f, 0); // Gravity
    newParticle.life = 1.0f; // 1 second lifespan
    newParticle.color = glm::vec4(1.0f, 0.5f, 0.0f, 1.0f); //
    Orange color

    particles.push_back(newParticle);
}
```

Update Particles: Update each particle's position based on its velocity and apply forces like gravity.

```cpp
```

```cpp
void updateParticles(std::vector<Particle>& particles, float dt)
{
    for (Particle& p : particles) {
        p.velocity += p.acceleration * dt; // Apply gravity or
        other forces
        p.position += p.velocity * dt; // Update position based
        on velocity
        p.life -= dt; // Decrease life

        // If particle has expired, reset it
        if (p.life <= 0) {
            p.life = 1.0f; // Reset for reuse
            p.position = glm::vec3(rand() % 10, 10, rand() %
            10); // New position
        }
    }
}
```

Rendering the Particles: Once the particles have been updated, render them using OpenGL. For efficient rendering, particles are often drawn as **point sprites,** which are textured 2D sprites that always face the camera.

```cpp
cpp

glBegin(GL_POINTS);
for (const Particle& p : particles) {
    glColor4fv(glm::value_ptr(p.color)); // Set color based on
    particle properties
    glVertex3fv(glm::value_ptr(p.position)); // Render particle
    at its position
}
glEnd();
```

Shading and Particle Effects: For more advanced rendering, particle shaders can be used to add effects like fading, scaling, or changing colors based on particle life.

```cpp
#version 330 core
in float particleLife;
out vec4 FragColor;

void main() {
    float alpha = particleLife; // Fade out the particle over
    time
    FragColor = vec4(1.0, 0.5, 0.0, alpha); // Color with fading
    effect
}
```

3. Optimizations for Real-Time Simulations

Both fluid dynamics and particle systems can be computationally expensive, especially when simulating large systems with many particles or fluid cells. OpenGL offers several techniques for optimizing these simulations:

Instancing: For particle systems, instancing can be used to render multiple particles with a single draw call, reducing the overhead of individual rendering operations.

Compute Shaders: OpenGL's **compute shaders** allow for GPU-accelerated physics calculations. This is particularly useful for updating particle positions or solving fluid dynamics equations in parallel on the GPU.

Level of Detail (LOD): For large-scale simulations, use **LOD techniques** to reduce the detail of objects or particles that are far from the camera. This helps reduce the number of calculations required for distant objects.

Use of Textures: Instead of storing and processing large amounts of data for each particle or fluid point individually, textures (such as **3D textures** for fluid simulations) can be used to store simulation data in a compact form that can be quickly accessed by shaders.

355

In this chapter, we've explored how OpenGL can be used to create powerful, real-time visualizations and simulations. By leveraging OpenGL's flexibility and performance, scientists and engineers can visualize complex data and run simulations that help solve problems across many domains, from fluid dynamics to particle systems.

As you progress with your own simulations and visualizations, remember that performance is key. Efficient data management, optimization techniques, and leveraging GPU capabilities through shaders will be crucial for making your simulations run smoothly and interactively in real time.

Rendering Large Datasets with OpenGL for Real-Time Interaction

Rendering large datasets in real-time is one of the most challenging aspects of scientific visualizations. Whether you are working with molecular data, geospatial data, or environmental simulations, OpenGL provides the tools needed to handle and visualize large datasets with high performance.

However, to efficiently render large datasets, several strategies need to be employed, such as **level of detail (LOD) management**, **data compression**, **efficient memory management**, and **rendering techniques** tailored for large-scale data. In this section, we will explore how to efficiently render large datasets in real-time, ensuring high interactivity and smooth performance.

1. Key Strategies for Rendering Large Datasets

When rendering large datasets, the key to maintaining performance is **optimization**. The following strategies will help you achieve smooth, real-time performance with minimal lag and stuttering:
- **Level of Detail (LOD) Techniques**
- **Efficient Data Management**
- **Using Geometry Instancing**
- **Efficient Shading Techniques**

- **Offloading Computation to the GPU**

2. Level of Detail (LOD) Techniques

Level of Detail (LOD) is a crucial technique for optimizing rendering performance when working with large datasets. The idea behind LOD is that objects in the distance require less detail to appear correctly, whereas objects near the camera should be rendered with high detail.

Basic LOD Concepts:

- **Distant Objects**: For objects far from the camera, a simpler version (or a lower resolution) of the model can be used.
- **Near Objects**: Objects closer to the camera should be rendered in their highest resolution, with more detail and geometry.

This reduces the number of vertices and complex shaders required for objects that are far away and therefore less visible. By selectively rendering only the most important details, you can maintain performance while still providing a detailed visualization.

Implementing LOD in OpenGL:

You can implement LOD by creating multiple versions of the same model at different levels of detail. As the camera moves closer or farther from an object, you can switch between these versions using distance-based criteria.

```cpp
// Compute distance from the camera to the object
float distanceToCamera = glm::length(cameraPosition -
objectPosition);

// Choose which LOD model to use based on the distance
int lodLevel = 0; // Default LOD
if (distanceToCamera > farThreshold) {
```

```
    lodLevel = 2; // Low detail
} else if (distanceToCamera > mediumThreshold) {
    lodLevel = 1; // Medium detail
} else {
    lodLevel = 0; // High detail
}

// Load and render the corresponding LOD model
renderLODModel(lodLevel);
```

You can create multiple versions of each object using different vertex densities (e.g., high, medium, and low poly versions) and choose the appropriate model based on the camera's position.

3. Efficient Data Management

When working with large datasets, managing memory efficiently is critical to maintaining performance. This includes using **Vertex Buffer Objects (VBOs)**, **Index Buffer Objects (IBOs)**, and **textures** that store large amounts of data but are only updated when necessary.

Using VBOs and IBOs for Large Data Sets:

- **Vertex Buffer Objects (VBOs)**: VBOs store vertex data (positions, colors, normals, etc.) in GPU memory, making it faster to access and render large amounts of data. This is much more efficient than repeatedly uploading data to the GPU every frame.
- **Index Buffer Objects (IBOs)**: IBOs allow you to reuse vertex data for different objects by referencing vertex indices instead of duplicating data. This reduces the size of the data that needs to be stored in memory and lowers the computational cost.

cpp

358

```
GLuint VBO, IBO;
glGenBuffers(1, &VBO);
glBindBuffer(GL_ARRAY_BUFFER, VBO);
// Upload vertex data to GPU memory

glGenBuffers(1, &IBO);
glBindBuffer(GL_ELEMENT_ARRAY_BUFFER, IBO);
// Upload index data to GPU memory

// Render the object using VBO and IBO
glDrawElements(GL_TRIANGLES, numIndices, GL_UNSIGNED_INT, 0);
```

These techniques significantly reduce the memory footprint, allowing the system to handle larger datasets.

4. Using Geometry Instancing

For large datasets where many objects share the same geometry but have different transformations (such as position, rotation, and scale), **geometry instancing** is an effective optimization technique. By instancing, you can render multiple objects with a single draw call, drastically reducing the number of GPU calls.

For example, in a simulation of stars in a galaxy, each star would have the same mesh but a different position. Rather than issuing a draw call for each star, you can batch all of the stars into a single instanced draw call.

```cpp
// Generate model matrices for instancing (e.g., positions for
each object)
std::vector<glm::mat4> modelMatrices =
generateInstanceTransforms(numObjects);

// Set up instancing
glBindVertexArray(vao);
glBindBuffer(GL_ARRAY_BUFFER, instanceVBO);
glBufferData(GL_ARRAY_BUFFER, modelMatrices.size() *
```

359

```
sizeof(glm::mat4), &modelMatrices[0], GL_STATIC_DRAW);

// Render all instances with a single draw call
glDrawArraysInstanced(GL_TRIANGLES, 0, numVertices, numObjects);
```

This approach significantly reduces the number of draw calls and increases rendering efficiency, making it ideal for large-scale simulations.

5. Efficient Shading Techniques

Shaders are crucial when rendering large datasets, but they can also be a bottleneck if not optimized. To render large datasets efficiently, use **simplified shaders** for distant objects or low-detail objects and **optimized shaders** that use minimal computations per pixel.

Shader Optimization Tips:

- **Avoid complex conditionals** in fragment shaders that can reduce performance.
- Use **texture atlases** for efficient texture sampling, especially when multiple objects share the same textures.
- **Precompute lighting and other calculations** when possible, or move computations to the vertex shader where appropriate.

```cpp
#version 330 core

// Simplified fragment shader for distant objects
in vec3 fragColor; // Color from vertex shader
out vec4 finalColor;

void main() {
    finalColor = vec4(fragColor, 1.0); // Simple color
    pass-through
```

```
}
```

By reducing the number of calculations performed per fragment and simplifying shaders, you can greatly improve rendering performance, especially for large datasets.

6. Offloading Computation to the GPU

One of the most powerful aspects of OpenGL is the ability to offload computational work to the GPU. This can be particularly useful when dealing with large datasets or simulations that involve many calculations.

Using Compute Shaders:

Compute shaders allow you to perform general-purpose computations on the GPU. You can use compute shaders to precompute data, such as physics simulations or complex mathematical operations, and then transfer that data to the GPU for rendering.

```cpp
#version 430 core
layout (local_size_x = 16, local_size_y = 16) in;

buffer Data {
    float values[];
};

void main() {
    uint index = gl_GlobalInvocationID.x;
    // Perform calculations here (e.g., update fluid simulation)
    values[index] = values[index] * 0.99; // Example computation
}
```

By offloading simulations or data processing tasks to the GPU using compute shaders, you can free up the CPU for other tasks and take full advantage of the parallelism offered by modern GPUs.

7. Optimizing Data Loading and Streaming

In scientific visualizations, data sets can often be too large to load all at once into memory. **Streaming data** from disk or other storage solutions (such as cloud storage) is essential for rendering large datasets.

Streaming Techniques:

- **Paged Data Loading**: Load data in "chunks" or "tiles" based on the camera's position or the region of interest. For example, if visualizing terrain, load only the portion of the terrain visible in the camera's view frustum.
- **Data Compression**: Compress the data on disk and decompress it in real-time as it's needed for rendering.

By using these techniques, you can keep memory usage low and only load the data necessary for rendering at any given time.

Rendering large datasets in real-time with OpenGL requires careful consideration of performance and memory management. By employing techniques such as Level of Detail (LOD), geometry instancing, efficient texture management, and offloading computation to the GPU, you can achieve interactive frame rates even with large datasets. Additionally, optimizations such as using VBOs, IBOs, and compute shaders will allow you to process and render complex scientific visualizations with high efficiency.

Ultimately, mastering the ability to render large datasets in real-time is a critical skill for scientific visualization and simulation, and OpenGL provides the tools to do so effectively.

Virtual Reality with OpenGL

Setting up OpenGL for VR Applications (Oculus, HTC Vive, etc.)

Virtual Reality (VR) is one of the most immersive technologies available today, offering users a fully interactive and engaging experience. With the rise of consumer-grade VR hardware, like the **Oculus Rift**, **HTC Vive**, and **PlayStation VR**, developers have the opportunity to create sophisticated VR applications and games that leverage the capabilities of OpenGL for high-performance rendering and real-time interactivity.

In this chapter, we will dive into how to set up OpenGL for VR applications. We will cover the essentials of working with VR hardware, including creating VR-ready applications with OpenGL, integrating with popular VR SDKs, and optimizing performance for an immersive experience. Whether you are developing for **Oculus**, **HTC Vive**, or other VR platforms, understanding the underlying principles and tools for VR development will allow you to create high-quality, smooth, and responsive virtual environments.

1. Introduction to VR Development with OpenGL

Virtual reality applications often require real-time rendering of immersive 3D environments with high frame rates, low latency, and accurate motion tracking. While OpenGL is a powerful tool for creating 3D environments, VR development introduces additional challenges such as stereoscopic rendering, motion sickness reduction, and handling VR hardware features like controllers and head tracking.

Unlike traditional 3D graphics development, VR development typically involves rendering to two distinct views (one for each eye) and synchronizing these views with the head movements of the user. Additionally, VR applications demand high frame rates—ideally 90Hz or more—to ensure a smooth, comfortable experience. This chapter will walk you through setting up OpenGL for VR development, starting with the necessary VR hardware and SDKs.

2. Understanding the Basics of VR Hardware

To set up OpenGL for VR applications, it's essential to understand how VR hardware works. While the specifics may vary depending on the headset (Oculus Rift, HTC Vive, etc.), most VR systems share common components:

- **Headset**: The headset provides a stereoscopic display and tracks the movement of the user's head. Each eye has a separate screen, and the two screens are rendered with slightly different views to simulate depth and create a 3D effect.
- **Motion Tracking**: VR headsets use sensors (such as gyroscopes, accelerometers, and external cameras) to track the movement of the user's head. This tracking data is crucial for adjusting the rendered scene to match the user's perspective in real time.
- **Controllers**: VR controllers allow users to interact with the virtual world. These controllers are tracked in space and provide input in terms of position, orientation, button presses, and touchpad interactions.
- **Cameras and Sensors**: In systems like the HTC Vive, external cameras or sensors are used to track the user's movement within a play area, allowing for room-scale VR experiences.

The goal of setting up OpenGL for VR is to ensure that the rendering pipeline is optimized for these hardware components and that the user has a fluid, realistic experience.

3. Required SDKs for VR Development

To interact with VR hardware through OpenGL, you'll need to work with an appropriate SDK (Software Development Kit). Different VR platforms offer SDKs that abstract away the complexity of hardware interactions and make it easier to render 3D environments.

1. Oculus SDK

The Oculus SDK is specifically designed to work with Oculus headsets (like the **Oculus Rift** and **Oculus Quest**). It provides tools for handling head tracking, controller input, rendering for the Oculus display, and more.

Key features of the Oculus SDK:

- **Tracking**: Includes head tracking and controller tracking.
- **Rendering**: Provides functions for stereoscopic rendering, asynchronous timewarp, and foveated rendering.
- **Input**: Handles input from Oculus Touch controllers and the Oculus Remote.

To set up OpenGL with the Oculus SDK, you would typically:

- Initialize the Oculus SDK and create an **Oculus Rift** runtime environment.
- Set up **distortion rendering** (for the lens distortion effect) to improve image quality on the curved display.
- Handle stereo rendering (two separate views for each eye).

cpp

```
#include <OVR_CAPI.h>
ovr_InitParams initParams = {0};
ovr_Initialize(&initParams);

// Create Oculus session
ovrSession session;
ovr_Create(&session, nullptr);
```

```cpp
// Retrieve tracking information
ovrTrackingState trackingState = ovr_GetTrackingState(session,
0.0);
```

2. HTC Vive SDK (SteamVR)

The HTC Vive is one of the most popular VR headsets, and it uses the **SteamVR** SDK for integration with OpenGL. SteamVR provides an easy-to-use interface for interacting with the HTC Vive's head tracking and controller input.

Key features of the SteamVR SDK:

- **Tracking**: Tracks the headset and controllers.
- **Controller Input**: Provides access to controller positions, button states, and touchpad inputs.
- **Room-Scale VR**: Supports Vive's room-scale tracking and boundary systems.

To set up OpenGL with SteamVR, you'll:

- Initialize SteamVR and set up the VR compositor for rendering.
- Retrieve tracking data for the headset and controllers.
- Handle multiple eye buffers and render two separate views for stereoscopic vision.

```cpp
cpp

#include <openvr.h>
vr::IVRSystem* vr_system;
vr::VR_Init(&vr_system, vr::VRApplication_Scene);

// Set up the camera matrices for each eye
```

```cpp
vr::HmdMatrix44_t leftEyeProjection =
vr_system->GetProjectionMatrix(vr::Eye_Left, nearClip, farClip);
```

3. Other VR SDKs (e.g., Windows Mixed Reality)

Other platforms like **Windows Mixed Reality** or **PlayStation VR** also offer SDKs tailored to their specific hardware. These SDKs typically include similar functionality for tracking, rendering, and input handling.

For example, the **Windows Mixed Reality SDK** provides integration with **Microsoft's MR headsets** and enables VR development for the **Windows Store**. The SDK offers tools for spatial awareness, input from controllers, and immersive rendering.

4. Setting Up OpenGL for Stereo Rendering

One of the primary challenges of VR is rendering two distinct views: one for each eye. This is known as **stereoscopic rendering**, and OpenGL must be configured to handle the rendering of each eye independently while maintaining high performance.

Stereo Rendering Setup:

In OpenGL, stereo rendering typically involves:

- **Setting up two viewports**: One for the left eye and one for the right eye.
- **Adjusting projection matrices**: The left and right eyes have slightly different perspectives, so the projection matrix must be adjusted accordingly.
- **Rendering two scenes**: Render the same scene twice, once for each eye, ensuring that the camera position is adjusted to create depth.

Code Example: Stereo Rendering Setup

cpp

```
// Set up left and right eye viewports
glViewport(0, 0, screenWidth / 2, screenHeight);
renderLeftEyeView();

glViewport(screenWidth / 2, 0, screenWidth / 2, screenHeight);
renderRightEyeView();
```

To ensure the two eyes have the correct perspective, modify the camera matrix to slightly offset each view (known as **IPD**, or **Interpupillary Distance**, which is the distance between the eyes). The goal is to create a convincing 3D effect by rendering each scene with the right perspective for each eye.

5. Optimizing VR for Performance

VR applications require high frame rates (typically 90 frames per second or higher) to ensure smooth and comfortable experiences. OpenGL offers several optimization techniques to meet this demand:

- **Foveated Rendering**: This technique renders the area in the center of the screen at full resolution while reducing the resolution in the peripheral regions, where the user's eyes have lower visual acuity.
- **Asynchronous Timewarp**: This technique allows for adjusting the image based on the user's head movements after rendering, reducing latency and improving the sense of immersion.
- **Multi-threading**: Offloading the rendering pipeline and physics calculations to multiple threads can significantly improve frame rates in VR applications.
- **Reducing Draw Calls**: Use techniques such as **geometry instancing** to reduce the number of draw calls for static objects.

6. Handling User Input in VR

Interaction is key to a successful VR experience, and OpenGL can be used in conjunction with VR SDKs to handle input from VR controllers and head tracking. The SDKs typically provide functions to access controller

368

positions, button presses, and gestures.

For instance, in the Oculus SDK, the position and orientation of controllers are returned as **OVRInput** objects, which can be used to update objects in the scene or trigger interactions.

Setting up OpenGL for VR applications requires an understanding of both VR hardware and the tools required to interact with it effectively. By utilizing the right SDKs, setting up stereoscopic rendering, and optimizing your application for real-time performance, you can create fully immersive and interactive VR experiences. Whether you are developing for Oculus, HTC Vive, or other VR systems, OpenGL provides a robust platform for rendering high-quality, real-time 3D graphics in virtual reality.

Best Practices for VR Rendering and Performance Optimization

Virtual reality (VR) applications require not only high-quality rendering but also exceptional performance to maintain immersion and prevent discomfort such as motion sickness. Achieving this in VR is challenging because the experience demands **high frame rates (at least 90 FPS)** and **low latency**, which means rendering two separate views (one for each eye) at an even higher frame rate. In addition, minimizing the time between user input and corresponding visual feedback is crucial to avoid disorientation.

In this section, we will discuss **best practices for VR rendering** and **performance optimization** using OpenGL to ensure smooth, immersive, and responsive VR experiences.

1. Achieving High and Consistent Frame Rates

To ensure a smooth VR experience, it's essential to maintain a consistent frame rate of **90 frames per second (FPS)** or higher for both eyes. The typical VR headset has a refresh rate of 90Hz, meaning the display is refreshed 90 times per second, and if the frame rate drops below this, it can cause **motion sickness** or discomfort for users.

Optimizing for High Frame Rates:

- **Efficient Scene Management**: Keep the complexity of the scene manageable by reducing the number of objects and the complexity of their meshes. This means using **Level of Detail (LOD)**, **instancing**, and **culling** (such as **frustum culling**) to render only the objects visible to the camera.

- **Async Timewarp**: Use techniques like **asynchronous timewarp** or **asynchronous reprojection**, which adjust the rendered frame based on the head movements after the rendering process. This helps in reducing latency, especially when the frame rate drops below 90 FPS. It allows for maintaining smooth head tracking even if the rendering frame rate falls short temporarily.

- **Lower Quality for Distant Objects**: Objects that are far from the viewer should be rendered with lower quality (using low-resolution textures or simpler meshes), as they contribute less to the perceived detail.

```cpp
// Example: LOD selection based on camera distance
float distance = glm::length(cameraPosition - objectPosition);
if (distance > LOD_threshold) {
    renderLOD_low();  // Use simplified geometry for distant
    objects
} else {
    renderLOD_high();  // Use high-detail models for close
    objects
}
```

Avoiding Frame Rate Drops:

- **Use efficient shaders**: Avoid complex calculations in fragment shaders, as they can become a bottleneck. For instance, avoid using too many dynamic lighting models when the object is far away or simple.

- **Optimize physics simulations**: Offload heavy physics calculations to compute shaders or use simplified physics models when high precision isn't necessary.

2. Reducing Latency and Improving Responsiveness

In VR, **latency** refers to the delay between the user's action (such as head movement or controller input) and the corresponding visual update in the VR environment. High latency causes a disconnection between the user's actions and the visuals, which can lead to **motion sickness**.

Strategies for Reducing Latency:

- **Double/Triple Buffering**: Use **double buffering** or **triple buffering** to avoid waiting for the GPU to finish rendering before the next frame is processed. This allows for smoother transitions between frames and reduces tearing, a common artifact in VR.

cpp

```cpp
// Use triple buffering for smoother frame transitions in VR
glfwSwapBuffers(window);
```

- **Asynchronous Reprojection**: Many VR SDKs (like **Oculus SDK** and **SteamVR**) support **asynchronous reprojection**. This technique allows the system to adjust the rendered frames after the fact to compensate for dropped frames and minimize latency. Make sure to enable this feature in your VR application to avoid visual stutter.
- **Render Head Movements Separately**: For minimizing latency when tracking head movements, **asynchronous timewarp** is crucial. It allows the application to render new frames even before the full GPU rendering pipeline is finished. This ensures that the user's head movements are reflected quickly.
- **Controller Input Handling**: Ensure that controller inputs are

processed and reflected immediately on the screen to maintain the sense of presence. Using **haptic feedback** can also improve immersion and reduce latency in input recognition.

3. Optimizing Stereo Rendering

Since VR requires rendering two views (one for each eye), it's important to optimize **stereo rendering** to avoid unnecessary computations and to ensure that the GPU doesn't become overwhelmed with redundant rendering tasks.

Best Practices for Stereo Rendering:

- **Optimized Projection Matrices**: In VR, the projection matrices for both eyes need to be adjusted slightly for the inter-pupillary distance (IPD). When rendering each eye's view, OpenGL should adjust the camera's frustum or projection matrix to simulate the separation between the eyes and provide depth to the scene.

cpp

```
// Example of adjusting the projection matrix for each eye
glm::mat4 leftEyeProjection =
glm::perspective(glm::radians(90.0f), aspectRatio, nearClip,
farClip);
leftEyeProjection[3][0] -= ipd / 2.0f;  // Adjust for left eye

glm::mat4 rightEyeProjection =
glm::perspective(glm::radians(90.0f), aspectRatio, nearClip,
farClip);
rightEyeProjection[3][0] += ipd / 2.0f;  // Adjust for right eye
```

- **Avoid Redundant Drawing**: Use techniques such as **instancing** or **frustum culling** to avoid rendering the same objects twice or drawing objects that are not visible to either eye. This minimizes GPU overhead by rendering only visible portions of the scene.

- **Separate Viewports**: Use OpenGL's glViewport function to render each eye to its respective viewport. This allows you to optimize the rendering for both eyes without drawing redundant data.

```cpp
// Set up the viewport for the left eye
glViewport(0, 0, screenWidth / 2, screenHeight);
renderLeftEyeView();

// Set up the viewport for the right eye
glViewport(screenWidth / 2, 0, screenWidth / 2, screenHeight);
renderRightEyeView();
```

4. Minimizing Motion Sickness

Motion sickness in VR is primarily caused by **visual mismatches** between the user's head movements and what's rendered on the screen, or by low frame rates. To minimize discomfort, it is essential to provide fluid motion, stable head tracking, and prevent any visual jitter.

Reducing Motion Sickness:

- **High Frame Rate**: Consistently maintaining a high frame rate (90 FPS or higher) is essential for a smooth experience. Any drop in frame rate can lead to **motion blur** or **stuttering**, which contributes to motion sickness.
- **Smoothing Head Movement**: Ensure that head tracking is as smooth as possible. Use **smoothing algorithms** or **timewarp techniques** to interpolate between frames and avoid abrupt shifts.
- **Visual Stabilization**: Implement **foveated rendering**, where the area around the user's gaze is rendered in higher detail, while peripheral regions are rendered with lower resolution. This both reduces the computational load and improves visual quality in areas where the user is most focused, improving comfort.

- **Comfort Mode and Boundaries**: Implement a **comfort mode** in your VR applications that lets users feel more in control. For example, when the player moves too quickly or experiences jerky movements, you can provide an option to reduce the intensity of movement or implement a **boundaries system** that informs them of the edges of the play area.

5. Performance Optimization Techniques

In addition to rendering optimizations, you should also consider performance strategies specific to VR, which require both low latency and high rendering performance.

Performance Tips for VR:

- **Render in Batches**: Group objects that share the same materials into batches, and draw them all at once, reducing the number of draw calls.
- **Use Simplified Shaders**: For objects that are far away or less important, use simpler shaders. Avoid high-precision calculations in fragment shaders and limit the number of complex lighting models, as these can significantly reduce performance.
- **Efficient Asset Management**: Load and manage large assets efficiently. For VR applications, texture streaming and compressed assets can save a significant amount of memory and improve load times. Use **mipmap levels** for textures to ensure the right level of detail is applied based on the object's distance from the camera.
- **GPU-Accelerated Computation**: Use **compute shaders** to offload non-graphical computations (such as physics calculations or AI logic) to the GPU. This can free up CPU resources for rendering and other tasks.

Optimizing VR rendering and performance is crucial to delivering high-quality, immersive experiences. By ensuring a consistent frame rate, reducing latency, and using advanced techniques like stereo rendering, motion sickness minimization, and GPU optimizations, you can create VR applications that are not only visually stunning but also smooth and comfortable for users.

Incorporating these best practices into your OpenGL-based VR development will help you overcome common challenges and create a seamless, responsive virtual reality experience. By striking the right balance between visual fidelity and performance, you can ensure that your VR application runs smoothly across various hardware platforms, keeping users engaged without discomfort.

Building a Simple VR Application with OpenGL

Now that we've covered the foundational principles of VR rendering and performance optimization, it's time to walk through the process of building a simple VR application using OpenGL. This application will render a basic 3D scene in VR, allow user interaction via motion controllers, and handle head tracking. We'll build this application step-by-step using **Oculus** (or **SteamVR**) and **OpenGL**.

In this tutorial, we'll focus on setting up a simple VR scene with a **VR headset**, rendering to the **stereoscopic display** (one for each eye), and handling basic input like head tracking and controller interaction.

We will assume you already have **OpenGL** set up and are familiar with 3D rendering concepts. The goal is to create a foundational VR app that you can extend and build upon as you become more familiar with VR development in OpenGL.

1. Prerequisites and Tools

Before starting, you'll need to set up the following tools and SDKs for VR development:

- **VR Hardware**: Oculus Rift, HTC Vive, or other supported VR headsets.
- **VR SDK**: For Oculus, the **Oculus SDK**; for HTC Vive, the **SteamVR SDK**.
- **OpenGL**: Ensure that you have an OpenGL development environment set up and functional.
- **GLFW or SDL**: A window management library that supports VR SDK integration.

We'll be using **GLFW** here to manage the window and input, along with **Oculus SDK** for Oculus Rift, but the process is very similar for other platforms like **HTC Vive** and **SteamVR**.

2. Initializing the VR SDK

The first step in building a VR application is to initialize the VR SDK. This involves setting up the VR runtime environment and ensuring that the VR headset is connected and ready for use.

For Oculus (Oculus SDK):

Here's how you can initialize the Oculus SDK:

```cpp
#include <OVR_CAPI.h>  // Oculus SDK header

ovrSession session;
ovrGraphicsLuid luid;
if (OVR_FAILURE(ovr_Initialize(nullptr))) {
    std::cerr << "Oculus SDK initialization failed!" <<
    std::endl;
    return -1;
}

if (OVR_FAILURE(ovr_Create(&session, &luid))) {
    std::cerr << "Failed to create Oculus session!" << std::endl;
    ovr_Shutdown();
```

```
    return -1;
}
```

For SteamVR (HTC Vive):

For HTC Vive, SteamVR SDK is commonly used. To initialize SteamVR with OpenGL, you would typically use the **SteamVR SDK**:

cpp

```
#include <openvr.h>  // SteamVR SDK header

vr::IVRSystem* vrSystem;
vr::EVRInitError eError = vr::VRInitError_None;
vrSystem = vr::VR_Init(&eError, vr::VRApplication_Scene);
if (eError != vr::VRInitError_None) {
    std::cerr << "SteamVR Initialization Failed!" << std::endl;
    return -1;
}
```

3. Setting Up OpenGL for Stereoscopic Rendering

Once the VR headset is initialized, the next step is to set up OpenGL for stereoscopic rendering. This involves rendering two views: one for the left eye and one for the right eye. Each eye needs to see a slightly different view to create the illusion of depth and immersion.

Render Loop:

In the render loop, you need to create two **viewports** (one for each eye) and ensure that the scene is rendered from two slightly different perspectives. Below is a simple example for rendering with Oculus.

cpp

```
// Get the eye poses for the left and right eyes
ovrEyeRenderDesc leftEyeDesc = ovr_GetRenderDesc(session,
ovrEye_Left, EyeFov);
ovrEyeRenderDesc rightEyeDesc = ovr_GetRenderDesc(session,
```

```
ovrEye_Right, EyeFov);

// Set up projections and views for each eye
ovrMatrix4f leftEyeProjection =
ovrMatrix4f_Projection(leftEyeDesc.Fov, 0.1f, 100.0f,
ovrProjection_LeftHanded);
ovrMatrix4f rightEyeProjection =
ovrMatrix4f_Projection(rightEyeDesc.Fov, 0.1f, 100.0f,
ovrProjection_LeftHanded);

ovrMatrix4f leftEyeView = ovrMatrix4f_Translation(0.0f, 0.0f,
0.0f); // Set the view for the left eye
ovrMatrix4f rightEyeView = ovrMatrix4f_Translation(0.0f, 0.0f,
0.0f); // Set the view for the right eye

// Create frame buffers for both eyes
GLuint leftEyeFrameBuffer, rightEyeFrameBuffer;
glGenFramebuffers(1, &leftEyeFrameBuffer);
glGenFramebuffers(1, &rightEyeFrameBuffer);

// Render the scene for the left eye
glBindFramebuffer(GL_FRAMEBUFFER, leftEyeFrameBuffer);
glViewport(0, 0, width / 2, height);
renderScene(leftEyeProjection, leftEyeView);

// Render the scene for the right eye
glBindFramebuffer(GL_FRAMEBUFFER, rightEyeFrameBuffer);
glViewport(width / 2, 0, width / 2, height);
renderScene(rightEyeProjection, rightEyeView);
```

In the example above, we render the scene to two different framebuffers, one for each eye, using OpenGL's **framebuffer objects (FBOs)**. After rendering the scene for both eyes, the next step is to combine the results into a final stereo image.

4. Handling User Input (Controller and Head Tracking)

VR applications require handling various types of input, such as head movements and controller actions. VR headsets use **motion tracking** to

378

detect head movements, and controllers (like the **Oculus Touch** or **HTC Vive controllers**) allow users to interact with the environment.

Head Tracking:

Head tracking is typically already provided by the VR SDK (such as **Oculus SDK** or **SteamVR**), and it can be accessed to update the user's viewpoint based on their head movements.

cpp

```cpp
// Get the current head pose (position and orientation)
ovrPosef headPose = ovr_GetTrackingState(session, 0).HeadPose;

// Extract the position and orientation
glm::vec3 headPosition = glm::vec3(headPose.Position.x,
headPose.Position.y, headPose.Position.z);
glm::quat headOrientation = glm::quat(headPose.Orientation.w,
headPose.Orientation.x, headPose.Orientation.y,
headPose.Orientation.z);

// Apply head movement to the camera view
cameraPosition = headPosition;
cameraOrientation = headOrientation;
```

Controller Input:

Controller input is crucial for interaction in VR. For Oculus, controllers are tracked and provide data about button presses, touchpad input, and spatial tracking.

cpp

```cpp
// Get input data from Oculus controllers
ovrControllerType controllerType =
ovr_GetConnectedControllers(session);
ovrInputState controllerState = ovr_GetInputState(session,
controllerType);

// Process input for action (e.g., button press or motion)
```

```
if (controllerState.Buttons & ovrButton_A) {
    // Handle "A" button press
}
```

5. Rendering the Final Scene

Once the left and right-eye views have been rendered, the final step is to display these frames on the headset. You can do this by submitting the rendered frames to the **VR SDK** for display.

For Oculus:

cpp

```cpp
// Submit the left and right eye frames to the Oculus SDK for
display
ovr_CommitTextureSwapChain(session, leftEyeTexture);
ovr_CommitTextureSwapChain(session, rightEyeTexture);
```

For HTC Vive (SteamVR):

cpp

```cpp
// Submit left and right eye render targets to SteamVR
vrSystem->Submit(vr::Eye_Left, leftEyeTexture);
vrSystem->Submit(vr::Eye_Right, rightEyeTexture);
```

Building a simple VR application with OpenGL involves several steps, from initializing the VR SDK to rendering stereoscopic images and handling user input. By following these practices, you can develop a basic VR environment that leverages OpenGL's powerful graphics rendering capabilities and provides an immersive experience for users.

As you become more familiar with the VR development process, you can add more advanced features such as **interactive objects, real-time**

physics, **advanced lighting**, and more, but this foundational knowledge will give you a strong starting point for all future VR applications.

Debugging and Profiling OpenGL Applications

Common OpenGL Errors and How to Troubleshoot Them

Developing OpenGL applications can sometimes be a challenging process, particularly when dealing with complex scenes, advanced rendering techniques, or performance bottlenecks. OpenGL, like many graphics APIs, has its own set of pitfalls that developers need to identify and troubleshoot. Debugging OpenGL applications effectively is crucial for achieving high-quality, efficient, and error-free rendering.

In this chapter, we will explore some of the most common OpenGL errors you might encounter during development, as well as techniques and tools to troubleshoot them efficiently. From misconfigured shaders to performance issues and rendering artifacts, understanding how to identify and fix OpenGL problems is essential for any graphics programmer.

1. Understanding OpenGL Error Reporting

OpenGL has a set of mechanisms for error reporting, but its default error handling system can be somewhat minimalistic. The API itself doesn't throw exceptions or provide detailed error messages. Instead, it sets an error flag that can be queried using the function **glGetError()**.

This function returns an **error code** that represents the type of error encountered. If there are no errors, it returns **GL_NO_ERROR**. If an error has occurred, it returns an appropriate error code, such as:

- **GL_INVALID_ENUM**: An unacceptable enum value was provided.
- **GL_INVALID_VALUE**: A numerical value out of range was used.
- **GL_INVALID_OPERATION**: The function was called in an inappropriate context.
- **GL_OUT_OF_MEMORY**: The operation cannot be completed due to insufficient memory.

How to Use glGetError() Effectively:

To check for errors in OpenGL, you should periodically call **glGetError()** in your application to identify issues. This is especially useful after function calls that could potentially trigger errors, such as those that set state or allocate resources.

```cpp
GLenum error = glGetError();
if (error != GL_NO_ERROR) {
    std::cerr << "OpenGL Error: " << error << std::endl;
}
```

However, **glGetError()** can be somewhat slow if used excessively in the main rendering loop. As a result, it's typically best used during the debugging phase or in parts of the application where you suspect issues.

2. Debugging Shaders

Shaders are often the source of many OpenGL issues. Problems in shaders can manifest as incorrect rendering, broken visuals, or crashes. Here are some common shader-related errors and how to troubleshoot them.

Shader Compilation Errors

A shader will fail to compile if there's an issue with its syntax or structure. You can retrieve detailed error messages using **glGetShaderiv()** and **glGetShaderInfoLog()** functions, which provide insight into the cause of the error.

Here's an example of how to check for shader compilation errors:

cpp

```cpp
GLuint shader = glCreateShader(GL_VERTEX_SHADER);
const char* shaderSource = "your shader code here";
glShaderSource(shader, 1, &shaderSource, nullptr);
glCompileShader(shader);

// Check for compilation errors
GLint success;
glGetShaderiv(shader, GL_COMPILE_STATUS, &success);
if (!success) {
    GLchar infoLog[512];
    glGetShaderInfoLog(shader, 512, nullptr, infoLog);
    std::cerr << "Shader Compilation Failed: " << infoLog <<
    std::endl;
}
```

This will output the exact error messages related to shader compilation.

Linking Errors

After compiling shaders, you must link them into a program. If there's a mismatch between the attributes and uniforms, or other issues, linking will fail. Use **glGetProgramiv()** and **glGetProgramInfoLog()** to check for errors in linking.

cpp

```cpp
GLuint shaderProgram = glCreateProgram();
glAttachShader(shaderProgram, vertexShader);
glAttachShader(shaderProgram, fragmentShader);
glLinkProgram(shaderProgram);

// Check for linking errors
GLint success;
glGetProgramiv(shaderProgram, GL_LINK_STATUS, &success);
```

```
if (!success) {
    GLchar infoLog[512];
    glGetProgramInfoLog(shaderProgram, 512, nullptr, infoLog);
    std::cerr << "Program Linking Failed: " << infoLog <<
    std::endl;
}
```

Common Shader Issues:

- **Attribute Mismatches**: Ensure that the attributes in your vertex shader (e.g., position, color, normal) match those in the vertex array and buffer.
- **Uninitialized Uniforms**: Always check that all uniforms (e.g., transformation matrices, lighting parameters) are initialized before use.

3. Debugging OpenGL State Issues

OpenGL is a **state machine**, meaning it operates based on a series of states that can affect subsequent rendering calls. Problems arise when OpenGL's state is not what you expect it to be. Common issues include:

- Incorrect **blend mode** settings.
- **Depth testing** being turned off when it should be on.
- **Culling** settings leading to unwanted faces being drawn.

Checking OpenGL States:

To troubleshoot OpenGL state issues, you can manually query the current OpenGL state using **glIsEnabled()** or **glGet()** functions.

Example: Checking if **depth testing** is enabled:

cpp

```
if (!glIsEnabled(GL_DEPTH_TEST)) {
    std::cerr << "Depth testing is disabled!" << std::endl;
}
```

Additionally, tools like **OpenGL Debug Output** and **OpenGL Profiler** (available in most graphics card drivers) allow you to automatically capture state changes and any error messages related to OpenGL commands.

4. Common Rendering Issues

In OpenGL applications, various rendering issues can arise from incorrect settings or faulty code. These issues can be hard to pin down, but understanding common problems can help.

Black or Blank Screen:

This is a frequent issue when rendering in OpenGL, typically caused by one of the following:

- **Improper projection or view matrices**: Make sure your view and projection matrices are correctly configured.
- **Clear color not set**: If you forget to set the clear color, OpenGL might not properly clear the buffer.

```cpp
glClearColor(0.0f, 0.0f, 0.0f, 1.0f);  // Set clear color to
black
glClear(GL_COLOR_BUFFER_BIT | GL_DEPTH_BUFFER_BIT);  // Clear
the color and depth buffers
```

Textures Not Showing:

If textures are not being applied correctly, the issue might be with:

- **Incorrect texture coordinates**: Ensure that your 3D model has proper texture coordinates and the correct shader is being used to apply them.
- **Texture unit binding**: Ensure that the texture is bound to the correct texture unit before use in the shader.

386

```cpp
glActiveTexture(GL_TEXTURE0); // Activate texture unit 0
glBindTexture(GL_TEXTURE_2D, textureID);  // Bind the texture
```

Z-Fighting (Depth Issues):

When two objects are very close to each other in the Z-axis, OpenGL may have difficulty determining which one is in front, leading to flickering or z-fighting. You can solve this by:

- **Adjusting near and far clipping planes**.
- **Disabling depth writes** for certain objects if not necessary.

```cpp
glDepthFunc(GL_LESS);  // Use "less" depth comparison for proper
z-buffering
```

5. Tools for Debugging and Profiling OpenGL Applications

To streamline debugging and profiling OpenGL applications, several tools and libraries are available:

OpenGL Debug Output

This feature is available in modern OpenGL implementations and allows you to capture debug messages from OpenGL. By enabling it, you can receive real-time feedback from the OpenGL driver about issues like invalid state changes, performance bottlenecks, and more.

```cpp
glEnable(GL_DEBUG_OUTPUT);
glDebugMessageCallback(myDebugCallbackFunction, nullptr); // Set
your debug callback function
```

387

Graphics Debuggers

- **RenderDoc**: A powerful graphics debugger that allows you to capture OpenGL frames and inspect the state of your application at any point during rendering.
- **gDEBugger**: A tool for OpenGL and OpenCL debugging, providing detailed insight into OpenGL state changes and error messages.
- **NVIDIA Nsight**: A profiling and debugging tool that provides performance metrics, OpenGL-specific debugging, and the ability to trace GPU commands.

GPU Profilers

- **NVIDIA Nsight** and **Intel GPA** provide performance profiling tools to measure GPU activity and optimize your rendering pipeline.
- **OpenGL Timer Queries**: Use **timer queries** to measure how long certain rendering operations take, which is especially useful for identifying bottlenecks.

```cpp
GLuint query;
glGenQueries(1, &query);
glBeginQuery(GL_TIME_ELAPSED, query);
// Render commands you want to profile
glEndQuery(GL_TIME_ELAPSED);
```

Debugging and profiling OpenGL applications can be complex, but with the right approach and tools, it becomes significantly easier. By understanding common errors, using OpenGL's error reporting mechanisms, and integrating debugging tools into your workflow, you can efficiently identify and resolve issues in your OpenGL applications. This chapter has covered essential strategies for debugging shaders, handling OpenGL states, and optimizing rendering performance. By adopting these best practices, you'll be well-equipped to build robust, high-performance OpenGL applications.

Using OpenGL Debugging Tools (e.g., gDEBugger, RenderDoc)

Debugging OpenGL applications can be complex, especially when dealing with advanced rendering techniques or performance issues. Fortunately, there are several powerful tools available that can help developers gain deeper insights into the behavior of OpenGL applications and identify problems at a much more granular level. These tools allow for real-time inspection of OpenGL states, resource management, frame-by-frame debugging, and more. Two of the most popular OpenGL debugging and profiling tools are **gDEBugger** and **RenderDoc**.

In this section, we will discuss how to use these tools to streamline your debugging process and resolve OpenGL issues more effectively.

1. gDEBugger

gDEBugger is a powerful OpenGL debugger and profiler that allows you to trace OpenGL calls and analyze their effects on rendering and performance. It provides a comprehensive set of features for debugging shaders, identifying performance bottlenecks, and inspecting OpenGL objects.

Key Features of gDEBugger:
- **OpenGL Call Tracing**: gDEBugger logs all OpenGL calls made by your application, showing detailed information about every function call, its parameters, and the state changes triggered by it.
- **Shader Debugging**: gDEBugger allows you to inspect, debug, and step through shaders (both vertex and fragment shaders). This is invaluable for tracking down rendering errors that might be caused by incorrect shader logic.
- **Resource Inspection**: You can view and analyze OpenGL resources

389

such as textures, buffers, shaders, and framebuffers. This allows you to spot issues like incorrect texture bindings, uninitialized buffers, or problems with resource usage.

- **State Inspector**: gDEBugger provides a state inspector that lets you inspect the current state of OpenGL objects and configurations, such as the active texture units, shader programs, framebuffers, etc. This is useful for understanding why something may not be rendering as expected.

Using gDEBugger:

To use gDEBugger, you'll typically need to:

1. **Install gDEBugger**: Download and install gDEBugger from the official website (note that it is no longer actively maintained but still works well for debugging OpenGL applications).
2. **Integrate gDEBugger with Your Application**: During development, you can link your application with gDEBugger's SDK, or you can launch your application from gDEBugger directly.
3. **Enable OpenGL Tracing**: Once integrated, gDEBugger can trace OpenGL calls, track your resource usage, and analyze your shaders as they execute.
4. **Analyze the Results**: gDEBugger provides detailed logging for each OpenGL function call, which you can use to identify potential issues. For example, you can check if OpenGL errors are triggered after specific function calls or identify excessive GPU memory usage.

Example Use Case:

Suppose you notice a strange graphical artifact in your OpenGL application. By using gDEBugger, you can track each OpenGL call leading to the artifact and inspect the state changes involved. You can also check if any OpenGL errors were raised during rendering.

2. RenderDoc

RenderDoc is another highly popular and widely used graphics debugger that focuses on frame capturing, GPU state inspection, and shader debugging. It's an open-source tool that supports not only OpenGL but also other APIs like Vulkan, DirectX, and Metal. RenderDoc allows you to capture and analyze individual frames, providing a detailed snapshot of everything happening during rendering.

Key Features of RenderDoc:

- **Frame Capture and Replay**: One of RenderDoc's most powerful features is its ability to capture a single frame from your application and replay it. This enables you to analyze how the scene was rendered, step through OpenGL calls, and inspect GPU resources like textures and buffers at any point in the frame.
- **Shader Debugging**: RenderDoc lets you pause the execution of a frame and examine the shaders as they are compiled and executed. You can step through each instruction in a shader, inspect input/output variables, and identify issues with shader logic.
- **GPU State Inspection**: RenderDoc provides a detailed breakdown of the GPU's state at any point during frame rendering. You can inspect things like bound shaders, textures, buffers, and uniform values. This helps identify issues with resource bindings or incorrect state configurations.
- **Performance Analysis**: RenderDoc includes some basic profiling features that help you spot performance bottlenecks, such as expensive OpenGL calls or inefficient resource usage. It can show how long each GPU operation took and how resources were accessed.

Using RenderDoc:

1. **Install RenderDoc**: Download and install RenderDoc from its official GitHub page or website.
2. **Capture a Frame**: After launching your OpenGL application with RenderDoc, use the tool's hotkey (typically F12) to capture a frame.

COMPUTER GRAPHICS WITH OPENGL

This will pause your application and allow you to inspect all the OpenGL calls made during that frame.

3. **Inspect the Frame**: RenderDoc will provide a frame-by-frame view of the OpenGL state at the time of capture. You can use the GUI to navigate through all the OpenGL calls, inspect the state of each object, and check the contents of textures, buffers, and framebuffers.

4. **Shader Debugging**: If the issue is shader-related, RenderDoc lets you inspect the compiled GLSL code and even step through the shader's execution. You can check the values of inputs and outputs at each stage of the shader pipeline.

5. **Performance Profiling**: RenderDoc also shows how much time each OpenGL operation took during the frame. This can help you identify GPU bottlenecks, such as expensive draw calls or inefficient resource accesses.

Example Use Case:

Let's say you are working on a 3D scene and you're noticing performance issues, but you aren't sure whether the problem lies in the shaders, the draw calls, or texture management. By using RenderDoc, you can capture a frame, inspect the shader code and GPU state, and identify whether a specific draw call is taking too long or whether textures are being accessed inefficiently. This detailed analysis allows you to optimize the rendering pipeline.

3. Other OpenGL Debugging and Profiling Tools

While gDEBugger and RenderDoc are two of the most well-known tools, there are several other useful utilities for debugging OpenGL applications:

- **OpenGL Debug Output**: OpenGL 4.3 and later versions include the **Debug Output** functionality. This feature allows OpenGL to report errors and warnings automatically to the application through a callback. You can enable this by calling **glEnable(GL_DEBUG_OUT PUT)** and setting up a callback function to handle messages.

```cpp
glEnable(GL_DEBUG_OUTPUT);
glDebugMessageCallback(MessageCallback, nullptr);

// Define a simple debug callback function
void APIENTRY MessageCallback(GLenum source, GLenum type, GLuint
id, GLenum severity,
                              GLsizei length, const GLchar*
                              message, const void* userParam)
{
    std::cerr << "OpenGL Debug Message: " << message <<
    std::endl;
}
```

- **NVidia Nsight**: Nsight is a suite of profiling and debugging tools available from NVIDIA for debugging OpenGL, Vulkan, and CUDA applications. It includes GPU performance counters, memory inspection, and shader debugging.
- **Intel GPA (Graphics Performance Analyzers)**: Intel GPA is another powerful tool for profiling and optimizing graphics applications. It provides frame-by-frame performance analysis, helping you identify bottlenecks and inefficient GPU operations.

Debugging OpenGL applications can be challenging, but with the right tools and techniques, you can effectively identify and resolve issues. By using tools like **gDEBugger** and **RenderDoc**, you can track OpenGL calls, inspect resources, debug shaders, and analyze performance bottlenecks with a high level of detail. Additionally, utilizing built-in OpenGL features like **debug output** can streamline your debugging process.

393

Profiling OpenGL Applications for Performance Bottlenecks

Performance profiling is one of the most critical aspects of optimizing OpenGL applications. In complex 3D rendering applications, performance bottlenecks can arise from various sources such as inefficient shaders, excessive draw calls, poor memory management, and unoptimized resource management. Profiling helps you identify these bottlenecks and enables you to take corrective action, ensuring that your application runs efficiently even under heavy workloads.

In this section, we'll explore how to profile OpenGL applications for performance issues and how to leverage profiling tools to track down and resolve bottlenecks.

1. Why Profiling is Important

Profiling allows developers to analyze the execution of their OpenGL code and pinpoint areas that negatively impact performance. Without profiling, it's easy to optimize blindly or make assumptions about where performance issues are originating. By gathering data on GPU utilization, frame rendering times, and resource usage, profiling offers clear insights into where improvements are needed.

Key metrics you should track during profiling include:

- **Frame Time**: The amount of time it takes to render one frame. This is a key metric for ensuring smooth, real-time performance.
- **GPU Utilization**: The amount of time the GPU is actively processing commands and rendering frames.
- **Draw Calls**: The number of individual rendering commands issued by the CPU to the GPU.
- **Memory Usage**: The amount of GPU and CPU memory used for textures, buffers, shaders, and other resources.
- **Shader Performance**: The time spent in the vertex and fragment shaders, including any inefficiencies like redundant operations.

By understanding these metrics, you can identify the most resource-intensive parts of your application and prioritize optimizations accordingly.

2. OpenGL Performance Profiling Tools

Several tools can be used to profile OpenGL applications and identify performance bottlenecks. These tools typically allow you to capture detailed performance data for your OpenGL calls and inspect the GPU's state. Some of the most widely used tools for OpenGL profiling include:

A. OpenGL Profiler

The **OpenGL Profiler** is a built-in feature of the macOS platform that allows developers to analyze the performance of OpenGL applications. It provides detailed statistics about frame rendering time, resource usage, and GPU performance, making it ideal for troubleshooting performance issues.

Key features of the OpenGL Profiler:

- **Frame Analysis**: You can capture a frame and analyze its performance, including how much time was spent on each stage of the pipeline (vertex processing, fragment shading, etc.).
- **Resource Usage**: The profiler provides detailed memory usage statistics for buffers, textures, and shaders, helping to identify memory leaks or inefficient resource allocation.
- **GPU Time Profiling**: It shows how much time is spent in various GPU operations, such as drawing primitives, processing shaders, and rasterization.

B. NVIDIA NSight

NVIDIA NSight is a powerful performance analysis and debugging tool designed for CUDA and OpenGL applications running on NVIDIA GPUs. It provides in-depth insights into both the CPU and GPU aspects of your application, allowing you to track GPU utilization, memory bandwidth, and shader execution times.

Key features of NSight:

- **GPU Trace**: It captures the GPU's execution timeline, which allows you to visualize the relationship between CPU commands and GPU execution.
- **Shader Profiling**: You can drill down into individual shader stages to analyze execution times, idle times, and how well your shaders are performing.
- **Frame Debugging**: Just like RenderDoc, NSight can capture and replay frames, allowing you to isolate performance bottlenecks in specific scenes.

C. AMD Radeon™ GPU Profiler

The **AMD Radeon GPU Profiler** is a tool designed for AMD GPUs that enables developers to monitor and optimize the performance of their OpenGL applications. It allows you to measure key performance indicators like GPU usage, bottlenecks, and memory utilization.

Key features of the Radeon GPU Profiler:

- **Pipeline Analysis**: This tool breaks down the OpenGL pipeline into its constituent stages and provides detailed performance data for each stage, allowing you to isolate the source of performance issues.
- **Shader and Pipeline Optimization**: The profiler shows the time taken by shaders and pipeline stages, helping you optimize shader code and improve overall performance.
- **Memory Usage**: The profiler tracks memory usage for buffers, textures, and other GPU resources, helping you detect memory leaks and inefficient resource allocation.

D. RenderDoc

Although **RenderDoc** is primarily a graphics debugger, it also includes powerful profiling capabilities. RenderDoc can capture and replay frames while providing detailed information on GPU resource usage and performance bottlenecks.

Key features of RenderDoc for profiling:

- **Frame Capture**: RenderDoc allows you to capture an individual frame and analyze the GPU state, helping you understand how resources are being used and where time is spent.
- **GPU Metrics**: It displays GPU performance metrics such as time spent on shader execution, memory usage, and the time spent in each stage of the OpenGL pipeline.
- **Shader Performance**: RenderDoc can show the time spent in each shader stage, enabling you to identify expensive or inefficient shader code that may be impacting performance.

3. Profiling Common Performance Bottlenecks

Once you've chosen your profiling tool, the next step is to focus on the most common performance bottlenecks in OpenGL applications. Here are some of the most frequent issues you might encounter:

A. Excessive Draw Calls

Each draw call issued by the CPU involves a switch in OpenGL state, which can cause performance overhead. Excessive draw calls can result in lower performance, especially if the objects being rendered share common properties (e.g., textures, shaders).

How to troubleshoot:

- Use **instancing** to render many identical objects with a single draw call.
- Use **batching** techniques to group similar objects together before rendering.
- Use **occlusion culling** to avoid rendering objects that are not visible in the current view.

B. Inefficient Shaders

Shaders that perform complex or redundant calculations can become performance bottlenecks. Inefficient vertex or fragment shaders may cause high execution times or unnecessary GPU power consumption.

How to troubleshoot:

- Use **shader profiling** tools like **gDEBugger**, **NVIDIA Nsight**, or **RenderDoc** to check shader performance.
- Look for opportunities to simplify shader operations or precompute values on the CPU.
- Avoid heavy loops or conditionals in shaders and prefer simpler, optimized math operations.

C. Texture and Buffer Binding

Frequent texture or buffer binding changes can slow down performance by forcing the GPU to reallocate resources or invalidate caches. This is particularly problematic if textures or buffers are frequently bound and unbound in a render loop.

How to troubleshoot:

- Minimize texture and buffer state changes by grouping similar resources together.
- Use **texture atlases** to pack multiple textures into a single texture, reducing binding overhead.
- Batch resources so that you minimize the number of binding operations.

D. Inefficient Memory Usage

Improper use of GPU memory, such as allocating too many buffers, using too much texture memory, or failing to clean up resources properly, can lead to poor performance. Memory bandwidth is often a limiting factor, especially in high-resolution scenes or complex simulations.

How to troubleshoot:

- Use memory profiling tools to check GPU memory usage and identify potential leaks or unnecessary allocations.
- Make sure to clean up unused resources by deleting textures, buffers, and shaders when they're no longer needed.
- Optimize your data layout and access patterns to reduce memory

access latency.

4. Performance Optimization Techniques

Once you've identified the bottlenecks in your OpenGL application, it's time to implement optimizations. Here are some key techniques that can help you boost performance:

- **Batching and Instancing**: Reduces the number of draw calls, which can drastically improve performance in scenes with many objects.
- **Level of Detail (LOD)**: Reduces the complexity of objects that are farther away from the camera, decreasing GPU load.
- **Frustum Culling**: Ensures that only visible objects are rendered, preventing unnecessary computations for objects outside the camera view.
- **Use of VAOs and VBOs**: Optimizes vertex and index buffer usage to minimize CPU-GPU communication overhead.
- **Multithreading**: Offloads non-OpenGL tasks to separate CPU threads to ensure that the rendering thread remains focused on drawing.

Profiling and debugging OpenGL applications is an essential skill for any graphics programmer. By using powerful tools like **gDEBugger**, **RenderDoc**, and other GPU profiling tools, you can pinpoint and address performance bottlenecks that would otherwise be difficult to identify. Whether you're optimizing draw calls, shaders, or memory usage, the key to efficient OpenGL development is a systematic approach to performance analysis.

Optimizing Shader Code and Reducing Runtime Overhead

Shaders are a critical component in OpenGL applications, particularly in complex 3D graphics and games. They are executed on the GPU, and their performance can significantly affect the overall rendering efficiency of your application. Optimizing shader code is essential to ensure that shaders run as efficiently as possible, especially when targeting high-performance applications or VR environments where low latency and smooth rendering are paramount.

In this section, we will discuss various strategies and techniques for optimizing your shader code and reducing the associated runtime overhead. We'll cover both vertex and fragment shaders, as well as general best practices that can be applied across all types of shaders.

1. Minimize Shader Complexity

One of the most direct ways to optimize shader performance is by minimizing the computational complexity of the code. Complex calculations in shaders can introduce unnecessary overhead, especially in cases where they are executed many times per frame (for instance, during the rendering of large numbers of objects or particles).

A. Reduce Expensive Operations

Certain operations are more computationally expensive than others. It's important to minimize their use or replace them with more efficient alternatives wherever possible. For example:

- **Avoiding Division**: Division is significantly slower than multiplication or addition. If you need to perform a division in a shader, try to factor out common terms or use a reciprocal (e.g., 1.0 / x) instead.

```glsl
// Avoid division by using a reciprocal
float invX = 1.0 / x;
```

- **Simplify Mathematical Expressions**: Operations such as square roots, trigonometric functions, and logarithms can be costly on the GPU. Whenever possible, try to approximate these functions or look for ways to avoid their use in performance-critical paths.

```glsl
// Instead of using sqrt, approximate with a faster method
float invSqrt = inversesqrt(x);
```

- **Minimize Conditionals**: Branching statements (such as if or switch) can lead to divergent execution on modern GPUs, where different threads in a warp (group of threads) may follow different paths. This can result in performance penalties. Try to reduce the use of conditionals, or replace them with mathematical functions such as mix() or step(), which are more GPU-friendly.

```glsl
// Instead of if statements, use mix
float result = mix(a, b, condition);
```

B. Precompute and Cache Results

If your shader performs expensive computations that don't change between frames or objects, consider precomputing these values on the CPU and passing them as uniforms to the shader. For example, if you're calculating a lighting model that doesn't change over time, calculate it once on the CPU and avoid recalculating it in the fragment shader each frame.

```glsl
// Instead of calculating this value per-fragment, calculate it
on the CPU
uniform mat4 precomputedMatrix;
```

2. Optimize Texture Sampling

Texture sampling is an integral part of shader programming, but it can become a bottleneck if not optimized properly. High-resolution textures or excessive texture fetches can severely impact performance.

A. Mipmap Usage

Mipmaps are precomputed versions of textures at various levels of detail (LOD). Using mipmaps improves performance by reducing the number of texture fetches and ensures better visual quality at a distance. OpenGL automatically chooses the appropriate mipmap level, but explicitly specifying the use of mipmaps in your shaders can further optimize texture sampling.

```glsl
// Use mipmaps to sample at the appropriate level of detail
vec4 textureColor = texture(textureSampler, texCoords);
```

B. Texture Fetching Efficiency

Minimize the number of texture fetches in a shader, as each fetch introduces latency. Use techniques such as **texture atlases** (combining multiple textures into one larger texture) to reduce the number of texture binds and fetches. This is especially useful for 2D sprite rendering or when applying multiple textures to a single object.

```glsl
// Use a texture atlas to sample multiple textures with a single fetch
vec4 texColor = texture(textureAtlas, texCoords);
```

C. Avoiding Unnecessary Texture Access

If a texture is not essential to a shader's calculations (for example, if the result of a texture fetch is not used in later computations), avoid accessing it. This reduces unnecessary texture loads that can add up quickly in a complex scene.

402

```glsl
// Only sample textures when needed
if (useTexture) {
    vec4 texColor = texture(textureSampler, texCoords);
}
```

3. Use Early Fragment Tests and Depth Pre-Pass

In many rendering applications, especially those involving complex scenes, not every fragment (pixel) will end up visible on screen. By performing early depth and stencil tests, you can avoid doing unnecessary work in the fragment shader for fragments that are occluded by other geometry.

A. Early Depth Testing

You can enable depth testing to reject fragments that are occluded by closer geometry early in the pipeline, which helps reduce the workload on your fragment shaders.

```cpp
glEnable(GL_DEPTH_TEST);  // Enable depth testing to avoid
processing hidden fragments
```

B. Depth Pre-Pass

In complex scenes, especially with transparent or high-poly objects, you might perform a **depth pre-pass** before rendering the full geometry. This involves rendering only the depth information of objects in the scene, which allows you to perform an additional depth test when you render the actual objects, rejecting unnecessary fragments early on.

```cpp
// Depth pre-pass: render only depth values first
glClear(GL_DEPTH_BUFFER_BIT);
glDepthFunc(GL_LESS);
```

```
renderGeometry();
```

4. Minimize State Changes

State changes in OpenGL (such as changing shaders, textures, or buffers) can be expensive because they require the GPU to reconfigure or reload resources. Minimizing state changes in your shader code and OpenGL calls can improve performance significantly.

A. Batch Draw Calls

Try to batch multiple objects with the same shader and texture into a single draw call. This reduces the number of state changes that OpenGL must handle during the rendering process.

cpp

```
// Batch multiple objects with the same texture and shader
glUseProgram(shaderProgram);
glBindTexture(GL_TEXTURE_2D, textureID);
// Draw multiple objects
drawObject1();
drawObject2();
```

B. Efficient Resource Management

Make sure to only change the resources (textures, buffers) that need to be updated. For instance, avoid switching shaders or textures unnecessarily if they are already in the correct state. Minimize the number of state changes to improve performance.

5. Use Profiling Tools to Optimize Shaders

Using profiling tools is essential to ensure that your shader optimizations are actually improving performance. Tools like **NVIDIA NSight**, **RenderDoc**, and **gDEBugger** allow you to measure shader execution time, track GPU memory usage, and inspect the efficiency of each shader stage.

- **Shader Profiler**: Use shader profilers to analyze how much time each stage of your shader takes to execute (vertex, fragment, geometry). Focus optimization efforts on the stages that take the most time.

- **GPU Time Metrics**: Monitor how much time the GPU spends processing different parts of the pipeline. If your fragment shaders are taking a significant amount of time, it's a sign that optimization is needed.

- **Overdraw Metrics**: Overdraw happens when fragments are rendered multiple times in a single pixel, which is often due to poor culling, transparency issues, or inefficient geometry. Profiling tools can highlight overdraw, allowing you to optimize the scene and reduce GPU workload.

6. Optimizing GLSL Code for the GPU

OpenGL shaders are executed in parallel by many threads on the GPU, and the performance of your shaders depends on how well you write them. GPUs are designed to handle many lightweight operations concurrently, but they are not suited for large, complex operations that require frequent communication between threads. Here are a few tips for optimizing GLSL code:

- **Use Vector Types**: GLSL has built-in support for vector and matrix types, which allow you to perform operations on multiple components at once. This is much more efficient than performing individual scalar operations.

- **Avoid Redundant Calculations**: If a value is calculated multiple times, store it in a variable instead of recalculating it each time. This reduces unnecessary computations and improves performance.

- **Leverage GPU Parallelism**: Break down calculations into smaller, independent operations that can be processed in parallel by different threads.

Optimizing shader code is essential for achieving high performance in OpenGL applications. By minimizing shader complexity, reducing texture sampling overhead, and applying best practices like early fragment tests and efficient state management, you can ensure that your shaders run as efficiently as possible. Profiling tools like **gDEBugger**, **RenderDoc**, and **NVIDIA NSight** are invaluable for identifying performance bottlenecks and guiding optimization efforts. Ultimately, careful attention to shader performance will help you achieve smooth, high-quality rendering for your applications.

Best Practices for Writing Efficient OpenGL Code

Writing efficient OpenGL code is not just about performance; it also involves creating code that is clean, maintainable, and reusable. By adhering to best practices for structuring and organizing your OpenGL code, you can reduce complexity, improve debugging and testing, and ensure that your applications can scale effectively as they grow.

In this chapter, we will discuss best practices for writing modular, reusable, and maintainable OpenGL code. These practices are particularly important for large-scale applications, such as games or simulations, where the rendering pipeline can become complex and the codebase can quickly grow unwieldy.

1. Modularizing Your OpenGL Code

Modularity is one of the key principles of writing maintainable and efficient code. By organizing your OpenGL code into logical, self-contained modules, you can improve both code readability and maintainability. Instead of writing large, monolithic functions, break your code into smaller, focused components that each handle a specific responsibility.

A. Organize Code by Functionality

Group related code into separate files or classes. For example, you might want to have distinct modules for:

- **Shader management**: A class or module dedicated to loading,

compiling, and managing shaders.
- **Resource management**: Code responsible for managing textures, buffers, and other OpenGL resources.
- **Rendering logic**: A separate set of classes for rendering objects, handling the drawing pipeline, and applying transformations.

This approach helps avoid cluttering your main application logic with unrelated OpenGL functions, making the codebase easier to navigate and extend.

B. Use Object-Oriented Programming (OOP) Principles

OpenGL itself is a state machine, but organizing your code with object-oriented principles can help keep track of the many states and resources OpenGL uses. For instance, you can use classes to represent entities like:

- **ShaderProgram**: A class that encapsulates the loading, compilation, and usage of vertex and fragment shaders.
- **Mesh**: A class representing a 3D object, storing its vertex data, indices, and textures.
- **Camera**: A class responsible for managing the view and projection matrices, as well as controlling the camera's movement.

OOP principles such as encapsulation, inheritance, and polymorphism can help keep your OpenGL code organized, modular, and easier to extend or refactor.

2. Reusable Code Design

When working with OpenGL, it's common to write code that performs similar tasks in multiple places, such as setting up shaders or managing buffers. To avoid duplicating code, you should aim to write reusable components and functions.

A. Write General-Purpose Utility Functions

Instead of re-implementing the same logic across your application, write utility functions that handle common tasks such as:

- **Loading and binding shaders**: A reusable function for compiling shaders, linking them into a program, and checking for errors.

cpp

```cpp
GLuint LoadShader(const char* vertexPath, const char*
fragmentPath) {
    // Load, compile, and link shaders
    GLuint vertexShader = CompileShader(GL_VERTEX_SHADER,
    vertexPath);
    GLuint fragmentShader = CompileShader(GL_FRAGMENT_SHADER,
    fragmentPath);
    return LinkProgram(vertexShader, fragmentShader);
}
```

- **Buffer creation**: Create functions that handle buffer generation, binding, and cleanup for vertex buffers, index buffers, etc.

cpp

```cpp
GLuint CreateBuffer(GLenum target, const void* data, GLsizeiptr
size) {
    GLuint buffer;
    glGenBuffers(1, &buffer);
    glBindBuffer(target, buffer);
    glBufferData(target, size, data, GL_STATIC_DRAW);
    return buffer;
}
```

- **Texture loading**: Write a single, reusable function that loads textures from files into OpenGL.

cpp

```
GLuint LoadTexture(const char* texturePath) {
    // Load the texture from file and create OpenGL texture
    object
    GLuint texture;
    glGenTextures(1, &texture);
    glBindTexture(GL_TEXTURE_2D, texture);
    // Load texture image here and set texture parameters
    return texture;
}
```

By writing these reusable functions, you reduce the need for repeated code, making your application easier to maintain and extend.

B. Use Abstractions for Shader Programs and Buffers

Shaders and buffers are central to OpenGL applications, so it's crucial to handle them in a way that maximizes reusability and minimizes boilerplate. Instead of manually binding and using shaders or buffers every time you need them, create abstractions that make your code cleaner and more modular.

For example, create a **ShaderProgram** class that handles both the loading and usage of shaders:

cpp

```
class ShaderProgram {
public:
    ShaderProgram(const char* vertexPath, const char*
    fragmentPath) {
        programID = LoadShader(vertexPath, fragmentPath);
    }

    void Use() const {
        glUseProgram(programID);
    }

private:
```

```cpp
    GLuint programID;
};
```

Now, instead of manually calling OpenGL functions to load and use shaders, you can simply instantiate the ShaderProgram class and call Use():

cpp

```cpp
ShaderProgram shader("vertex_shader.glsl",
"fragment_shader.glsl");
shader.Use();
```

3. Resource Management

Managing OpenGL resources, such as buffers, textures, and shaders, efficiently is key to creating a performant and maintainable application. When resources are not properly managed, it can lead to memory leaks, excessive GPU usage, or incorrect rendering.

A. Use RAII for Resource Management

RAII (Resource Acquisition Is Initialization) is a technique used to manage resource lifecycles by binding the resource management to the lifetime of an object. In C++, this is accomplished by placing OpenGL resources (such as textures or buffers) inside classes, ensuring that resources are automatically cleaned up when they go out of scope.

For example, a Texture class might automatically load and clean up OpenGL texture objects:

cpp

```cpp
class Texture {
public:
    Texture(const char* texturePath) {
        glGenTextures(1, &textureID);
        glBindTexture(GL_TEXTURE_2D, textureID);
        // Load texture data
    }
```

411

```cpp
~Texture() {
    glDeleteTextures(1, &textureID);
}

void Bind() const {
    glBindTexture(GL_TEXTURE_2D, textureID);
}

private:
    GLuint textureID;
};
```

With this approach, when a Texture object goes out of scope, the destructor will automatically delete the texture, ensuring there are no memory leaks.

B. Manage Buffer Objects Efficiently

To avoid unnecessary performance hits, buffer objects should be managed efficiently. For instance, use **Vertex Array Objects (VAOs)** and **Vertex Buffer Objects (VBOs)** to group together attributes (like positions, normals, and texture coordinates) for efficient rendering. This minimizes the number of OpenGL calls and reduces overhead.

```cpp
cpp

GLuint VAO, VBO;
glGenVertexArrays(1, &VAO);
glBindVertexArray(VAO);

glGenBuffers(1, &VBO);
glBindBuffer(GL_ARRAY_BUFFER, VBO);
glBufferData(GL_ARRAY_BUFFER, sizeof(vertices), vertices,
GL_STATIC_DRAW);

// Set up vertex attributes
```

In larger applications, you may want to organize your resources into **resource managers** that keep track of textures, buffers, and shaders, ensuring they are reused efficiently and cleaned up when no longer needed.

4. Optimizing Draw Calls and State Changes

Reducing the number of draw calls and state changes can have a significant impact on rendering performance. Every time OpenGL switches shaders, textures, or other states, it incurs a performance cost. Therefore, minimizing these changes can greatly improve efficiency.

A. Batch Draw Calls

Try to group objects that share the same state (e.g., shaders, textures) into a single draw call. For example, if you're rendering multiple objects with the same shader and texture, you can draw them all in one batch, reducing the number of draw calls.

```cpp
// Bind shader and texture once
shader.Use();
texture.Bind();

// Batch multiple objects
for (auto& object : objects) {
    object.Draw();
}
```

B. Minimize State Changes

Whenever possible, try to minimize the frequency of state changes. For example, avoid binding new textures or changing shaders frequently during rendering. Instead, organize your rendering loop to ensure that state changes are made infrequently and only when necessary.

5. Documentation and Comments

Good documentation and clear comments are essential for maintaining OpenGL code, especially when working in teams or revisiting code after a long period. Be sure to document:

- **Shader code**: Explain complex shader logic, especially if you're using advanced techniques like lighting models, post-processing, or custom effects.
- **Code structure**: Outline how different parts of the codebase interact, especially when using abstractions or design patterns like OOP or RAII.
- **Performance considerations**: Document any optimizations or trade-offs made to improve performance.

By following these best practices for writing modular, reusable, and efficient OpenGL code, you will significantly improve both the performance and maintainability of your OpenGL applications. With a well-structured codebase, you can ensure that your application will be scalable, easier to debug, and ready for future enhancements or optimizations.

Code Organization and Structure for Large Projects

When working on large-scale OpenGL projects, efficient code organization becomes essential for both scalability and maintainability. As the project grows, keeping the codebase clean, modular, and well-structured will help developers manage the complexity and ensure that the application remains flexible to accommodate future changes. In this section, we will explore the best practices for organizing and structuring your OpenGL code in large projects, with an emphasis on maintainability, readability, and performance.

1. Organizing Your Project Directory Structure

The structure of your project directory is one of the first things you'll need to decide when working with OpenGL. A well-organized directory structure provides clear separation between different components of your application, making it easier to locate files, add new features, and maintain the project over time. Below is a typical structure for an OpenGL project:

A. Suggested Directory Layout

```plaintext
/ProjectName │ ├──────
 /assets            # Textures, models, and other
 assets │ ├──────
   /textures │ ├─────
   /models │ └─────
   /shaders │ ├──────
 /src              # Source code files │ ├───────
   /core           # Core OpenGL functions, utilities, and
   abstractions │ ├──────
   /renderer       # Code for managing the rendering
   pipeline │ ├──────
   /resources      # Code for managing assets (e.g., shaders,
   textures) │ ├──────
   /math           # Mathematical utilities (e.g., matrices,
   vectors) │ ├──────
   /input          # Code for handling user input (keyboard,
   mouse, etc.) │ └──────
   /physics        # (Optional) Physics simulation
   code │ ├──────
 /include          # Header files for the above
 components │ ├──────
   /core │ ├──────
   /renderer │ ├──────
   /resources │ ├──────
   /math │ ├──────
   /input │ └──────
   /physics │ ├──────
 /libs             # External libraries and
```

```
dependencies  ├──────
/bin                      # Executable files and compiled
binaries      └──────
/docs                     # Documentation
```

B. Separation of Concerns

Each folder in this structure has a clear responsibility, making it easy to extend and modify the application without interfering with unrelated parts of the code. For example:

- **/core**: This folder contains core functionalities, such as OpenGL context initialization, window creation, and utilities for managing shader programs or buffers.
- **/renderer**: Here you will put all the code related to the actual rendering pipeline, such as managing the camera, applying transformations, and drawing objects.
- **/resources**: This folder handles asset loading and management, such as texture loading, shader compilation, and model parsing. It abstracts away the complexity of resource management, allowing the rest of your application to access resources seamlessly.
- **/math**: Store all utility code for mathematics, like matrix and vector operations, in a dedicated directory. This allows you to keep mathematical functions isolated, making the code more reusable across different parts of the project.
- **/input**: A separate folder for managing user input makes it easier to handle different types of input devices (keyboard, mouse, gamepad) and to modify or extend input logic.

2. Use of Header Files for Modular Code

In large OpenGL projects, it's important to keep the interface (header files) and implementation (source files) separate. This allows for better modularity and the ability to quickly locate and modify code. Header files should contain the declarations of functions, classes, or variables,

416

while the source files (with the .cpp or .c extension) should contain the implementation details.

A. Creating Header Files

Each module (e.g., renderer, shader manager, input handler) should have its own header file where you define the interface that other parts of the application will interact with. For example, in the shader.h header file, you might declare functions like:

```cpp
// shader.h
#ifndef SHADER_H
#define SHADER_H

#include <string>
#include <GL/glew.h>

class Shader {
public:
    Shader(const std::string& vertexPath, const std::string&
    fragmentPath);
    ~Shader();

    void use();
    GLuint getID() const;

private:
    GLuint shaderID;
    void compileShader(const std::string& source, GLenum type);
    void checkCompileErrors(GLuint shader, const std::string&
    type);
};

#endif
```

B. Implementing Functions in Source Files

In the corresponding .cpp file, you implement the functions defined in the header:

cpp

```cpp
// shader.cpp
#include "shader.h"
#include <fstream>
#include <sstream>
#include <iostream>

Shader::Shader(const std::string& vertexPath, const std::string&
fragmentPath) {
    // Load, compile, and link shaders
    compileShader(vertexPath, GL_VERTEX_SHADER);
    compileShader(fragmentPath, GL_FRAGMENT_SHADER);
}

void Shader::compileShader(const std::string& path, GLenum type)
{
    // Implementation for shader compilation...
}

void Shader::use() {
    glUseProgram(shaderID);
}

GLuint Shader::getID() const {
    return shaderID;
}
```

By separating declarations and implementations, you can improve code readability and avoid unnecessary recompilation, which is particularly useful in large projects.

3. Dependency Management and External Libraries

In large OpenGL projects, you'll likely need to use external libraries for things like math operations (e.g., **GLM** for matrices and vectors), window/context management (e.g., **GLFW** or **SDL**), or asset loading (e.g., **Assimp** for 3D models). To ensure these libraries don't complicate your

418

project structure, follow these practices:

A. Use a Package Manager

Using a package manager like **vcpkg** or **Conan** can help manage and integrate external libraries with your project. These tools automatically download, build, and link libraries, making it easier to keep dependencies up-to-date and manage them in a consistent manner.

```plaintext
vcpkg install glfw3 glm assimp
```

This way, you don't have to manually download or link libraries—**vcpkg** handles it all.

B. Link Libraries Modularly

When using external libraries, avoid having them interspersed throughout your codebase. Instead, link them in specific modules where they are necessary. For example, a renderer module might include **GLM** and **GLFW**, while an asset_loader module might include **Assimp**. This allows for greater flexibility if you decide to swap out or modify one of these libraries in the future.

4. Maintainability and Code Reusability

Writing modular code is not just about reducing complexity; it's also about ensuring that the code remains reusable and easy to maintain over time. The following practices help achieve this:

A. Use Smart Pointers for Resource Management

In modern C++, use **smart pointers** (e.g., std::unique_ptr, std::shared_ptr) to manage OpenGL resources, such as buffers, textures, and shaders. This reduces the risk of resource leaks and ensures that resources are automatically cleaned up when no longer needed.

cpp

```
std::unique_ptr<Shader> shader =
std::make_unique<Shader>("vertex.glsl", "fragment.glsl");
```

B. Document Your Code

Even in a well-structured project, clear documentation is vital. Use comments and documentation to explain the purpose of each module, function, and class. When working in teams, documenting assumptions, decisions, and key concepts can help other developers understand the code without needing to spend hours deciphering it.

5. Version Control and Collaboration

For larger projects, version control is a must. Using **Git** or other version control systems ensures that your codebase can scale with collaboration and allows for easy management of branches, releases, and feature development.

A. Maintain a Consistent Branching Strategy

Adopt a branching strategy that suits your team. Common strategies include **Gitflow** or **feature branching**, where each feature or bug fix is developed in its own branch and merged back into the main branch once complete.

B. Continuous Integration/Continuous Deployment (CI/CD)

Set up a CI/CD pipeline to automate the build and testing process. This ensures that the codebase remains stable even as new features are integrated.

Efficiently structuring and organizing your OpenGL project from the outset is crucial for ensuring long-term maintainability, scalability, and performance. By writing modular, reusable code, keeping a clean directory structure, using proper resource management, and adopting good coding practices, you can significantly improve both the development process and the performance of your OpenGL applications. Following these best practices ensures that your codebase remains flexible, extensible, and optimized, allowing you to tackle even the most complex graphics projects with confidence.

Tips for Keeping Your OpenGL Code Clean and Maintainable

Maintaining clean and efficient code is crucial for the long-term success of any OpenGL project, especially as the codebase grows. As with any complex software development, adhering to best practices in code organization, naming conventions, and documentation will improve the readability, reusability, and maintainability of your OpenGL code. This section will cover practical tips that will help you write clean, manageable OpenGL code.

1. Follow Consistent Naming Conventions

Naming conventions are a simple but powerful way to maintain clarity and consistency throughout your code. Following a naming pattern allows developers to quickly understand the purpose of variables, functions, and classes without needing to read through their implementation details.

A. Naming Variables, Functions, and Classes

- **Variables**: Use meaningful names that describe what the variable represents, and keep them concise. For example, use viewMatrix instead of vm.
- **Functions**: Functions should be named according to what they do, and they should start with a verb to indicate an action (e.g., loadShader(), drawMesh()).
- **Classes/Structs**: Classes and structs should be named using Pascal-Case, which capitalizes the first letter of each word (e.g., ShaderProgram, MeshRenderer).

B. Avoid Ambiguity and Overloading

Ensure that variable and function names are specific to their purpose

421

and avoid using overly general names such as data or temp. Ambiguous names can lead to confusion, particularly when scaling up a project.

2. Keep Your Functions Small and Focused

In OpenGL, as with any programming task, keeping functions small and focused on a single task is essential for readability and reusability. Each function should do one thing and do it well. Large functions that handle multiple tasks can be difficult to understand and prone to errors.

A. Single Responsibility Principle (SRP)

Adhere to the **Single Responsibility Principle**, which states that a function (or class) should have only one reason to change. For instance:

- A function that loads a texture should only be responsible for loading the texture, not for managing how textures are displayed on objects.
- A shader program class should manage the shader compilation and linking process but should not handle input or camera transformations.

If you find a function becoming too large, consider splitting it into smaller, more manageable functions.

cpp

```cpp
// Instead of one large function, break it down into smaller
parts
void LoadTexture(const char* filename) {
    GLuint textureID = LoadImage(filename);
    BindTexture(textureID);
    ConfigureTextureSettings();
    ...
}
```

3. Use Comments and Documentation Wisely

While writing self-explanatory code is important, there are times when a little explanation can go a long way, especially when dealing with complex OpenGL concepts like shaders, matrices, or advanced rendering techniques.

Good comments can save hours of debugging and help others understand your code.

A. Explain Why, Not Just What

Comments should primarily explain *why* something is done in a particular way, not just *what* is happening. For example, when performing a non-obvious optimization or using a specific OpenGL extension, document the reasoning behind it.

cpp

```
// Using a non-linear projection matrix for better depth
precision in large scenes
viewProjectionMatrix = glm::perspectiveFov(glm::radians(60.0f),
width, height, 0.1f, 1000.0f);
```

B. Use Docstrings for Classes and Functions

For more complex functions or classes, provide a brief docstring that explains the purpose, parameters, and expected output. This is particularly useful in large projects, where developers may come back to a piece of code months or years later.

cpp

```
/**
 * Loads and compiles a vertex and fragment shader from
 specified file paths.
 * @param vertexPath: The file path to the vertex shader.
 * @param fragmentPath: The file path to the fragment shader.
 * @return The OpenGL shader program ID.
 */
GLuint LoadShader(const char* vertexPath, const char*
fragmentPath) {
    ...
}
```

C. Keep Comments Up-to-Date

Outdated comments are often worse than having no comments at all.

When making changes to the code, be sure to update comments to reflect those changes.

4. Avoid Magic Numbers

Magic numbers (literal values used without explanation) can make code harder to understand and maintain. In OpenGL, this is particularly important when dealing with shader parameters, texture coordinates, and other settings that require numerical constants.

A. Define Constants or Enumerations

Instead of using magic numbers in your code, define them as constants or enumerations. This improves readability and allows you to easily update values in one central location.

cpp

```
// Instead of using 0.1f directly in the code
#define Z_NEAR 0.1f
#define Z_FAR 100.0f

glm::mat4 projection = glm::perspective(glm::radians(45.0f),
aspectRatio, Z_NEAR, Z_FAR);
```

B. Use Enums for State and Mode Management

For OpenGL-specific settings (such as blending modes, culling settings, or texture filtering), use enums to improve clarity and reduce errors.

cpp

```
enum class BlendMode {
    Opaque = GL_SRC_ALPHA,
    Transparent = GL_BLEND_SRC_ALPHA
};

SetBlendMode(BlendMode::Transparent);
```

5. Separate OpenGL Logic from Application Logic

Keeping OpenGL-specific code separate from your game or application logic is crucial for maintaining flexibility. This separation helps you change how OpenGL interacts with the rest of your application without modifying your core logic.

A. Abstract OpenGL Calls

Create abstraction layers that hide OpenGL calls, making it easier to replace or modify OpenGL-related functionality. For example, if you decide to switch from OpenGL to Vulkan or Metal in the future, abstracting OpenGL-specific code into modules like Renderer or GraphicsManager will make such a transition easier.

cpp

```
class GraphicsManager {
public:
    void RenderMesh(const Mesh& mesh) {
        BindMeshBuffers(mesh);
        DrawMesh(mesh);
    }
    // Other OpenGL related methods
};
```

6. Use OpenGL Extensions Judiciously

OpenGL is a large and complex API with a variety of extensions that provide access to additional features and optimizations. While extensions can be powerful, they can also lead to issues with portability, as not all hardware supports all extensions.

A. Check for Extension Availability

Before using an OpenGL extension, ensure that it is supported on the target hardware. Use glGetString(GL_EXTENSIONS) or platform-specific methods to query supported extensions at runtime.

cpp

```
if (glewIsSupported("GL_ARB_texture_compression")) {
    // Use compressed textures
}
```

B. Provide Fallbacks for Missing Extensions

In case an extension is not supported, provide fallback implementations that will allow your application to run without the feature, even if it runs less efficiently.

7. Regular Refactoring and Code Reviews

Refactoring is an ongoing process of improving the internal structure of your code without changing its external behavior. As your OpenGL project evolves, it's essential to periodically refactor your code to remove redundant logic, improve modularity, and enhance performance.

A. Code Reviews

Code reviews are an essential part of maintaining code quality. Regular reviews help identify inefficiencies, catch potential bugs, and ensure that coding standards are consistently applied. In OpenGL projects, where performance is crucial, peer reviews can help spot areas where optimizations might be missed.

B. Refactor for Efficiency

Whenever possible, look for opportunities to optimize code and reduce redundancy. Refactoring also allows you to apply new best practices as they evolve and helps maintain a high level of code quality throughout the development lifecycle.

8. Performance Considerations for Clean Code

While clean code is important, it's also crucial to consider performance when designing your OpenGL code. Performance optimizations, such as minimizing state changes, reducing draw calls, and optimizing buffer usage, should be balanced with the need for maintainable and readable code. Remember that code cleanliness doesn't always have to come at the expense of performance—find ways to achieve both.

By adhering to these best practices for organizing and maintaining your OpenGL code, you'll set your project up for long-term success. Well-organized code is easier to debug, optimize, and extend, and it's also more approachable for other developers who may join the project later.

www.ingramcontent.com/pod-product-compliance
Lightning Source LLC
LaVergne TN
LVHW081511050326
832903LV00025B/1443